GREEKS AND PRE-GREEKS

By systematically confronting Greek tradition of the Heroic Age with the evidence of both linguistics and archaeology, Margalit Finkelberg proposes a multi-disciplinary assessment of the ethnic, linguistic and cultural situation in Greece in the second millennium BC. The main thesis of this book is that the Greeks started their history as a multi-ethnic population group consisting of both Greek-speaking newcomers and the indigenous population of the land, and that the body of 'Hellenes' as known to us from the historic period was a deliberate self-creation. The book addresses such issues as the structure of heroic genealogy, the linguistic and cultural identity of the indigenous population of Greece, the patterns of marriage between heterogeneous groups as they emerge in literary and historical sources, the dialect map of Bronze Age Greece, the factors responsible for the collapse of the Mycenaean civilisation and, finally, the construction of the myth of the Trojan War.

MARGALIT FINKELBERG is Professor of Classics at Tel Aviv University. Her previous publications include *The Birth of Literary Fiction in Ancient Greece* (1998).

GREEKS AND PRE-GREEKS

Aegean Prehistory and Greek Heroic Tradition

MARGALIT FINKELBERG

CAMBRIDGE
UNIVERSITY PRESS

CAMBRIDGE UNIVERSITY PRESS
Cambridge, New York, Melbourne, Madrid, Cape Town, Singapore, São Paulo

Cambridge University Press
The Edinburgh Building, Cambridge CB2 2RU, UK

Published in the United States of America by Cambridge University Press, New York

www.cambridge.org
Information on this title: www.cambridge.org/9780521852166

First published 2005

Printed in the United Kingdom at the University Press, Cambridge

A catalogue record for this book is available from the British Library

ISBN-13 978-0-521-85216-6 hardback
ISBN-10 0-521-85216-1   hardback

TO THE MEMORY OF MY PARENTS
τοὺς ζωοὺς κατέλειπον ἰοῦσ᾽ ἐς ᾿Ίλιον ἱρήν

Contents

Maps

Figures

Preface

It is almost impossible for a Homerist not to become involved, at one stage or another, in the world that the *Iliad* and the *Odyssey* purport to describe. My own interest in Aegean prehistory was first aroused by reading Denys Page's *History and the Homeric Iliad* many years ago. Gradually, the unqualified acceptance of Page's interpretation and conclusions as regards the relationship between the Homeric tradition and the Aegean Bronze Age gave way to systematic questioning of the assumptions from which he proceeded, which eventually led to conclusions diametrically opposed to those arrived at by Page. This, however, does not diminish the impact that his singularly stimulating book had on my work.

This book was long in the making. A number of the arguments found in it have appeared in various publication venues since 1988, but it was not until 1998 that they combined to form a larger thesis. The active participation in discussions which took place on AegeaNet, a discussion group on the prehistoric Aegean moderated by John Younger, during this very year was undoubtedly one of the factors that stimulated me to consolidate the ideas from which this book developed, and it was in 1998 again, at the Seventh International Aegean Conference held in Liège, that its main thesis was first presented. I am also much indebted to the Institute for Advanced Studies, Jerusalem, where I spent six months in 1999 as a member of the international research group on Mechanisms of Canon-Making in Ancient Societies. The exposure to the canonical texts of other civilisations and historical periods, as well as the exchange of ideas with scholars in other fields that I experienced during this period, enlarged my horizons and gave me a fuller understanding of the role of Homer as both the custodian of the past and its creator.

The first draft of this book was completed during my term as a Visiting Fellow at All Souls College, Oxford, in 1999–2000. I have no doubt that the amiable atmosphere and the ideal working conditions provided by the College, as well as the first-class scholarly facilities of the University of

Oxford, were the very factors that allowed me to bring my work to completion, and I am taking this opportunity to express my gratitude to the Warden and Fellows of All Souls. Martin West was the first to read the manuscript and to comment on it; in many respects his criticism and suggestions determined the directions in which the original version was subsequently revised. Aryeh Finkelberg read each one of the new versions that appeared in the subsequent years, and his thorough and often devastating criticism was in fact the main reason why these new versions continued to emerge. Deborah Boedeker, Benjamin Isaac, Emily Lyle, David Shulman and Calvert Watkins read either the entire manuscript or parts of it, and shared with me their suggestions and queries. Among those with whom different aspects of my argument were discussed, and sometimes disputed, the points made by Elizabeth Barber, Robert Drews, Irad Malkin, Sarah Morris, Thomas Palaima, Itamar Singer and Judith Weingarten have proved especially helpful; more specific contributions of other colleagues are acknowledged in the footnotes to the relevant sections of the text. I am grateful to audiences in Tel Aviv, Jerusalem, Oxford, Edinburgh, Princeton, St John's and Halifax, before whom different parts of this book were presented, for their discussion and comments. I am also grateful to the Cambridge University Press team – Sinead Moloney, Anna-Marie Lovett, Jackie Warren and others whose names I do not know – for their devoted work on the production of this difficult volume, and especially to Bernard Dod for his collaboration, which went far beyond the original target of copy-editing and has led to many improvements in my argument and presentation of the material. My special thanks go to Michael Sharp, whose creative editorship has resulted in what I see as a considerable improvement of the whole book and eventually to the present version.

I am grateful to the Austrian Academy of Sciences for the permission to reproduce Maps 1a, b and 2a, b ('Suffixes -*ss*- and -*nd*- in Anatolia and Greece'), first published in Fritz Schachermeyr, *Ägäis und Orient* (Österreichische Akademie der Wissenschaften. Philosophisch-Historische Klasse. Denkschriften, 93. Bd.: Graz and Vienna, 1967), pp. 13–15, and the University of California Press for the permission to reproduce Map 5 ('Greece according to the Homeric Catalogue of Ships'), first published in Denys Page, *History and the Homeric Iliad* (University of California Press: Berkeley, 1959), between pp. 124 and 125.

Some of the material of this book first appeared in the following publications:

'Ajax's entry in the Hesiodic *Catalogue of Women*', *CQ* 38 (1988): 31–41;
'Royal succession in heroic Greece', *CQ* 41 (1991): 303–16;
'The dialect continuum of ancient Greek', *HSCPh* 96 (1994): 1–36;
'Anatolian languages and Indo-European migrations to Greece', *CW* 91 (1997): 3–20;
'The Brother's Son of Tawananna and others: the rule of dynastic succession in the Old Hittite Kingdom', *Cosmos* 13 (1997): 127–41;
'Bronze Age writing: contacts between East and West', in *The Aegean and the Orient in the Second Millennium*, ed. E. H. Cline and D. Harris-Cline (Liège, 1998): 265–72.
'Greek epic tradition on population movements in Bronze Age Greece', in *POLEMOS. Warfare in the Aegean Bronze Age*, ed. R. Laffineur (Liège, 1999): 31–6;
'Homer as a foundation text', in *Homer, the Bible and Beyond. Literary and Religious Canons in the Ancient World*, ed. M. Finkelberg and G. Stroumsa (Leiden, 2003): 75–96.

All translations are my own unless otherwise specified.

Abbreviations

AA	Archäologischer Anzeiger
AASOR	Annual of the American Schools of Oriental Research
AF	Altorientalische Forschungen
AJA	American Journal of Archaeology
AS	Anatolian Studies
BAR	Biblical Archaeology Review
BASOR	Bulletin of the American Schools of Oriental Research
BMCR	Bryn Mawr Classical Review
CA	Classical Antiquity
CAH	Cambridge Ancient History
CAJ	Cambridge Archaeological Journal
CPh	Classical Philology
CQ	Classical Quarterly
CRAI	Comptes rendus de l'Académie des Inscriptions et Belles-Lettres
CS	Cretan Studies
CW	Classical World
HAB	F. Sommer and A. Falkenstein, Die hethitisch-akkadische Bilingue des Hattusili I (Munich, 1938)
HSCPh	Harvard Studies in Classical Philology
IEJ	Israel Exploration Journal
IF	Indogermanische Forschungen
JCS	Journal of Cuneiform Studies
JESHO	Journal of the Economic and Social History of the Orient
JHS	Journal of Hellenic Studies
JIES	Journal of Indo-European Studies
JSOT	Journal for the Study of the Old Testament
KBo	Keilschrifttexte aus Boghazkoi (Leipzig and Berlin)
KUB	Keilschrifturkunden aus Boghazkoi (Berlin)
MH	Museum Helveticum

M-W   R. Merkelbach and M. L. West, *Fragmenta Hesiodea*
         (Oxford, 1967)
NYT   *New York Times*
OA   *Oriens Antiquus*
OJA   *Oxford Journal of Archaeology*
PCPhS *Proceedings of the Cambridge Philological Society*
REG   *Revue des Etudes grecques*
RHA   *Revue hittite et asianique*
SCI   *Scripta Classica Israelica*
SMEA   *Studi micenei ed egeo-anatolici*
ST   *Studia Troica*
TLS   *The Times Literary Supplement*
TPhS   *Transactions of the Philosophical Society*
ZPE   *Zeitschrift für Papyrologie und Epigraphik*

CHAPTER I

Introduction

LEGEND, LANGUAGE, ARCHAEOLOGY

The excavations of Troy and Mycenae initiated by Heinrich Schliemann
in the 1870s opened the great era of archaeological reconstruction of
Aegean prehistory. In 1900, the highly developed Minoan civilisation of
Crete began to be uncovered by Sir Arthur Evans and others. Especially
significant was the discovery of the Aegean scripts - Linear A, Linear B
and Cretan Hieroglyphic - which accompanied Evans' excavation. In the
years following these discoveries the Minoan was firmly believed to have
been the dominant civilisation of the Bronze Age Aegean. It was not until
1939, when the Pylos Linear B archives were discovered by Carl Blegen
and the Cincinnati expedition, that the majority of archaeologists realised
what had been clear to only a few, namely, that we should speak of two
Aegean civilisations rather than one: the Minoan civilisation of Crete and
the Mycenaean civilisation of mainland Greece. Although Mycenaean
Greece developed later and under considerable Minoan influence, it
eventually prevailed, and in the Late Bronze Age Crete turned into a
Mycenaean province. The former Minoan colonies became Mycenaean,
and after ca. 1450 BC Mycenaean influence replaced Minoan not only in
the Aegean but also in western Anatolia. In 1953, when the decipherment
of Linear B by Michael Ventris was made public, it was demonstrated
beyond doubt that the language of the Mycenaean civilisation was Greek.
As a result, an entirely new period, that of Mycenaean Greece, was added
to Greek history.

The impression made by the discovery of Troy was so strong that for a
long time most scholars took it for granted that for all practical purposes
the Homeric poems, which had directly stimulated Schliemann's excavations, should be approached as an authentic document originating in
Bronze Age Greece. Many a reconstruction of the religion, society,
economics and institutions of Mycenaean Greece published in the first

half of the twentieth century proceeded from this assumption. This period in Homeric scholarship produced such epoch-making studies as *The Mycenaean Origin of Greek Mythology* and *Homer and Mycenae* by M. P. Nilsson (1932 and 1933), *Homer and the Monuments* by H. L. Lorimer (1950), *From Mycenae to Homer* by T. B. L. Webster (1958), and was crowned with two great syntheses, *History and the Homeric Iliad* by Denys Page (1959) and *A Companion to Homer* by A. J. B. Wace and F. H. Stubbings (1962). Ironically, the years in which the two latter appeared were precisely the time when the pendulum of scholarly opinion as regards the historical value of the Homeric poems swung back.

In the 1950s, a radical shift began to take place in the evaluation of Homer's historic background. More than one factor was responsible for this development. The picture of Mycenaean society that emerged after the decipherment of Linear B led to an increasing understanding that the Homeric poems are by no means a direct reflection of that society; the study of the Homeric formulae showed that, contrary to what the pioneers of oral formulaic theory had believed, the traditional language is characterised by a high degree of flexibility and adaptation, so that it is absolutely out of the question that everything we find in Homer could have arrived untouched from the Bronze Age; finally, it was shown that the picture of society arising from the Homeric poems properly belongs to a later period. This last conclusion was almost entirely due to the work of M. I. Finley, whose articles and especially the book *The World of Odysseus* (1954) opened a new era in the historical study of Homer. As a result, a new consensus has arisen, which locates the historic background to the Homeric poems in the first rather than in the second millennium BC.

Finley himself placed the formative stage of the Homeric epics in the so-called 'Dark Age' (ca. 1050–ca. 800 BC). Yet, the argument that made it difficult to see in Homer a direct reflection of Mycenaean Greece also holds good as regards the hypothesis that a poet who presumably lived in the eighth or even seventh century BC was describing a society which preceded him by two hundred years. As Ian Morris put it in a seminal article, 'Trying to find tenth- and ninth-century societies in the *Iliad* and *Odyssey* is just as misguided as looking for the Mycenaeans.'[1] That is to say, if the Homeric epics do allow for the reconstruction of a consistent social and historical picture, this picture would rather belong to the time of the poet himself. That is why contemporary scholarly opinion tends to see the eighth century BC as providing the appropriate historic

---

1 I. Morris 1986: 127. Cf. Raaflaub 1991: 212; Bennet 1997.

background for the Homeric poems. Today, 130 years after Schliemann's discovery of Troy, the issue of 'Homer and Mycenae' is no longer considered substantial by the majority of scholars.[2]

At the same time, it seems that reaction to the older scholars' fundamentalist approach to the Greek heroic tradition has gone too far. It should not be forgotten that we owe our very knowledge of the existence of Mycenaean Greece to the stimulus that the poems of Homer furnished to Schliemann and others more than a hundred years ago. As Nilsson demonstrated in the 1930s, the cities identified by Homer as capitals of the kingdoms of heroic Greece were significant Mycenaean sites. In an article published in 1974 Antony Snodgrass convincingly argued that the contradictions in Homer's depiction of social institutions cannot be resolved and should be interpreted to the effect that, rather than reflecting a concrete historic society, the Homeric poems offer an amalgam created as a result of centuries-long circulation in oral tradition. If we also take into account that the language of Homer is a *Kunstsprache* consisting of different historic layers of the Greek language, including the earliest ones; that his formulae for weapons exhibit a combination of Bronze Age military technologies with those of the Archaic period; and that the same mixture of different historic periods is characteristic of his view of death and the afterlife, it would be difficult to avoid the conclusion that at least some parts of what we find in Homer must go back to earlier periods, including the Bronze Age.[3]

Finally, the comparative evidence makes it abundantly manifest that, whenever a heroic tradition can be correlated with written evidence, it can often be shown to have preserved a memory of momentous historic events, such as wars, migrations or foreign invasions. It would therefore be anachronistic to approach epic tradition with modern criteria of historicity and on the basis of this to deny it all historical basis whatsoever. To quote *The Chronology of Oral Tradition* by David P. Henige, the subtitle of which, *Quest for a Chimera*, speaks for itself: 'No one who has worked extensively with oral materials will deny their value as historical

---

2 This change of perspective is made immediately obvious from a comparison between the 1962 *Companion to Homer* by Wace and Stubbings on the one hand and *Zweihundert Jahre Homer-Forschung* by Joachim Latacz (1991) and *A New Companion to Homer* by Ian Morris and Barry Powell (1997) on the other. While all the historical chapters in the old *Companion* discuss various aspects of the Mycenaean background of Homer, only one contribution in each of the recent volumes deals with the Bronze Age.

3 Snodgrass 1974; cf. Finkelberg 1998b: 25–8. On language see e.g. Ruijgh 1967; on weapons Gray 1947; on death and afterlife Sourvinou-Inwood 1995: 12–13, 73–6, 89–92.

sources.'[4] A more detailed discussion as regards the historical value of traditional stories will be postponed until the next section. At this point, it suffices to say that to propose a more nuanced approach to the issue of the historicity of Greek tradition is one of the purposes of this book.

Similarly, the accumulation of data regarding the Bronze Age Aegean, and in particular its relationships with the contemporary civilisations of the Near East, has created a need for fresh approaches. While dramatic new insights have been achieved in the study of this topic in both archaeology and linguistics, relatively little has been done in terms of their integration into a larger picture. Moreover, and perhaps more important, very little attention has been paid to the fact that various processes in Western Asia on the one hand and the Eastern Mediterranean on the other did not develop independently of one another but are linked in a complex network of relationships. This concerns first and foremost the new assessment of the dispersion of Bronze Age Anatolian languages and its relevance to the issue of the so-called 'pre-Hellenic', or 'Aegean', substratum, one of the focal points of this book.

The study of the Anatolian languages is today about one hundred years old. Spectacular results have been achieved during this period in the discovery, decipherment and interpretation of documents written in Hittite, Palaic, Luwian, Lycian, Lydian and other Anatolian languages, and a new scholarly discipline, that of Anatolian studies, has emerged. At the same time, it would be no exaggeration to say that this discipline has not exerted any substantial influence on our construction of the prehistory of Greece. The contacts between Anatolian studies and Classics are only too rare and mostly affect isolated cases, such as the much-discussed '*Ahhiyawa* problem'. Many current theories of Greek prehistory still proceed from assumptions that can be traced to the end of the nineteenth century. However, the data thus far accumulated in the field of Anatolian studies are significant enough not only to throw a new light on these assumptions but perhaps even to challenge them.

As early as 1896, Paul Kretschmer drew scholarly attention to the fact that since the suffixes -*nth*- and -*ss*-, often attested in place-names in Greece, Crete and Asia Minor, cannot be identified as Greek, they should be taken as pointing to the existence of a pre-Hellenic linguistic substratum. In 1928, J. Haley and C. W. Blegen, in their seminal article 'The coming of the Greeks', showed that the distribution on the map of Greece of the geographical names identified by Kretschmer and others as

---

4 Henige 1974: 191. Cf. Hainsworth 1984: 112–13, Kirk 1990: 43–4; Finkelberg 1998c: 87–8.

belonging to the pre-Hellenic substratum closely corresponds to the map of distribution of Early Bronze Age archaeological sites.[5] This allowed the authors to associate the pre-Hellenic substratum with the people who inhabited Greece till the end of the Early Bronze Age and to move the date of the Greek arrival in Greece, formerly believed to have taken place ca. 1600 BC, to the beginning of the Middle Bronze Age (ca. 2050–2000 BC).[6]

But what about the linguistic identity of the Aegean substratum? It is well known that the suffixes -*nth*- and -*ss*- on the basis of which it was identified are closely paralleled by the suffixes -*nd*- and -*ss*- of the languages of Asia Minor attested in the Classical period, such as Lycian, Lydian and Carian. The discovery and decipherment of Hittite and other Bronze Age Anatolian languages has shown that they are closely related to the languages of Asia Minor and that the suffixes -*nth*- and –*ss* should be identified as typically Anatolian or, to be more precise, Luwian. Thus, the place-name *Parnassos* has consistently been analysed as a possessive adjective typical of the Luwian language, formed from a root which is likewise Luwian, for the word *parna* means 'house' in both Luwian and Lycian.[7] This evidently gives us a new perspective on the much-discussed issue of Near Eastern influences on Greek civilisation, which has recently received a substantial boost in M. L. West's *The East Face of Helicon*.[8] To the best of my knowledge, this perspective has not yet been fully explored.

Above all, however, the new assessment of the linguistic provenance of the Aegean substratum is directly relevant to the question of the identity of the population groups that inhabited Greece before 'the coming of the Greeks'. This question bears directly upon that of the terms in which the identity of the 'Hellenes' themselves is to be approached. Since the issues of ethnicity and ethnic identity in ancient Greece have recently become the focus of a lively scholarly discussion, I will address them separately in a later section.

---

5 Kretschmer 1896; Haley and Blegen 1928: 141–54. Cf. Caskey 1973: 139–40.
6 According to the minority opinion, represented by James Muhly, Robert Drews and others, the arrival of the Greeks should be synchronised with the emergence of the shaft graves of Mycenae at the end of the Middle Helladic period (ca. 1600 BC). Alternatively, John Coleman proposes abandoning the current dating of the 'coming of the Greeks', arguing that it was one of the waves of the Kurgan peoples that brought the Greeks to Greece ca. 3200 BC. See further Drews 1988: 16–24; Carruba 1995; Coleman 2000.
7 See Laroche 1957 and 1961; Heubeck 1961: 50–2; Palmer 1965: 30, 343, 348. Cf. Drews 1997: 153–7; Finkelberg 1997a: 7; Renfrew 1998: 253–4. Cf. also Parnes and Parnon, mountains in Attica and Laconia (I am grateful to Oliver Dickinson for drawing my attention to these names).
8 West 1997. See also Burkert 1992; S. Morris 1992.

Together with the issues of the ethnic, linguistic and cultural identity of the pre-Hellenic population of Greece, I will discuss the terms on which cultural interaction between Greeks and pre-Greeks was made possible, the duration of this interaction and its eventual impact on the civilisation of historic Greece. The book will address these questions by systematically confronting the Greek tradition of the Heroic Age with the evidence of linguistics and archaeology.

The analysis of the standard corpus of Greek genealogy carried out in Chapter 2 demonstrates that the heroic genealogies acted as an inventory not only of the 'descendants of Hellen' but also of other descent groups. At the same time, even those who did not count as descendants of Hellen were nevertheless considered 'Hellenes' in historic Greece. This hetero-geneity of Greek genealogy strongly suggests that, rather than founding their group identity on belief in a common descent, the body of 'Hellenes' as it is known to us from the historic period perceived itself as an ethnically heterogeneous group.

The even spread of the suffixes -ss- and -nth- over western Asia, Greece and Crete strongly suggests that the so-called pre-Hellenic populations of Greece were of Anatolian stock. If true, this would lead us not only to Anatolia but also farther east, for the simple reason that the Anatolians of Asia, Indo-Europeans though they were, cannot be taken separately from the great civilisations of the Near East. As the archaeological discoveries of recent years show, the Bronze Age Aegean was in close contact with these civilisations. The degree to which this new assessment of the linguistic and archaeological evidence at our disposal may affect the terms of the current discussion of the cultural identity of Aegean civilisation will be examined in Chapter 3.

The archaeological record shows little or no break in continuity in the material culture of Greece for the second millennium BC. To quote the standard account of the period as given by John Caskey, 'From the beginning of the Middle Bronze Age onward there was no real break in the continuity of cultural development, in spite of the several spectacu-lar advances and retreats that occurred, and therefore the people of Middle Helladic times must be looked upon as the first true Greeks in the land.'[9] At the same time, the 'coming of the Greeks' postulated by older scholars can hardly be envisaged as a single historic event. To quote Caskey again,

9 Caskey 1973: 139.

The process of change, which is reflected by archaeological evidence from many parts of the region, cannot have been simple. Rather, as was generally the case when migrations took place, the newcomers arrived in groups of various sizes, probably over an appreciable period of time. The people whom they found in possession also varied in the size and prosperity of their communities, some ready to resist while others deemed it necessary or prudent to make terms with the foreigners.[10]

Greek genealogical tradition suggests a similar picture. What it adds to the evidence of archaeology, however, is the element of fusion it implies between the Greeks and the indigenous population. The issue is obviously of crucial importance, and in Chapters 4 and 5 I will try to pursue it further by analysing the patterns of marriage between heterogeneous descent groups as they emerge in the literary and historical sources.

Large-scale migrations at the end of the Bronze Age transformed the dialect map of Greece into an irrational mosaic, where dialects with little linguistic overlap (e.g. Boeotian and Attic) inhabit contiguous territories, but closely related dialects such as Arcadian and Cyprian are geographically remote from each other. In view of this, it is hard to avoid the conclusion that the historic Greek dialects are no more than fragments of a whole which had ceased to exist before the political map of Greece as we know it was shaped. As I will argue in Chapter 6, the manner in which the principal dialect features are distributed among the historic dialects leads to the conclusion that before the collapse of Mycenaean Greece a dialect continuum characteristic of long-settled areas had spread without disruption over most of the territory of Greece. The evidence of the dialects thus agrees with archaeological evidence, in that both show that there was no break in continuity during the second millennium BC.

All this changes at the end of the second millennium. The destruction levels and depopulation attested at many Mycenaean sites testify to a sharp break in cultural continuity. There can be no doubt that we are facing the end of an era, and the same is true of other sites all over the Eastern Mediterranean. As I will argue in Chapter 7, the evidence supplied by the Greek dialects not only substantiates the picture drawn by archaeologists but, in that it unequivocally demonstrates the intrusive character of Doric and other West Greek dialects, also points towards the factors that effected the collapse of Mycenaean Greece. There can be little doubt that Greek tradition regarding the dramatic end of the Heroic Age and the migration of the last survivors of the Race of Heroes refers to

10 Caskey 1973: 117.

the same events. Furthermore, as I will argue in this chapter, the collapse of Mycenaean Greece ought to be brought into correspondence with recent archaeological discoveries in the Levant, which throw new light on the material culture of the Philistines.

Analysis of the epic tradition about the Trojan War allows us to suggest that certain events concerning the end of Mycenaean Greece did not make their way into the mainstream Greek tradition. This tradition, and above all the poems of Homer, either deliberately suppressed these events or moulded them anew in accordance with the contemporary agenda (Chapter 8). The latter consisted in answering the need for the consolidation of heterogeneous population groups that found themselves on the territory of Greece at the beginning of the first millennium BC. By creating a foundational myth that promulgated the idea of a common past, the new Greek civilisation established continuity between the Greece of the Heroic Age and historic Greece and thereby acquired the sense of common identity that it initially lacked.

The culmination of any historical enquiry is the point where the results of several disciplines coincide. 'The coming of the Greeks' by Haley and Blegen, which gave the hypothesis of the pre-Hellenic substratum a solid archaeological background, is the most conspicuous example of successful collaboration between linguistics and archaeology. That such major breakthroughs occur only too rarely should not deter us from trying to achieve meaningful correlations between different types of evidence, each with its own bias of survival and specific problems of interpretation. In recent years, such meaningful correlations between archaeology and linguistics have been established by Colin Renfrew, whereas Elizabeth Barber has shown that the dispersal of weaving technologies often supplies no less reliable evidence for population movements than the dispersal of languages.[11] Finally, although it is only recently that the research methods of genetics have begun to be applied to the study of population movements of the remote past, it has already become evident that, if consistently pursued, the application of genetics to the reconstruction of prehistory may well lead to the establishment of important correlations between genetics and historical linguistics.[12] It would be a pity if intellectual snobbery prevented the rich material supplied by myth and legend from

11 Renfrew 1987; Barber 1991, 1998, 1999, 2001. Cf., however, Renfrew 1998: 240: 'Despite these advances, I feel that archaeologists and historical linguists have not worked together with any very great effect to address some of the outstanding linguistic and archaeological problems.'
12 See esp. the linguistic sections in Cavalli-Sforza *et al.* 1996: 22–4, 164–7, 220–2, 263–6, 317–20, 349–51, 380–2. Cf. Renfrew 2001: 46–50.

becoming part of this joint effort. We have to consider every scrap of information that can throw light on human prehistory, for the simple reason that it is only such a multi-disciplinary approach that can give us a wider perspective of the past and guarantee real progress in the field.

MYTHS BETWEEN THE PAST AND THE PRESENT

The use of linguistic evidence for reconstructing the past hardly requires justification. The very fact of linguistic attribution of a given language or group of languages is a matter of great historical import. Thus, the conclusion that Greece was once occupied by non-Greek-speaking population groups only became possible as a result of analysis of the suffixes -*nth*- and -*ss*-. The same is true of population movements. The character of relationships between individual languages or dialects, in that it allows for coherent interpretation of these relationships in terms of geography, affords linguistics a much better vantage point for assessing the dispersal of populations than the one provided by archaeology. Thus, as we shall see in Chapter 7, while archaeology does not supply a clear picture as to the nature of the factors responsible for the collapse of Mycenaean Greece, analysis of the Greek dialects does offer such a picture.

The importance of the evidence provided by the ancient texts themselves is also immediately obvious. Unfortunately, as far as Aegean prehistory is concerned, only scarce textual evidence is available. Immensely important as the Linear B texts are, the historical information that they accumulate is not even remotely close to that contained in the documentary materials of the Near East. Some of these documents, such as the Hittite historical records relating to royal succession in the Old Hittite Kingdom, are addressed in the present book, but only as circumstantial evidence, as it were.

What the student of Greek prehistory has instead are literary sources originating in oral tradition. While it goes without saying that this tradition should not be treated on an equal footing with documentary sources nor used without being correlated with archaeological and linguistic evidence, it can nevertheless be employed with profit for the reconstruction of history. This is recognised even by those students of contemporary oral traditions who are best known for their critical attitude to the value of these historical traditions. Thus, according to Jan Vansina, 'Without oral traditions we would know very little about the past of large parts of the world, and we would not know them from the inside . . . Where there is no writing or almost none, oral traditions must bear the brunt of historical reconstruction.' In a similar vein, David Henige wrote: 'Regardless of this weakness, however, the body of oral tradition, real and potential, represents, together with archaeology and linguistics, nearly all that the historian of sub-Saharan Africa has to work with in his efforts to understand the more remote past.'[13] The question, however, is that of the terms on which the issue of the historicity of oral tradition should be approached.

There are two ways in which historical myth can be used for under- standing the past. First, it can be taken as telling us something about the past that it purports to describe; second, its historicity can be placed solely within the present, that is, within the period in which it was actually fixed. While older scholars favoured the first approach, the second is more widespread in our days. Within the last decade especially, the focus of attention has decisively shifted from the Mycenaean 'past' to the Archaic and Classical 'present' of Greek myth. This in itself is a welcome devel- opment, which compensates for earlier scholars' neglect of the myth's role as a vehicle for interpreting and legitimating historical circumstances in the present. What makes it difficult for me to adopt either unreservedly, however, is the extreme reductivism characteristic of both approaches. While one tends to see everything in historical myth as direct evidence of the past that the myth ostensibly describes, the other tends to deny to the myth any past dimension whatsoever. Yet the material at our disposal is much too complex to admit of such either/or assumptions.

Nobody today would deny that at any given moment historical myth functions as a cultural artefact representative of the period in which it circulates rather than the one which it purports to describe.[14] This would be even more true of traditional societies, in which the transmission of information is either entirely or predominantly oral. Thus, according to Jack Goody, the characteristic feature of such societies is the so-called homeostatic transformation, that is, a spontaneous process of adjusting the tradition to the society's contemporary circumstances.[15] However, this ought not to be taken to mean that, as is sometimes implied, the transformation of memory was total or that myths were invented anew each time they were told or enacted. Vansina's criticism of those anthropologists who, like T. O. Beidelman, deny all evidential value to traditions about the past, is directly relevant here:

13 Vansina 1985: 198–9; Henige 1974: 2–3.
14 On myth as cultural artefact see esp. J. Hall 1997: 40–2; Malkin 1998: 5–7; McInerney 1999: 29–30.
15 See e.g. Goody (2000), 42–6; Cf. Vansina (1985), 120–3. See also below, Chapter 8.

Beidelman cannot realistically claim that in every generation people invent a brand new past for themselves and believe it to be the past. His position goes against the dynamics of oral tradition and against the principle of selectivity and interpretation. Selectivity implies discarding certain information one has about the past and from that pool of information keeping only what is still significant in the present. However, the information that is retained, still comes from the past.[16]

Greek tradition could hardly be any different. Together with Ken Dowden, I cannot imagine that 'Greek mythology was invented as a whole new set of stories to replace what had gone before' and that 'in so traditional a society, stories were constantly being invented and discarded'.[17] Rather than inventing new stories, each generation reshaped the inherited myths anew according to its own cultural sensibilities and social agenda. But this reshaping had its limits. As Fritz Graf puts it, the myth is 'the stuff, a course of action fixed in general outline and with characters who are also fixed, which the individual poet can only vary within limits'.[18] In other words, if myths are cultural artefacts, we have also to postulate the materials out of which these artefacts were produced. To disentangle the original version of a myth from its later modifications, we have to ask ourselves why these modifications were introduced and what they came to replace.

To take only one example, in the First Olympian Pindar modifies what seems to be the traditional version of Pelops' story by offering one of his own making, more agreeable to the taste of the poet and his contemporaries: Pelops was taken to Olympus not to be dismembered, eaten and restored to life by the gods but because he was kidnapped by Poseidon, who fell in love with the handsome youth. Yet, as Walter Burkert showed in *Homo Necans*, the myth of dismemberment is a cultural reminiscence of a once widespread sacrificial practice.[19] In other words, however 'modernised' a given myth may be, we can often discern in it a residue of its past meaning. And, as far as Greek myth is concerned,

16 Vansina 1985: 190–1. Cf. also Vansina's criticism of Goody's earlier claim for total homeostasis, ibid. 121: 'In short there is congruence but there is no total congruence of content with the concerns of the present. Continuous selection of intentional historical accounts does not perfectly operate. The presence of archaisms in various traditions gives homeostasis the lie.'
17 Dowden 1992: 57. Cf. also the point made in Smith 1986: 177–9, that, rather than pure fabrication, even modern nationalist myths are as a rule made out of elements that had existed in an earlier tradition.
18 Graff 1991: 8: 'Der Mythos ist . . . der Stoff, ein in grossen Zügen festgelegter Handlungsablauf mit ebenso festen Personen, den der individuelle Dichter nur in Grenzen variiren kann.'
19 Pi. *O.* 1.26–7, 47–53; Burkert 1983: 93–103; cf. Graff 1991: 146–7.

it would invariably lead us to the Mycenaean civilisation of the second millennium BC.[20]

It may seem a truism to say that both dimensions of myth, the past and the present, are legitimate objects of scholarly research. However, some recent interpretations of Greek mythological tradition seem to proceed from the assumption that no study of the past dimension of myth is any longer possible or indeed legitimate. It is of course one thing to say 'I have little interest in myth as containing some kernel of truth',[21] and quite another to deny the study of the past dimension of myth the right to exist, as has become fashionable these days. Rather more often than not, this results in narrow interpretations which strip Greek myth (or any myth for that matter) of some of its most essential characteristics.

It is not only that the myths emerging from such a one-dimensional approach have no shadow, so to speak. Much more alarming is the fact that, while emphasising one important aspect of myth, namely its adaptation to changing circumstances, the approach in question tends to ignore the other, no less important one, namely the myth's essential stability. Accordingly, it fails to explain why the same myths were used and re-used for centuries in different social and historic circumstances. In that it fails to address the myth in its entirety, in the last analysis the non-essentialist approach to myth proves no less simplistic than the old fundamentalism that it came to replace. Yet, as any unprejudiced study of myth will show, myth is both changeable and stable at one and the same time, and these two aspects of it should be taken not as mutually exclusive but, rather, as mutually complementary. In Vansina's words, 'A body of tradition therefore reflects both the past and the present.'[22] This book is an attempt to do justice to both.

The main argument of this book is that the story of the Heroic Age as delivered in Pan-Hellenic tradition exhibits significant correlations with what archaeology and linguistics have to tell us about the situation in Greece in the second millennium BC. Whenever they disagree, this is usually due to the fact that the story of the Heroic Age is also a story of the time when the myth of the Heroic Age took on its standard form. This is especially true of the myth of the destruction of the Race of Heroes in the Trojan War. Significantly, it is at this point that we encounter a major discrepancy between Greek tradition and the archaeological and linguistic record. It is obvious indeed that the myth of the Trojan War, which is the principal explanation of the end of the Heroic Age adopted in

---

20 Cf. Dowden 1992: 60.   21 Malkin 1998: 7.   22 Vansina 1985: 122.

Pan-Hellenic tradition, cannot account for the fragmentation of the Greek dialects and the destructions that took place in mainland Greece at the end of the second millennium BC. We must therefore ask ourselves not only whether and to what extent the traditional story of the Heroic Age is reliable but also why this story was told at all. As I will argue in this book, while some aspects of the Greek myth of the Heroic Age preserve genuine traditions concerning the situation in Greece in the second millennium BC, others can only be properly understood when taken against the historic background of early Archaic Greece. In other words, there is no simple answer to the question whether the myth of the Heroic Age can be treated as a reliable source as regards the Bronze Age civilisation of Greece.

As we shall see in the next chapter, from the Archaic Age and up to the end of antiquity ancient poets and antiquarians operated with essentially the same mythological system. There can be little doubt that the main if not the only reason for this stability was the Pan-Hellenic character of the main body of Greek tradition. While the epichoric myths could well be tampered with for local or private purposes, the traditional stories that were in Pan-Hellenic circulation formed the generally agreed upon 'total system' (Dowden), and therefore were much less open to manipulation. As a result, the Pan-Hellenic tradition supplied the authoritative standard by which anomalies of any kind could effectively be checked. 'For each myth/subject, regardless of whether there is reference to a specific hypotext (this or that poet's telling), there is an intertext which, except in some peculiarly disputed or little-known myth, will amount to what Kullmann called *Faktenkanon*, a standard event-list.'[23]

An illuminating example of the verification of a local myth by bringing it into correspondence with the Pan-Hellenic tradition can be found in Pausanias' account of the early kings of Megara. Alkothoos son of Pelops killed the lion of Kithairon, married the daughter of the king Megareus, and became king in his stead. Yet Megareus had two sons of his own, Euippos and Timalkos. According to the Megarian version, Euippos was slain by the lion, whereas Timalkos, being one of the participants in the Dioscuri expedition, the purpose of which was to bring back Helen kidnapped by Theseus, was killed even earlier by the latter. Yet Pausanias shows that the Megarian version of the circumstances of Timalkos' death disagrees with the Pan-Hellenic tradition and therefore must be rejected as a local fabrication:

I wish I could write in accord with the Megarians, but am at a loss how to agree with them on everything they say. I do agree that the lion was killed on Kithairon by Alkathoos, but who wrote that Megareus' son Timalkos went to Aphidna with the Dioscuri? And how is he supposed to have fallen upon his arrival at the hands of Theseus when even Alcman, in his ode to the Dioscuri, says that they conquered Athens and took Theseus' mother prisoner but that Theseus himself was absent? And Pindar writes in the same manner . . . But it is clear to everyone who has ever dealt with genealogy that the Megarians know only too well that what they are doing is quite silly . . . As a matter of fact, they know the true story (τὸν ὄντα λόγον) but conceal it, for they would not admit that in the reign of Nisos their city was conquered, that Nisos' son-in-law Megareus succeeded him and that he himself was succeeded by his son-in-law Alkathoos.[24]

The distinction made by Vansina between official and private traditions seems to be directly relevant here: 'Most official traditions are accounts dealing with the history of the corporate group that keeps them. They were performed publicly, on occasions that had great meaning for that group and in the presence of the leaders of the group. They told the "truth" as guaranteed by the group . . . Private traditions only defend private interests and conformity with more general official tradition is not required.'[25] It is above all the conservative character of the mainstream tradition that allows us to approach even such late authors as Diodorus, Apollodorus or Pausanias as genuine representatives of the tradition in question.[26]

This is not to say that what I aspire to uncover are the historic facts behind each single traditional story. Rather, it is the study of the recurring patterns of behaviour which men and women of the past - no matter whether real or fictitious - were expected to follow under certain circumstances that is the focus of my attention. When a social practice becomes obsolete, but narrative patterns created by it continue to circulate in the popular tradition, it is only natural that the tradition, wherever it remains true to itself, should attempt to accommodate the inherited material to the social practices it now envisages as normal and recommendable. The divine intervention that prevents a human sacrifice in the extant versions of both the Sacrifice of Iphigenia and the Sacrifice of Isaac offers a good example. However, such accommodation almost never becomes absolute. 'Social change often leads to additions, not to suppression, leaving older

---

24 Paus. 1.41.4–5. See also below, pp. 67–8. On a similar case of drawing a clear-cut distinction between a local (the Spartan) and the Pan-Hellenic genealogical tradition see Hdt. 6.52–3.
25 Vansina 1985: 98. On the value of 'truth' in traditional poetry see e.g. Finkelberg (1998c), 69–93, 189–91, 151–60.
26 Cf. J. Hall 2002: 24–5. On the traditional character of Apollodorus' *Library* see also below, p. 28.

variants intact. Items that tend to be suppressed leave traces.'[27] And indeed, traces of the abandoned sacrificial practice are easily discernible in both the Greek and the Hebrew myth mentioned above.

In his 'Tyrannie et mariage forcé. Essai d'histoire sociale grecque' (1977) David Asheri demonstrated that a *casus fictus* preserved in the *Controversiae* of Seneca the Elder and describing the Greek tyrants' alleged custom of giving free-born women in marriage to their slaves is in fact a distant echo of a social practice which was deeply rooted in the realities of polis life and habitually set in motion in the emergency situation of *oligandria*, 'scantiness of men'. Asheri wrote in this connection:

In my opinion, the structural analysis of these myths and other similar phenomena, of traditions, aetiological and etymological legends, literary *Schablonen* and Utopias is not enough if it does not take into account the historic reality and social and ethical problematic of Greek societies afflicted by *oligandria* at the given historic period. In this case, as in many others, it is necessary to confront the problem of relationships between myth and history, without ever neglecting the possible existence of an infinity of intermediary mytho-historical stages. To treat myth as history would be as dangerous methodologically as to treat history as myth. All in all, it is wiser, I believe, to see in certain myths a reflection of history rather than to proceed in the opposite direction.[28]

One of my main objectives in this book is the identification within the mytho-historical continuum postulated by Asheri of recurrent patterns that can be shown to throw light on certain Bronze Age social practices – first and foremost the institution of royal marriage and the rule of succession – in order to restore at least some of them to their historic context. It would indeed be reasonable to suppose that, just as in later historic periods, prehistoric myths were also used to communicate meaningful messages by means of which the identities and social norms of those who took these myths as their own were articulated. In that they encapsulate in simple narrative structures the essentials of a given community's self-consciousness and routinely transmit these structures, however modified, from one generation to another, myths of the past are indispensable guides to the world in which the people who created them actually lived.

---

27 Vansina 1985: 122. See also below, Chapter 4.
28 Asheri 1977: 42. On criticism of the structuralist approach to historical traditions see also Vansina (1985), 161–5.

GROUP IDENTITY AND THE HELLENES

Throughout this book, I discuss various manifestations of group identity as articulated through shared self-identification, shared language, shared cult practices and the foundational myth. Alongside the identities of such population groups as the speakers of the so-called substratum languages of the Aegean or Late Bronze Age migrants to the Levant, I focus especially on the group whose identity is signalled by its self-identification 'Hellenes' and which broadly corresponds to what we mean today by 'ancient Greeks'. This subject, and particularly the question as to whether the modern category of ethnicity can be applied with profit to ancient Greek civilisation, has recently drawn much scholarly attention, especially in the studies of Edith Hall, Jonathan Hall, Irad Malkin and Jeremy McInerney, among others.[29] In what follows, I will try to define the place of the present book within the context of this discussion.

As the analysis of Greek genealogical tradition carried out in Chapter 2 shows, the population group that somewhere in the Archaic Age adopted the self-definition 'Hellenes' did not perceive itself as fully coextensive with 'the descendants of Hellen'. The latter designated a narrower sub-group based on a putative descent from the common ancestor. Although not without parallel in other traditional societies (see below, p. 35), such recognition by a population group of its own heterogeneity goes against the incorporating tendencies characteristic of systematic genealogy and should therefore be regarded as heavily marked. The awareness of the heterogeneity of 'Hellenes' can also be found in classical authors, especially Herodotus and Plato. The evidence they supply testifies to the fact that, rather than being based on common descent, belonging to the body of 'Hellenes' was articulated in social and juridical terms. The distinction drawn in Plato's *Menexenus* between 'Hellenes by nature' and 'Hellenes by convention' is especially pertinent (below, p. 37). This can only mean that the group identity 'Hellenes' was defined on broader grounds than those of common descent. As far as our evidence goes, it was expressed in common self-definition, common cult practices and the common foundational myth, all three having been self-imposed in the Archaic Age as part of the process of the thorough restructuring of Greek society to which classical scholars often give the name of Pan-Hellenism.[30]

29 E. Hall 1989; J. Hall 1997 and 2002; Malkin 1998 and 2003; McInerney 1999 and 2001.
30 On Pan-Hellenism see esp. Nagy 1979: 5–9 and 1990: 52–3; Strauss Clay 1989: 8–9; Slatkin 1991: 79–80; O'Brien 1993: 25, 30–1 and below, Chapter 8, but see already Rohde 1921: 39.

How would this assessment of Greek self-identification square with recent studies of Greek ethnicity? *Ancient Perceptions of Greek Ethnicity* (2001), issuing from a colloquium organised by Irad Malkin in 1997, is by any standard the most authoritative representation of the gamut of opinions held by leading scholars in the field. While all the contributors agree that ethnicity is a construct, their assessment of how it functioned in ancient Greece is far from uniform. Three main concepts of Greek ethnicity emerge and are applied both synchronically and diachronically. According to the first, considered particularly relevant to Archaic Greece, ethnicity is based on belief in common descent; the second is 'oppositional ethnicity', which was triggered by confrontation with the Persians and became predominant in the Classical Age; finally, in the Hellenistic Age, when belonging to the body of the 'Hellenes' increasingly became determined by Greek *paideia*, 'cultural ethnicity' comes to the fore. Herodotus' famous definition of the conditions of Greekness as 'common blood and common language, shared altars of gods and shared sacrifices, as well as the common customs' is often referred to or elaborated on, as for example in McInerney's formulation of ethnicity as 'the sense of peoplehood arising from shared blood, history, territory, language and customs'.[31] On the whole, however, Greek ethnicity emerges as an elusive category, changing from contributor to contributor and from period to period.[32]

Since 'oppositional' and the 'cultural' ethnicity are considered particularly appropriate for the Classical and Hellenistic periods, these constructions of ethnicity are less relevant to the present discussion. Not so in the case of ethnicity based on belief in shared descent. As we have seen, this form of ethnicity is generally recognised to have been predominant in early Greece. To quote what Jonathan Hall, the most prominent representative of the descent-based interpretation of ethnicity, wrote in his pioneering book *Ethnic Identity in Greek Antiquity*: 'Above all else, though, it must be the myth of shared descent which ranks paramount among the features that distinguish ethnic from other social groups, and, more often than not, it is proof of descent that will act as a defining criterion of ethnicity'.[33] I find Hall's definition both appropriate and helpful, in that it proposes a clear-cut criterion for identification of the ethnic group. This is not yet to say that Hall's construction of ethnicity

---

31 Hdt. 8.144.2 τὸ Ἑλληνικόν, ἐὸν ὅμαιόν τε καὶ ὁμόγλωσσον, καὶ θεῶν ἱδρύματά τε κοινὰ καὶ θυσίαι ἤθεά τε ὁμότροπα. Cf. McInerney 2001: 51.
32 See e.g. the review by M. C. Miller in *BMCR* (12 August 2002).
33 J. Hall 1997: 25; cf. J. Hall 2002: 9–19.

works particularly well when applied to Archaic Greece. We have seen indeed that, rather than basing the group identity 'Hellenes' on a myth of common descent, Greek heroic genealogy envisaged it as being shared by more than one descent group (see also Chapter 2). This incompatibility of the descent-based conception of ethnicity with the manner in which the early Greeks actually perceived themselves has been recognised by Irad Malkin. 'If genealogies mattered as defining ethnicity', he asks, 'why do we not find efforts to rework them in order to fit in the exceptions?'[34] The descent-based conception of Greek ethnicity supplies no answer to this question.

Malkin himself favours approaching ethnicity in cultural terms, ascribing especial importance to the 'shared foundational historical experience'.[35] In that it does justice both to the heterogeneity of Greek heroic genealogy and to the role that the myth of the Trojan War played in the formation of Greek identity, Malkin's approach more adequately represents the way in which the Greeks actually conceived of their identity than the narrower descent-based approach advanced by Hall.[36] At the same time, Malkin's cultural definition falls short of Hall's definition of ethnicity from the methodological point of view, in that it fails to draw a clear-cut distinction between ethnic identity and other culturally based group identities (for example, nation). That is, while one definition adequately describes ethnicity but is not applicable to the Greeks, the other is applicable to the Greeks but cannot serve as an exclusive definition of ethnicity. This is what makes me doubt that 'ethnicity' and 'ethnic group' are appropriate terms for describing the population group that identified itself as 'Hellenes'. The model of a regional federation, or *koinon*, as developed by Jeremy McInerney in his study of land and identity in ancient Phocis, seems much more promising in this respect.[37]

While territory is often referred to as an essential component of ethnic identity,[38] it is only too rarely that its role in the formation of the collective identity of a given population group has been the focus of scholarly attention. By analysing the epichoric myths of Phocis, McInerney has drawn a convincing picture of how, in virtue of their being bound by common territory, heterogeneous population groups who traced their

34 Malkin 2001: 11. This point is further elaborated on in Malkin 2003: 60–6.
35 Malkin 2003: 66.
36 Cf. e.g. the criticism by Antonaccio 2001: 115.
37 McInerney 1999. See also McInerney 2001.
38 See esp. J. Hall 1997: 2, 25, 32. Malkin 2003: 15, however, does not give this factor much importance.

descent to different origins eventually created a regional identity of their own, the most salient expression of which was the emergence of the eponymous hero (actually, two heroes) named Phocus:

> The Phocian *koinon* would come into existence only a generation before the Persian War, after the overthrow of Thessalian sovereignty. Thereafter the Phocians' federal body met at the Phocicon, minted federal coinage, and celebrated the victory over the Thessalians at the festival of Artemis Elaphebolos. But before this final political transformation could take place a Phocian identity had to be constructed. This was done through the myths associated with both heroes named Phocus, rendering in narrative form a process of state formation marked by territorial conflict and the establishment of borders.[39]

McInerney defines the Phocian regional identity as ethnic. Yet, just like the cultural definition discussed above, the territorial definition of ethnic identity does not stand the test of being a criterion of identity exclusive to an ethnic group. Moreover, as McInerney himself shows, Phocian collective identity lacks such an essential parameter of ethnicity as the belief in common descent: 'A more important feature of the story, however, is that the eponymous hero was not remembered as a progenitor. The Phocians were not blood descendants of Phocus but the inhabitants of a region named by him. Rather than being a divine ancestor, Phocus is an *archegetes*, making the creation of Phocis a process analogous to the founding of a colony.'[40] This is not what would be recognised as an ethnic group by Jonathan Hall and those other scholars who correctly see in descent the criterion that allows to distinguish effectively between ethnic and other social groups.[41] At the same time, the Phocian identity seems to be precisely the kind of group identity that can be compared with profit to the group identity of 'Hellenes'.

As McInerney's study makes clear, it is the results obtained in African anthropology rather than those drawn from the study of modern societies that are especially relevant to the group identity that is the subject of his discussion. The collection of essays *From Tribe to Nation in Africa. Studies in Incorporation Processes* (1970), edited by the anthropologists Ronald Cohen and John Middleton, seems especially relevant in this respect. In this collection, Cohen and Middleton set out to shift the focus of their colleagues' attention from ethnic to multi-ethnic groups:

---

39 McInerney 2001: 67.
40 McInerney 2001: 64.
41 Cf. e.g. Ronald Cohen's definition quoted in McInerney 2001: 67 n. 1: 'Ethnicity then is a set of descent-based cultural identifiers used to assign persons to groupings that expand and contract in inverse relation to the scale of inclusiveness and exclusiveness of the membership.'

Indeed we should like to recast the conceptualization of ethnicity itself through the understanding of processes which are involved in its emergence and change. To do this we have tried to indicate that ethnic units as clear-cut entities are sociological abstractions from situations that very often, especially in Africa, involve multi-ethnicity both traditionally and in the contemporary setting. If such is the case, we then need some concept to describe situations or groupings that are not homogeneous ethnically; and to such situations we would apply the term 'plural'.[42]

The case of multi-ethnic integration that has received most scholarly attention is naturally that of the nation-state. Yet, as Cohen and Middleton emphasise, among the studies in their book 'there are cases of non-state integration, that of societies that voluntarily or involuntarily find themselves to be parts of larger congeries of peoples'; such societies are based on intermarriage, common residence, membership in common cult groups and traditions of the common past.[43] As far as I can see, this would be a fair description not only of Phocian identity but also of the group identity of Hellenes. In recent years, Robert Fowler and Jonathan Hall have made a strong case for seeing the regional identity formed by the Pylaic Amphictiony, organised around the cult of Demeter at Anthela and later incorporated into the Delphic League, as the hard core of the identity of Hellenes.[44] Hall has also shown that this was the starting point of the process that culminated in the consolidation of Hellenic identity around the cult of Zeus at Olympia.[45] I would suggest, together with Malkin, that the myth of the common past as promulgated in the poems of Homer played no less important a role in the formation of Hellenic identity than common territory, common self-definition and common cult practices. On the whole, however, the picture of the 'Hellenes' as a heterogeneous population group integrated on the basis of common residence and membership in common cults that emerges from Hall's reconstruction closely corresponds to non-state integration observed in African societies.

I would also suggest that abstaining from the use of the categories 'ethnicity' and 'ethnic identity' would render Hall's reconstruction even more compelling. I find it symptomatic in this connection that Hall gives the title 'The Birth of a Nation' to a section that concludes his discussion

42 Cohen and Middleton 1970: 9.
43 Cohen and Middleton 1970: 7, 17; cf. Aidan Southall's contribution to the same volume: Southall 1970: 75–82.
44 Fowler 1998; J. Hall 2002: 144–54. See also Chapter 2.
45 J. Hall 2002: 154–71.

of the consolidation of Hellenic identity around the Olympian festival, and that a similar characterisation of Hellenic identity in national rather than ethnic categories can also be found in Malkin's latest book.[46] This is not to say I propose that in the ongoing discussion of Hellenic identity the category of 'ethnic group' should be replaced with that of 'nation', which certainly presents numerous terminological pitfalls of its own.[47] Yet, in virtue of the fact that it allows for the inclusion of heterogeneous ethnic components and embraces the sense of solidarity based on shared history and values, in some of its aspects 'nation' seems to suit the complex character of Hellenic identity much better than 'ethnic group' does.

However that may be, throughout this book I will be applying the term 'ethnic' only to the population groups that can be identified on the basis of common descent, either putative or otherwise, and the term 'multi-ethnic' to the units constituted by two or more population groups identified on the basis of common descent. When such descent-based identification cannot be shown to be relevant, I will use the general term 'population group'. And I will use the term 'descent group' when dealing with units identified on the basis of direct kinship, either putative or otherwise, such as, for example, clans.[48] I hope that these precautions will diminish the danger of a priori assumptions regarding the type of identity of the population groups under discussion.

Side by side with the construction of Hellenic identity, I will discuss the factors responsible for the specific form taken by it. It is indeed reasonable to suppose that, rather than being created *ex nihilo*, any given group identity emerges in response to external stimuli whose nature varies from one historic situation to another. Identity, in David Konstan's words, is 'a reactive phenomenon' and, as emphasised by Malkin, it does not write its past arbitrarily.[49] In other words, identity is not created in a vacuum, and therefore not everything about it is a construct. This would be especially true where, as in the historic situation discussed in the present book, one population group becomes partly replaced and partly absorbed by another. This comes close enough to what Carla Antonaccio

---

46 J. Hall 2002: 168; Malkin 2003: 66.
47 See e.g. Smith 1986: 6–18.
48 Cf. Morgan 2001: 83: 'Myth-historical claims of consanguinity form part of a continuing discourse of identity evident from Homer on and quite distinct from the kinship that primarily defines status and office in a tribal system (although this too is as much a social as a biological phenomenon).'
49 Konstan 2001: 30; cf. Malkin 2001: 16. Cf. also Smith 1986: 177–9.

observed for the situation in Sicily after Greek colonisation. She wrote in this connection:

It is, however, possible to establish an indigenous or local culture by proceeding from an examination of pre-Greek culture. This establishes baselines for difference, since local populations and their cultures existed before colonization and their identities are not wholly constructs of the colonizers. We can therefore use Smith's notion of 'coherence', provided by an examination of a 'full' past, Greek and indigenous, which limits the scope of ethnic invention and at the same time encompasses more than a selection of criteria. A full past accounts for all the data that exist rather than attending to only one discourse.[50]

There is an additional reason why those elements in the identity of population groups that go beyond their own self-awareness ought not to be neglected in scholarly research. The issue of Anatolian languages, one of the focal points of this book, provides an illustration. Anatolian languages have recently drawn much international attention, triggered by the article 'Language-tree divergence times support the Anatolian theory of Indo-European origin' published by the evolutionary biologists Russel Gray and Quentin Atkinson in *Nature* in November 2003.[51] Using computational methods derived from evolutionary biology, Gray and Atkinson arrived at results that ostensibly corroborate the so-called Indo-Hittite hypothesis as formulated by the American linguist E. H. Sturtevant in the 1940s. According to this hypothesis, rather than being sister-languages of Greek, Italo-Celtic, German, Slavic, Indo-Iranian and other languages constituting the Indo-European family, Anatolian languages separated from the proto-Indo-European unity at a very early period and therefore represent a much less advanced stage in the development of Indo-European. More specifically, Gray and Atkinson claimed that the results they obtained corroborate the hypothesis that Colin Renfrew advanced in *Archaeology and Language* (1987): according to this hypothesis, the first European farmers that arrived from Anatolia in the course of the so-called Neolithic Revolution (the seventh millennium BC) were Indo-European speakers (see also below, Chapter 3).

Both the validity of the results obtained by Gray and Atkinson and the question whether scientific methods drawn from another discipline are applicable to the study of languages are now a matter of scholarly debate.[52]

---

50 Antonaccio 2001: 125. Cf. Smith 1986: 177–9.
51 Gray and Atkinson (2003).
52 See e.g. M. Balter, 'Early date for the birth of Indo-European languages', *Science* 302 (28 November 2003): 1490–1 and 'Search for the Indo-Europeans', *Science* 303 (27 February 2004), 1323–6; N. Wade, 'A biological dig for the roots of language', *NYT* (16 March 2004).

Yet reports of this publication have also made their way into the popular press and earned such ill-informed headlines as 'Origin of the English language comes from Turkey' or even 'Auckland University researchers have stunned academics worldwide by tracing the origins of the English language to Turkish farmers'.[53] Moreover, the article by Gray and Atkinson was also discussed by right-wing groups on the Internet, and the claim was made that both the article and especially the press reaction to it are all part of a large international conspiracy to brainwash the public into believing that 'white people' (that is, Indo-Europeans) are descended from 'Turks' (that is, from Anatolia).[54] This is the 'full past' as constructed outside the academy. Whether we like it or not, the past never remains empty, and if we shrink from proposing 'full' hypotheses of it, reducing our construction to some aspects of the past at the expense of others, the vacuum thus produced will be filled by sensational news stories that encourage the spread of bigotry and ignorance.

53 I owe this reference to J. Clackson, 'What I do in Hittite', *TLS* (5 March 2004): 29.
54 See the thread '[Indo-European] language tree "rooted in Anatolia"' at www.stormfront.org/forum/showthread.php?t=101896&page=4&pp (Stormfront White Nationalist Community), November 2003–March 2004.

CHAPTER 2

The heterogeneity of Greek genealogy

GREEK GENEALOGICAL TRADITION

Like traditional poetries of other peoples, the traditional poetry of the Greeks celebrated the Heroic Age.[1] This was the time when men were bigger and stronger, and they performed marvellous feats of prowess. Their weapons were made of bronze and not of iron, and they were ruled by kings. Mycenae, a small town in historic times, was the capital of a great kingdom. The gods not only kept company with mortals, but even consorted with mortal women and conceived children with them. This is why the heroes of Greek legend, mortal though they were, were considered divine offspring, 'demigods', and belonged to the Race of Heroes. The Heroic Age came to an end in two great wars - the Theban and the Trojan, which were especially designed by Zeus to put an end to the Race of Heroes. Introducing a terminology strikingly similar to that used in modern archaeology, Hesiod placed the Heroic Age between the Bronze Age and the Iron Age, the poet's own time.[2] This was how the Mycenaean Greek civilisation of the second millennium BC was remembered in historic Greece.

Two distinct epic traditions specialised in perpetuating the memory of the Heroic Age. Side by side with the heroic epic proper, mostly associated with the name of Homer, there also flourished the tradition of the didactic epic, whose most prominent representative was Hesiod. The two traditions approached the Heroic Age from different perspectives. Genealogical lore, only marginal for the heroic epic, constituted the very core of the didactic tradition, its true *raison d'être*. In the eyes of the Greek audience, the dry and apparently uninspiring material of the genealogies was hardly less important than the poems of Homer. To demonstrate this,

---

1 On the comparative aspects of the myth of a Heroic Age see Chadwick 1912; Chadwick and Chadwick 1932: 13–18.
2 *Cypria* fr. 1 Bernabé; Hes. *Erga* 159–73; Hes. Fr. 204.95–105 M-W. See also below, Chapter 7.

it is enough to recall that when the first prose compositions of historical character, those of the so-called 'logographers', began to appear towards the end of the sixth century BC, they dealt almost exclusively with preparing what would be described today as critical editions of heroic genealogies. Hecataeus of Miletus dealt with the legends of Heracles and Deukalion and their descendants, as well as with other families that claimed heroic or divine descent; Acusilaus of Argos concentrated on Argive genealogies and traced the origin of the human race back to the Argive hero Phoroneus rather than to Deukalion, the founder of the human race in the mainstream tradition; Pherecydes of Athens brought heroic genealogies down to the Athenian families of his own times; finally, in his *Deukalioneia, Phoronis, Atlantis, Asopis* and *Troika* Hellanicus of Lesbos covered the entire range of traditional genealogy. Oral perform-ances of heroic genealogies enjoyed enormous prestige at least up to the time of Plato,[3] and traditional genealogical learning formed the core of what was later to become the standard corpus of Greek mythology in both Greece and Rome.

Preservation of the genealogies has always been a matter of great importance in traditional societies. The genealogies not only served as the most effective means for defining an individual's identity but also guaranteed one's rights and social status. As late as the end of the nineteenth century, the first question asked when two Kirghiz met was 'Who are your seven fathers-ancestors?', and every seven-year-old Kirghiz boy could recite his ancestors for at least six generations.[4] Genealogy also served for the articulation of collective identities of entire population groups. Among the Alur of Central Africa, more than a dozen ruling lines trace their descent to a single line of chiefs twelve generations ago; the beginning of the line corresponds to the group's first entry into the country upon their crossing of the Nile about three centuries ago. Traditions relating to the arrival from the Hawaiki homeland of the Great Fleet of seven canoes and their settlement of New Zealand in the fourteenth century are preserved among the Maori till today, to-gether with the names of six of the canoes and the genealogies of their leaders.[5]

3 See Pl. *Hipp.M.* 285b–e; cf. West 1985: 8; Thomas 1989: 173–5; Fowler 1998: 1; J. Hall 2002: 30.
4 On Central Asia see Chadwick and Chadwick 1940: 10, 140–1 and Chadwick and Zhirmunsky 1969: 18, 171–2; on a similar practice as attested for colonial Burundi see Vansina 1985: 182–3.
5 On the Alur see Southall 1970: 76–7; on the Maori see Walker 1992: 180; on Polynesia in general see Chadwick and Chadwick 1940: 235–9, 390–3. On a more nuanced approach to Maori traditions of the Great Fleet see Henige 1974: 22, 85–6, 100–2; his general scepticism

But there is always a point at which genealogical tradition merges into myth. To quote what the Chadwicks wrote in the *The Growth of Literature*, 'The family genealogies, especially those of royal lines, seem as a rule to be trustworthy for a certain number of generations before the time when they were first committed to writing . . . Beyond a certain point suspicious names usually appear; and the genealogies are extended into mythical elements.'[6] The same is true of king-lists. A list of Kuba rulers collected in 1908–9 contained no fewer than 121 names, of which only the last thirty-three represented a reasonably accurate account of the Kuba kings; the rest were eponyms, toponyms and patronyms. As Henige plausibly argued, the same explanation would also hold good of the genealogy of the First Dynasty of Babylon, of the twenty-eight names of which only the last nine are identical to the names of the first nine rulers of the dynasty and therefore can be regarded as reliable. According to the assessment of the genealogical tradition of the Asante by Jack Goody, 'The first king was followed directly by one in whose time the Asante threw off the yoke of Denkyira and became independent; that is, it jumps straight to the seventeenth century. The doings of later kings in such histories may be recalled by objects or skulls attached to the stool or the state drums.'[7] The Maori scholar Ranginui Walker characterises Maori tradition as follows:

While myth events were located in a remote past, traditions have a depth of twenty-six generations, or six and a half centuries. Yet despite this difference, the distinction between myth and tradition is not sharply demarcated. Undoubtedly the actors in the traditions were real men, but their activities have much in common with their mythological predecessors. That is to say, they were remote enough in time to be endowed with supra-normal powers. They also exhibited personality traits reminiscent of the heroes of mythology. The early traditions also transmitted myth-messages.[8]

Greek tradition was no exception. As in other traditional societies, for the ancient Greeks genealogy was the starting point from which they defined their identity and their relations to other peoples. Take for example the standard sequence that usually opens the Greek genealogies (Fig. 1): Deukalion → Hellen → Aiolos, Doros, Xouthos (or, according

notwithstanding, Henige recognises that there is a closer agreement between the archaeological and traditional evidence for New Zealand than for most of the other islands, see ibid. 40.
6 Chadwick and Chadwick 1940: 803.
7 Henige 1974: 46–7; Goody 2000: 31. Cf. Southall 1970: 76–7.
8 Walker 1992: 180.

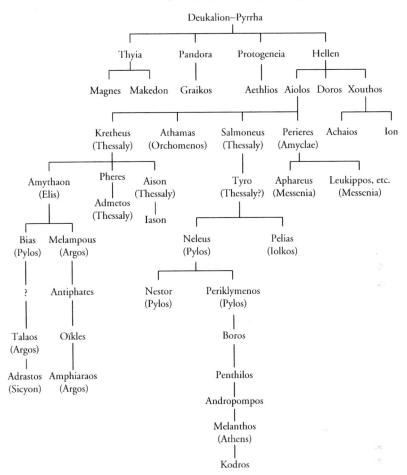

Figure 1. The descendants of Hellen (after West 1985 and Finkelberg 1999).

to Hecataeus fr. 13, Deukalion → Pronoos → Hellen).[9] But the tradition also credits Deukalion with three daughters - Thyia, Pandora and Protogeneia. All of them were impregnated by Zeus to become the mothers of Magnes and Makedon (Thyia), Graikos (Pandora) and Aethlios, the progenitor of the Aetolians (Protogeneia). The position of Magnes, Makedon, Graikos and Aethlios as sons of Hellen's sisters signals that although the Greeks did see themselves as closely related to the Magnetes, the Graikoi, the Macedonians and the Aetolians, they nevertheless

9 The genealogical stemmas adduced in Figs. 1 and 2 proceed from West 1985: 173–8.

regarded those tribes dwelling to their north as distinct from the Hellenes proper.[10]

The systematic character of the Greek genealogical tradition was fully realised only in 1967, with the publication of *Fragmenta Hesiodea* by Reinhold Merkelbach and Martin L. West. The major achievement of these scholars was the reconstruction of the structure of the *Catalogue of Women*, or *Ehoiai*, a comprehensive genealogical poem composed within the Hesiodic School sometime during the Archaic Age but undoubtedly belonging to the centuries-long genealogical tradition of the Greeks.[11] Study of the new material supplied by the papyri and analysis of both this material and the extant fragments of the poem against the general background of Greek genealogical tradition allowed Merkelbach and West to make sense of what had formerly existed as a bulk of disconnected fragments, and to reinstate the *Catalogue* as the most authoritative source on Greek genealogical lore. Another important result of the reconstruction was the realisation that the order of the Greek genealogies as represented in the later compendia, notably in Apollodorus' *Library*, is strictly traditional, which means that from the Archaic Age and up to Late Antiquity ancient antiquarians operated with approximately the same genealogical scheme.[12]

This would mean that, contrary to what many are inclined to believe, even a falsification of one's genealogical position could not be carried out arbitrarily, that is, without making it consistent in terms of the universally agreed upon system. 'It must not be supposed, however', the Chadwicks wrote about Polynesian genealogical lore, 'that this falsifying of the genealogies was an arbitrary or excessive aberration. . . Indeed both the conservation and the modification of the genealogies were guarded with the strictest jealousy, and often secrecy, by the most intellectual members of the community.'[13] That is to say, rather than changing the system, the

---

10 Cf. West 1985: 10: 'When Magnes and Makedon are made the sons of a sister of Hellen, this is a declaration that the Magnetes and Macedonians to the north of Thessaly are not Hellenes, not quite on a level with Hellenes, but akin to them.' On Makedon see also J. Hall 1997: 64: 'This line of descent *excludes* him from the Hellenic genealogy - and hence, by implication, the Macedonians from the ranks of Hellenism' (Hall's italics). On the Aetolians see J. Hall 1997: 47 and n. 104; on the question of the Greekness of the northwestern tribes in general see Malkin 1998: 142–50.

11 Janko 1982a: 85–7, places the *Catalogue of Women* in the seventh century BC, whereas West 1985: 136, argues for a later date in the middle of the sixth century. On the traditional character of the *Catalogue* see Finkelberg 1988: 32–5.

12 See West 1985: 45; Fowler 1998: 2.

13 Chadwick and Chadwick 1940: 392; cf. Finnegan 1977: 188–9. See also Vansina 1985: 38–9, on the *mwaaddy* of the Kuba, whose expertise was 'limited to questions of royal succession for which he had to know the precedents'. On the phenomenon as a whole see Goody 2000: 30–2.

experts who were responsible for the creation of new genealogies would modify their client's lineage so that it fitted into the pre-existing scheme. Thus, when in the fifth century BC Hellanicus made a claim that the Macedonians were Greeks by race, he made Makedon one of Aiolos' sons and thereby a descendant of Hellen; the Athenian tyrant Pisistratus' claiming descent from the Neleids of Pylos, from whom the kings of Athens were also descended, obviously also belongs here.[14] 'Greek mythology', as Dowden put it, 'is an "intertext", because it is constituted by all the representations of myths ever experienced by its audience and because every new representation gains its sense from how it is positioned in reality to this totality of previous presentations.'[15]

As a result, while individual and local genealogies could well fluctuate,[16] the Pan-Hellenic genealogical scheme largely remained untouched. However sophisticated the attempts to trace one's descent to the Heroic Age might be, this could not possibly affect the Pan-Hellenic genealogy, which never reached farther than the aftermath of the Trojan War. Neleus and Pelias, Amphiaraos and Adrastos were always represented as descendants of Aiolos, and Agamemnon and Menelaus as descendants of Pelops; Perseus was always a descendant of Lynkeus and Hypermestra, and Heracles was always Perseus' descendant. Had the entire body of Greek genealogy been totally reinvented each time when a new line was introduced, this would have resulted in a large number of mutually incompatible genealogical charts rather than in the reasonably stable system that we have at our disposal.

But how old is the scheme on which Greek genealogy is based? To quote the famous couplet which in all probability belonged in the introductory part of the *Catalogue of Women*,

"Ελληνος δ ' ἐγένοντο φιλοπτολέμου βασιλῆος
Δῶρός τε Ξοῦθός τε καὶ Αἴολος ἱππιοχάρμης.

'And Hellen, king fond of war, gave birth to Doros, Xouthos and Aiolos excelling in chariot-fighting.'[17] The fact, however, is that, beyond the genealogical scheme as such, Hellen does not function as a full-blooded mythological personage endowed with a distinctive 'life' of his own. The

---

14 Hellan. F 74 Jacoby; Hdt. 5.65.3–4. On Macedonian identity see now J. Hall 2001.
15 Dowden 1992: 8.
16 See e.g. Thomas 1989: 161–73, on the Philaid genealogy. On the distinction between the common and the local traditions see above, pp. 13–14.
17 Hes. Fr. 9 M-W.

explanation that most readily suggests itself is that he never was such a personage.

Everything points to the conclusion that the name 'Hellenes' was adopted as a self-definition of the Greeks not earlier than the Archaic Age. Homer applies it only to the inhabitants of Achaia Phthiotis in southern Thessaly, and it is in Achaia Phthiotis again that Hellen was generally believed to have been king.[18] Judging by the evidence of the epic tradition, the Greeks of the Heroic Age were identified as 'Argives', 'Danaoi' and, above all, 'Achaeans'. All this was well known to Thucydides:

> For it appears that Hellas never did anything in common before the Trojan War. And it seems to me that Hellas as a whole did not yet bear this name then, and that even the name 'Hellenes' did not exist at all before the time of Hellen, the son of Deukalion . . . Homer is the best witness to this: although he lived long after the Trojan War, he never uses this name ['Hellenes'] generally but applies it exclusively to the men of Achilles who came from Phthiotis. These were the first Hellenes; otherwise, the names that he uses in his poems are 'Danaoi', 'Argives' and 'Achaeans' . . . Thus, owing to their weakness and the lack of contact, all those separate Hellenic states which had a common language (ἀλλήλων ξυνίεσαν) and were afterwards called by a common name never embarked on a common enterprise before the Trojan War.[19]

It is not out of the question that the choice of Achaia Phthiotis as the homeland of Hellen was mainly due to the close proximity of Thermopylae, the place of the Pylaic Amphictiony out of which the Delphic Amphictiony most probably evolved. In Robert Fowler's words, 'The period of growth [of the Pylaic Amphictiony] corresponds exactly to the period in which the term "Hellas" was first extended. Even more suspiciously, the boundaries of this newly extended "Hellas" and those of the amphiktyony largely overlapped. This does not seem coincidental.'[20]

---

18 It is notoriously difficult to draw a clear-cut distinction between Homeric Phthia, historical Achaia Phthiotis and Hellas in which Deukalion and Hellen are said to have dwelt. See esp. Str. 9.5.6, p. 431: 'Some say that Phthia is the same as Hellas and Achaia and that of the two parts into which Thessaly as a whole is divided these form the other, the southern, one; but others distinguish between them.' Cf. *Il.* 2.530, 9.395, 447, 478, 16.595.

19 Thuc. 1.3. Cf. *Il.* 2. 684; Str. 8.6.6, p. 370. On Hellen's whereabouts see West 1985: 53 n. 43, 57; Kirk 1985: 202 (on *Il.* 2.529–30), 229 (on *Il.* 2.683–4); Fowler 1998: 9–11 (with bibliography); J. Hall 2002: 125–34.

20 Fowler 1998: 11. On the Pylaic Amphictiony see Roux 1979: 1–4; Lefévre 1998: 13–16; McInerney 1999: 162–5; on its association with the diffusion of the terms 'Hellas' and 'Hellenes' see J. Hall 2002: 144–54, esp. 152: 'The first *amphiktyones* are located in precisely the area that is named "Hellas" in the *Iliad*.'

It is not only Hellen himself who appears to be a post-factum genealogical construct with no background in the Heroic Age. The same would also be true of the other members of the initial group, namely, Hellen's sons Aiolos, Doros and Xouthos, and Xouthos' sons Ion and Achaios. All of them, with the possible exception of Xouthos,[21] are obviously hardly more than products of genealogical speculation meant to account for historic divisions among the Greeks of later periods.

Side by side with such late additions, there are also some significant gaps. Compare, for example, the case of the Phrygians. The Phrygians spoke an Indo-European language closely related to Greek, which allows us to suppose that their position as regards the Greeks could not have differed much from that of the Macedonians.[22] Yet, no ancestor of the Phrygians is mentioned in Greek genealogies on a par with Makedon and Graikos. This 'structural amnesia' was obviously due to the fact that, as distinct from the Macedonians who remained in their original habitat in southeastern Europe, the Phrygians moved to Anatolia in the time of the great migrations at the end of the Bronze Age.[23] Analogous processes apparently resulted in certain peoples, like the Medes or the Latini, who under no circumstances could have been known to the Greeks of the Bronze Age, becoming attached to Greek genealogies only because they came to be a conspicuous part of the Greek cultural horizon at later periods.[24]

---

21 Xouthos has some mythological substance as the hero who helped the Athenian king Erechtheus in his war against Euboea, married his daughter and became king. Eur. *Ion* 57–64, 289–98; Str. 8.7.1, p. 383; Paus. 7.1.2.

22 Note that some of the ostensibly isolated Greek words, which are often associated with the so-called pre-Hellenic substratum, in fact have parallels in Macedonian or Phrygian. Thus Greek *thalassa*, 'sea', and *wanakt-*, 'ruler', are the same as Macedonian *dalangkha* and Phrygian *vanakt-*: cf. Lejeune 1972: 108; Neumann 1979: 824. On the pre-Hellenic substratum see below, Chapter 3.

23 Hdt. 7.73; Str. 14.5.29, pp. 680–1; Xanthus 765 F 14 Jacoby. Cf. Mellink 1991: 621. Linguistic considerations speak against the argument expounded in Drews 1993a: 65–6 and 1993b: 9–26, that the tradition of the Phrygian migration from Europe to Asia is a fifth-century BC invention. Of all the languages of the East Indo-European group only Greek, Macedonian and Phrygian are *centum* languages, that is, they did not develop the palatalisation of the velar consonants characteristic of the other East Indo-European languages (Armenian, Albanian, Indo-Iranian, the Slavic and Baltic languages). This common retention can only be accounted for if we assume that the Greeks, Macedonians and Phrygians jointly separated from the proto-Indo European unity and left before the Balkans before satemisation of the rest of the East Indo-European languages had taken place. Had Greek and Phrygian separated before the arrival of the Greeks in the Balkans, Phrygian should have been related to Greek approximately as are Armenian or Iranian, which also belong to the Eastern group of Indo-European languages and are quite close to Greek. On East Indo-European and Greek see Mallory 1989: 108; cf. West 1997: 2 n. 2. On 'structural amnesia' see Henige 1974: 27.

24 Medeios, eponym of the Medes, Hes. *Th.* 1000–1; Latinos, eponym of the Latini, Hes. *Th.* 1011–13. Cf. West 1966: 430, 436 and 1985: 130–1. On Latinos see also Jameson and Malkin 1998.

All this strongly suggests that, contrary to the message that it ostensibly transmits, the overarching genealogical scheme on which the standard corpus of Greek genealogy is based cannot be traced back to the Heroic Age. This does not mean, however, that it did not incorporate genealogical traditions much older than the genealogy of Hellen proper. To see that this was indeed the case it will be sufficient to turn to the stemma of Aiolos.

'Wherever the family tree becomes bushy, instead of tracing only a stem, wherever it remains relatively unpatterned, it may well be valid, especially when the various ancestral figures do not all become founders of social groups now recognised as communities.'[25] As distinct from the stemmas of Hellen's other sons, that of Aiolos is not only 'bushy' but also abounds in mythological material relating to the Heroic Age.[26] Thus, all the protagonists of the Argonautic saga (Athamas, Pelias, Aison, Iason) are envisaged as descendants of Aiolos. Other early Aiolids are Sisyphos, an important mythological figure in his own right, and his grandson Bellerophon; Tyro, mother of Neleus and Pelias, a consort of Poseidon and one of the most prominent female figures in Greek genealogy; Neleus, who became the progenitor of an important line which included Homeric Nestor; Admetos, famous for his friendship with Apollo and for the self-sacrifice of his wife Alkestis, herself a descendant of Aiolos; the seer Melampous and his brother Bias who became the founders of the royal dynasty of Argos; their descendants Amphiaraos and Adrastos, who played leading parts in the concluding stages of the Theban saga, and Amphiaraos' sons Amphilochos and Alkmaon, both among the leaders of the Epigoni.[27]

Considering that the descendants of Aiolos are associated with such prominent centres of Mycenaean civilisation as Iolkos, Pylos, Amyclae and others, we can conclude that it was above all this stemma that was envisaged as standing for the people whom we identify today as the Mycenaean Greeks.[28] Their post-factum identification as 'descendants of

---

25 Vansina 1985: 183.

26 Cf. J. Hall 1997: 48; McInerney 1999: 135.

27 Oddly enough, not many descendants of Aiolos participated in the Trojan War, and those who did were not very prominent. Among those whose descent from Aiolos is certain are Nestor and his son Antilochos; Amphilochos and Alkmaon sons of Amphiaraos (non-Homeric); Adrastos' nephew Euryalos; Eumelos son of Admetos and Alkestis and the northerners Protesilaos and Podarkes.

28 One can only wonder to what degree this picture depended on the Aeolian tradition on which the mainstream Greek epic tradition was substantially based. On the Aeolian tradition see e.g. West 1988: 162–5.

Hellen' reveals Greek awareness about the fact that the ethnic group that in the Archaic Age began to identify itself in this way had been present on the territory of Greece also in the periods in which the eponym 'Hellen' had not yet been available. As the decipherment of Linear B has shown, this would be a fair assessment of the situation in Greece in the second millennium BC.

'HELLENES BY NATURE' AND 'HELLENES BY CONVENTION'

The remarkable fact about Greek genealogy, however, is that the stemma of Hellen does not cover the entire nomenclature of mythological person-ages associated with the Heroic Age. The standard Greek genealogy opens with the stemma of Deukalion, which includes Hellen and his descend-ants, then takes a fresh start by introducing the stemma of Inachos/Phoroneus and their descendants, and ends with minor stemmas of the descendants of Pelasgos (= the Arcadians); of Atlas; of Asopos, among them Achilles and Aias; of Kekrops (= the Athenians) and of Pelops, among them Agamemnon and Menelaus; it invariably ends with the description of the Trojan War and the Returns, the two events that concluded the Heroic Age.[29]

As this arrangement shows, by no means all the heroes of Greek legend were regarded as descendants of Hellen. The most prominent of the stemmas that do not derive from Hellen was without doubt that of the river Inachos and his son Phoroneus. Characteristically, this stemma can be traced back much farther than that of Deukalion: eighteen gener-ations before the Trojan War as against nine in the case of the descendants of Hellen (Fig. 2). It can hardly be doubted that both the length of the stemma and especially its origins in a river communicate a message of its 'more or less' indigenous character.[30] This would not be surprising had the stemma of Inachos represented a local genealogy, as for example in the case of Athens, where since the fifth century BC autochthony and Hellenic descent were alternately used to advance the Athenians' claim to superior-ity.[31] We have seen, however, that the stemma of Inachos is an integral

---

29 For the comprehensive genealogical charts see West 1985: 173–82.
30 Cf. Dowden 1992: 75: 'To be son of a river is a statement of autochthony.' On being 'more or less indigenous' see Cohen and Middleton 1970: 12: 'By this term we mean that any group which has occupied a territory longer is "indigenous" with respect to the other one.'
31 See Konstan 2001: 32–41, esp. 40: 'Autochthony in general depended on local rather than Pan-Hellenic myths.' On the contradictory character of the Athenian claims see J. Hall 1997: 51–6; Isaac 2004: 111–13.

Greeks and Pre-Greeks

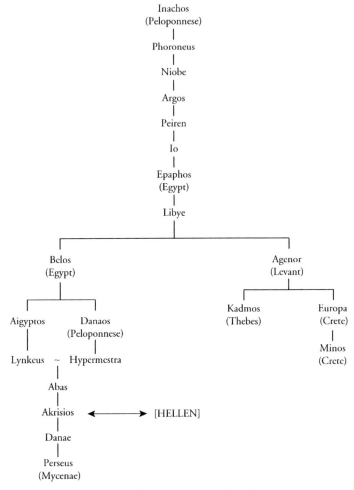

Figure 2. The descendants of Inachos.

part of the Pan-Hellenic genealogical system, which can only mean that both the heterogeneity of its origins and its claim to autochthony were generally agreed upon. Moreover, the stemma of Inachos was also a particularly ramified one. It was envisaged as spreading as far as Egypt and the Levant and associated with such important centres of the Mycenaean civilisation as Mycenae, Tiryns, Thebes and Knossos. Finally, it included such well-known personages of Greek legend as Io, Danaos, Kadmos, Minos, Oedipus, Perseus and Heracles, to mention only a few.

Yet, no effort was made to subsume the descendants of Inachos or, for that matter, many other illustrious men and women of the Heroic Age under the stemma of Hellen.

Thus, in the final analysis, the standard Greek genealogy emerges as an aggregate of mutually unconnected stemmas, each of them traced to a separate progenitor of its own: a far cry indeed from a unified genealogical tree, such as that of the descendants of Noah. The heterogeneous character of Greek genealogy is made especially clear by the fact that several non-Hellenic stemmas even offer alternative candidates for the role of 'Noah'. Thus, according to the Peloponnesian tradition, Phoroneus son of Inachos rather than Deukalion son of Prometheus was the only survivor after the Flood and therefore the founder of the human race, and a similar story was told of Aiakos, the progenitor of the Myrmidones.[32] In view of this, it is difficult to avoid the conclusion that Greek genealogical lore envisaged the population groups that inhabited heroic Greece as ultimately not of the same descent.

This compares well with some well-attested cases of ethnic incorporation studied by modern anthropology. Aidan Southall's work on the Alur of Central Africa seems to be especially relevant. The Alur are a people of the Lwoo group, divided among many chiefdoms and living on both sides of the boundary between Uganda and Zaire. At the same time, nearly all Alur traditions also include non-Lwoo ethnic groups. Some of the latter exist today as large tribes in their own right, with their own languages and cultures; that is to say, the incorporation by the Alur affected only parts of the ethnic groups in question. In addition, there are other non-Lwoo ethnic groups, some of them consisting of a number of separate sections scattered over Alurland and in different chiefdoms. Some of these groups, as for example Palei, found in several major chiefdoms, trace their origins to a legendary ruler whose descent line differs from that of Alur chiefs. 'This myth integrates a large number of themes', Southall writes. 'It establishes an august origin for Palei, which no one cares to deny. But it is an origin which is nonetheless clearly distinct from the patrilines of Alur chiefs. Yet no one would suggest that Palei were not Alur.'[33]

In a similar manner, even those who did not count as descendants of Hellen were nevertheless considered Hellenes in historic Greece. Thus,

---

32 Phoroneus: Acusilaus 2 F 23a Jacoby; Aiakos: Hes. Fr. 205 M-W; Str. 8.6.16, p. 375; cf. West 1985: 162–3.
33 Southall 1970: 72–3; cf. McInerney 1999: 27–8 and 2001: 60.

Herodotus tells us that the Athenian tyrannicides Harmodios and Aristogeiton were descendants of Kadmos, that is, ultimately, of Inachos; in the fifth century BC the Gephyraeans, a clan of Theban refugees to which the two belonged, continued to preserve their native cults, among them the cult of Demeter Achaiia, in which the Athenians, Ionians by race, were not allowed to participate.[34] Yet it is hard to imagine that this might mean that Harmodios and Aristogeiton did not count as Hellenes (for example, that they would not be admitted to the Olympian Games) or spoke a language other than Greek. Likewise, the only reason why the members of the Macedonian royal family became recognised as Hellenes was that they were able to trace their descent to Heracles, another representative of the non-Hellenic stemma of Inachos (see below). Herodotus' observation to the effect that, in so far as they belonged to the descent line of Inachos, both Heracles himself and the Dorian kings who claimed to be his descendants could not be regarded as Hellenes by race, is directly relevant here. His detailed account of the Pan-Hellenic tradition regarding the Dorian kings is especially illuminating:

In what follows I adduce the general tradition of the Greeks (κατὰ τὰ λεγόμενα ὑπ' Ἑλλήνων). Up to Perseus son of Danae (that is, without taking into account the god) the kings of the Dorians are correctly incorporated into Hellenic genealogy (καταλεγομένους . . . ὑπ' Ἑλλήνων) and correctly shown to be Hellenes, for even at this early date they had already become reckoned among Hellenes (ἐς Ἕλληνας . . . ἐτέλεον). The reason why I said 'up to Perseus' and did not start my count further up is that no name of a mortal father can be attached to Perseus like Amphitryon's name to Heracles . . . But one who goes up from Danae daughter of Akrisios and counts all her forefathers would discover that the leaders of the Dorians were in all probability genuine Aegyptians (Αἰγύπτιοι ἰθαγενέες). This is, then, Perseus' genealogy as given by the Hellenes (ταῦτα μέν νυν κατὰ τὰ Ἕλληνες λέγουσι γεγενεηλόγηται). Yet according to the Persian story Perseus himself was an Assyrian who became a Hellen (ἐγένετο Ἕλλην), but his ancestors did not.[35]

Herodotus' contention that, in spite of their being 'genuine Aegyptians', from Perseus' time onwards the ancestors of the Dorian kings 'became reckoned among Hellenes' is especially noteworthy. Generally speaking, the expression τελεῖν εἴς τινας applies to the cases in which an individual or a group of people becomes certified as a legitimate member of a larger body; the bestowing of citizenship provides the closest

---

34 Hdt. 5.57; 5.61.
35 Hdt. 6. 53–4. Cf. also 2.43: 'Both parents of Heracles, Amphitryon and Alkmena, were descended from Aigyptos and therefore were Aegyptians.' Cf. Thomas 2001: 220–2.

parallel.[36] That belonging to the body of the Hellenes could well be treated in the same terms follows also from another passage in Herodotus, where he tells how at the time when another non-Hellenic stemma, that of the Athenians, was in the process of becoming 'to be reckoned among Hellenes', the Pelasgians became their fellow inhabitants (*sunoikoi*) and as a result of this were also made Hellenes.[37] In yet another passage Herodotus says that the people of Attica, the Athenians included, changed their language simultaneously with their 'turning into Hellenes'.[38]

The above seems to indicate that 'Hellenes' and 'descendants of Hellen' should not be treated as full synonyms; even those who did not belong to the narrower body of the 'descendants of Hellen' could nevertheless count as 'Hellenes'. The following passage from Plato's *Menexenus* helps to bring this point home:

... we [the Athenians] are pure Hellenes, who have not mixed with barbarians (ἀμιγεῖς βαρβάρων). For we are not like descendants of Pelops or Kadmos, Aigyptos or Danaos, nor many others who, being barbarians by nature (φύσει) and Hellenes by convention (νόμῳ), dwell among us (συνοικοῦσιν ἡμῖν) – we reside here as genuine Hellenes, not as half-barbarians (μειξοβάρβαροι). . .[39]

The chauvinist rhetoric of the passage aside, it is evident that in admitting that the descendants of Pelops, Kadmos and Danaos are Hellenes 'by convention' rather than 'by nature' Plato testifies to the fact that Greek identity was defined on broader grounds than those of common descent.

We do not know when the non-Hellenic stemmas were first juxtaposed to the stemma of Hellen or, to put it in a different way, when the representatives of non-Hellenic descent groups began to be counted as Hellenes. Nonetheless, it is hard to avoid the impression that the establishment in the eighth century BC of the Pan-Hellenic cult of Olympian Zeus, accompanied by the initiation of the Olympian Games and the introduction of a new chronology, had something to do with it. Otherwise, it would be difficult to explain why the right of participation in the

36 Cf. e.g. τ. ἐς Βοιωτούς Hdt. 6.108; εἰς ἀστούς τ. S. *OT* 222, *et al.* See further LSJ s.v. II 3.
37 Hdt. 2.51: Ἀθηναίοισι γὰρ ἤδη τηνικαῦτα ἐς Ἕλληνας τελέουσι Πελασγοὶ σύνοικοι ἐγένοντο ἐν τῇ χώρῃ, ὅθεν περ καὶ Ἕλληνες ἤρξαντο νομισθῆναι. Cf. τ 57 ?
38 Hdt. 1.57.3: εἰ τοίνυν ἦν καὶ πᾶν τοιοῦτο τὸ Πελασγικόν, τὸ Ἀττικὸν ἔθνος, ἐὸν Πελασγικόν, ἅμα τῇ μεταβολῇ τῇ ἐς Ἕλληνας καὶ τὴν γλῶσσαν μετέμαθε. Cf. Thomas 2001: 222–5. It is curious that the elusive Pelasgians, frequently referred to in literary tradition as those who inhabited Greece before Hellen and his descendants, are genealogical non-entities. Pelasgos himself properly belongs to the stemma of the Arcadians (see West 1985: 179), but his descendants hardly play any part in Greek genealogy.
39 Pl. *Mx.* 245d. Plato's 'Hellenes by convention' (νόμῳ) may be compared to Ἕλληνες ἤρξαντο νομισθῆναι at Hdt. 2.51 (quoted in full above, in n. 37).

Games was a universally recognised certificate of Greekness, whether 'by nature' or 'by convention'.[40] However that may be, it is the Olympian Games that give us a telling illustration of the fact that in the last analysis the social conventions of identity carried more weight than mere common descent. As is well known, only freeborn Greeks who had committed no religious offence were entitled to participate in the Games. In the early fifth century the contestants in the foot-race refused to run against Alexander, son of the king of Macedon, claiming that 'it is Hellenes, not barbarians, who should participate in the competition' (οὐ βαρβάρων ἀγωνιστέων εἶναι τὸν ἀγῶνα ἀλλὰ Ἑλλήνων); only after Alexander had proved that the Macedonian royal house was ultimately descended from Argos, that is, from Heracles, was he recognised as a Hellen and admitted to the competition.[41] Now in strictly genealogical terms Makedon, son of a sister of Hellen, was much closer to the latter than Heracles, a descendant of Inachos. Yet, the Macedonians did not become, to use the expression of Herodotus, 'reckoned among Hellenes', whereas the Inachids did. As far as our evidence goes, this was the only thing that eventually counted.

It is far from clear why in the Archaic Age, when the overarching genealogical scheme purporting to account for the identity of the 'Hellenes' was created, no attempt was made to subsume the descendants of Inachos and representatives of the other non-Hellenic stemmas under the stemma of Hellen. According to Robert Fowler, the answer lies with the fact that Greece was a collection of city-states rather than a single tribal society: 'Had Greece been a single society, one can expect that over time this new understanding of their relationship to Hellen would have had a greater effect on the genealogies; Inachos, Kekrops, Kadmos and the others would have become Deukalionids. Instead, the independence of the cities produced a centrifugal force counteracting the desire for unity under the name "Hellenic".'[42] However, this explanation does not account for the fact that identification with a given descent group often crossed the boundaries between city-states. The *metroxenoi*, 'those born of an alien mother', discussed in Chapter 5, are one such example; the case of the Gephyraeans referred to above is another. We have seen indeed that, Athenian citizens as they certainly were, the Gephyraeans nevertheless identified themselves and were identified by others as descendants of

40 On the role of Olympia in the construction of Hellenic identity see esp. J. Hall 2002: 154–71.
41 Hdt. 5.22. Cf. Thomas 2001: 219.
42 Fowler 1998: 16.

Kadmos; other families who were identified in the same way were found at this period as far away from Athens as Thera, Cyrene and Akragas.[43]

In view of this, it seems likely that it was above all the non-Hellenic descent groups themselves who insisted on preserving their separate identities – their 'roots', as it were.[44] That Deukalion and Phoroneus continued to coexist peacefully side by side till the end of Greek civilisation allows us to suggest that even in historic times the descendants of Inachos and other non-Hellenic descent groups were influential enough to neutralise the incorporating tendencies characteristic of systematic genealogy. We have seen that as a rule Greek genealogical accounts did not deal with peoples who, like the Phrygians, were no longer part of the ethno-geographical milieu of the Greeks. That the descendants of Inachos and other non-Hellenic stemmas were treated differently signals that these stemmas were envisaged as accounting for the identity of descent groups which were still part of the Greek milieu in the historic period.[45] To form a fuller view of the processes involved, we must look at the genealogical scheme in the light of geography.

Both Aiolos himself and most of his sons are firmly associated with Thessaly. Nevertheless, two sons of Aiolos, namely, Athamas and Perieres, suddenly emerge outside Thessaly – in Boeotian Orchomenos and in Amyclae, respectively; both married into local ruling families and in due course became kings themselves (see Fig. 1). That this translocation of Aiolos' sons is far from accidental follows from the fact that in subsequent generations their descendants continue to emerge in various places all over the Peloponnese. Neleus and Amythaon went to Pylos and Elis, respectively, married into local families, and among their descendants appear such prominent figures of Greek legend as Nestor, Bias and Melampous. The descendants of the latter two spread further to Argos and Sicyon, and at the end of the Heroic Age we find some of them, notably Amphiaraos and Adrastos, among the rulers of these two cities (see also below, pp. 82–3). As for the Pylian dynasty of Neleus, it was generally believed that upon the fall of Mycenaean Greece it rose to new prominence in sub-Mycenaean Athens. This is neatly reflected in Hellanicus' genealogy of the Athenian king Kodros, who in his turn was seen as father of the founders of Ionian colonies in Asia Minor (Fig. 1).[46]

---

43 See Pi. *P*. 3.72–81; *I*. 7.1–15; *O*. 2.38–45; Hdt. 4.145–54; *SEG* ix. 3.
44 This explanation was suggested to me by Israel Shatzman.
45 Cf. Henige 1974: 96: 'Most king-lists and royal genealogies are political tools - those that have not proved useful in this regard are often rejected and forgotten.'
46 Hellan. F 125 Jacoby. Cf. Drews 1983: 10–20 and below, pp. 94–5.

In his discussion of migration accounts among the Kuba of Central Africa, Vansina refers to cases of recitation by king or council of the list of places where their forebears halted:

They have no social importance today. Such places are too far away to be the objects of claims over land, and they do not affect the legitimacy of the institutions that present them. Their main aim seems only historical. And yet it is not. They stress group consciousness (*Wirbewusstsein*) and, more importantly, they relate the group to the overall worldview of the community. The places do matter on the mental map of the world and they will be ordered to fit such a map.[47]

The initial association of the descendants of Aiolos with Northern Greece and their subsequent infiltration into the Peloponnese, inhabited by the descendants of Inachos and probably also other heterogeneous descent groups, points in the direction of a similar mental map. This map (which, among other things, accounted for the northern location of Mount Olympus, the abode of the Olympian gods) reveals a pattern the emergence of which could hardly be accidental. As far as I can see, this pattern only makes sense if we assume that the translocations of the descendants of Aiolos as described in Greek tradition were meant to commemorate the process of their gradual infiltration into the Bronze Age Peloponnese.

This concurs again with Southall's assessment of the processes of ethnic incorporation among the Alurs:

More than a dozen of the ruling lines extant at the end of the nineteenth century have an agreed upon common tradition which derives them all from a single line of chiefs twelve generations ago. It is obviously of significance that no agreed upon names of rulers are remembered before this point, which corresponds to the epoch-making crossing of the Nile by this group and their first entry into the country to the west of it . . . Oral tradition, ritual re-enactment, and the present spatial disposition of groups all lead us to envisage a gradual moving into Alurland by noble and commoner Lwoo together with some members of other ethnic groups some three or more centuries ago.[48]

As we saw above, the process of incorporation into the Alur body eventually involved also parts of population groups that continued to exist as independent ethnic entities with their own languages and cultures side by side with the Alurs.

Judging by the fact that the newcomers from the North are invariably represented in Greek tradition as intermarrying with local families, the

47 Vansina (1985), 92.
48 Southall 1970: 76–7.

process of their infiltration into the Peloponnese was obviously not envisaged as accompanied by violence. That is to say, it is the model of peaceful dispersal rather than one involving invasion, war and conquest that was seen in Greek tradition as properly accounting for the spread of the descendants of Aiolos over the Peloponnese during the Heroic Age.[49]

We have seen that Plato styled the descendants of Inachos *sunoikoi*, fellow inhabitants, of the descendants of Hellen, and that Herodotus claimed that the Pelasgians were made Hellenes by virtue of their status as the *sunoikoi* of the Athenians. Forming a political union, *sunoikia*, and contracting treaties of *epigamia*, or intermarriage, between heterogeneous population groups were both quite common in the ancient world.[50] As anthropological research shows, these are the very processes that lead to the emergence of overarching social unities on the basis of which new group identities are being created.[51] It may therefore be suggested that intermarriage and the ensuing social interaction with the indigenous population led to the emergence of new population groups that embraced both the indigenous population and the Greek-speaking newcomers from the North. If correct, this would mean that the standard corpus of Greek genealogy as described above acted as the inventory of both the 'descendants of Hellen' – that is, the population groups that can conventionally be referred to as 'ethnically Greek'[52] – and of those population groups with which they had mixed to form the body of 'Hellenes'. In other words, the ancient Greeks as we know them started their history as a multi-ethnic population group and the body of 'Hellenes' as known to us from the historic period was a deliberate self-creation. This hypothesis and its cultural implications will be pursued further in this book.

---

49 Cf. Finkelberg 1999.
50 Compare, for example, Strabo's description of 'the partnership in the throne and state' (κοινωνία τῆς ἀρχῆς καὶ πολιτείας) established between Romulus and Titus Tatius after the rape of the Sabine women, see Str. 5.3.2, p. 230; cf. Str. 5.3.4, p. 231; 5.4.7, p. 246; 6.2.3 p. 268. On the processes of accretion, assimilation and incorporation among historical Greek *ethnē* see McInerney 2001: 60–7.
51 See e.g Cohen and Middleton 1970: 18–21, on marriage and the incorporation process in Africa.
52 For the terms 'ethnically Greek' and 'objective ethnicity' see Malkin 1998: 144, 142. On my own use of the terms 'ethnic' and 'ethnicity' see above, p. 21.

CHAPTER 3

The pre-Hellenic substratum reconsidered

ANATOLIAN LANGUAGES AND THE AEGEAN SUBSTRATUM

Who were the Inachids, the Pelopids and the other population groups with whom the Greek-speaking tribes intermingled in the course of the second millennium BC? Until recently, the answer would have been that these were speakers of the unknown language or a group of languages to which the suffixes -*nth*- and -*ss*- belonged. However, today we seem to be in a position to give a more qualified answer to this question.

It has long been recognised that the suffixes -*nth*- and -*ss*-, the identification of which gave rise to the hypothesis of the pre-Hellenic Aegean substratum, are actually identical to the suffixes -*nd*- and -*ss*- of the languages of Asia Minor (see Maps 1 and 2). At the end of the nineteenth century, when Kretschmer drew scholarly attention to the suffixes in question, the languages of Asia Minor attested in the Classical period, such as Lycian, Lydian and Carian, were generally considered not to belong to the Indo-European family of languages. Accordingly, Kretschmer's conclusion was that the linguistic substratum he discovered should be identified as non-Indo-European. No one could have imagined that it would soon be shown that a language belonging to the Indo-European family was in use in Anatolia in the second millennium BC. Ironically, the new picture of Indo-European began to emerge precisely in the years that gave rise to the orthodoxy of the non-Indo-European pre-Hellenic substratum.

In 1891, the Amarna archives excavated by the British archaeologist Flinders Petrie produced, among numerous documents written in Akkadian, two letters in an unknown language. These, addressed to the king of a country called Arzawa, belonged with the rest of the archives to the short period between 1370 and 1350 BC during which Amarna was inhabited. Since they were cast in cuneiform script, the clay tablets on which the letters were written could be read, but nobody was able to interpret the

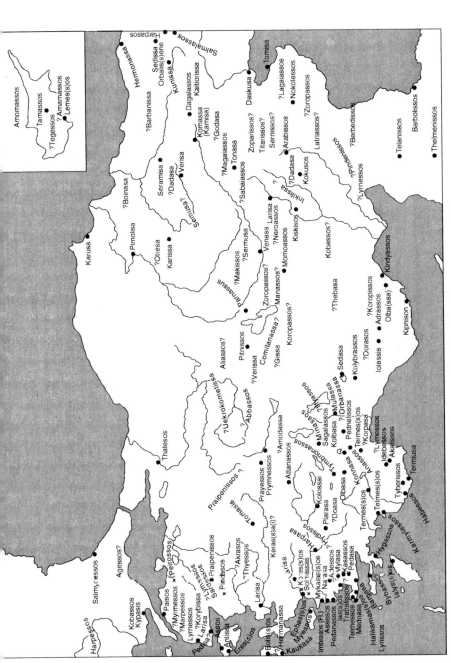

Map 1a. Suffix -ss- in Anatolia (after Schachermeyr 1967).

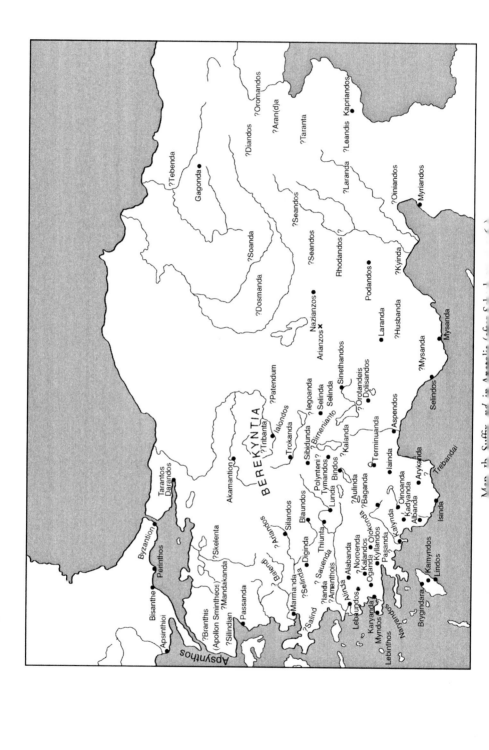

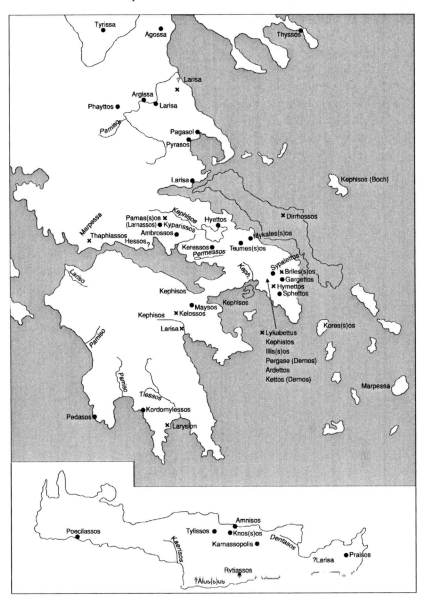

Map 2a. Suffix -ss- in Greece (after Schachermeyr 1967).

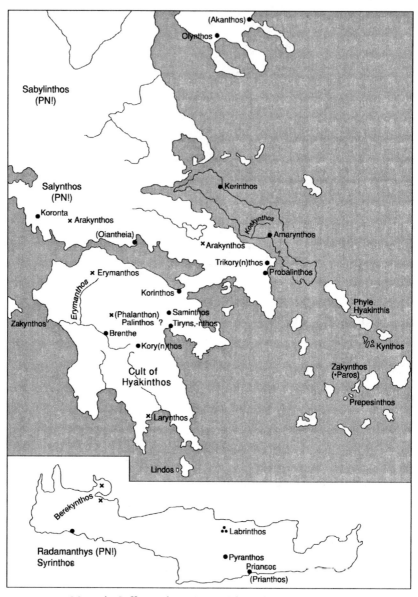

Map 2b. Suffix - *nth*- in Greece (after Schachermeyr 1967).

meaning of the words. Fragments of clay tablets written in the language later identified as 'Arzawan' had also been found some years earlier at the site of Boghazköy in northeast Anatolia. The German expedition that began to excavate Boghazköy in 1906 discovered large archives containing about ten thousand clay tablets. Some of them were written in Akkadian, and therefore could be read, so that the excavators soon realised that they had uncovered Hattusa, the capital of the empire of the Hittites, a people known from the Egyptian and Assyrian sources as well as from the Bible. The archives belonged to the period between 1600 and 1200 BC, and they produced numerous tablets in the 'Arzawan' language of Amarna, which was soon given the new name of Hittite.

Already in 1902 the Norwegian philologist J. A. Knudzon pointed out that there seemed to be a linguistic affinity between the language in which the two Amarna letters were written and the Indo-European languages. Yet it was not until 1915, the year of publication in *Mitteilungen der deutschen Orientgesellschaft* of 'The solution of the Hittite problem' by the Czech orientalist Bedřich Hrozný, that the Indo-European provenance of Hittite became established as a scientific fact. Unfortunately, Hrozný's extensive use of the etymological method, which often led him to ascribe to the Hittite words meanings based on a superficial similarity between these words and words in other Indo-European languages, to some degree obscured the value of his discovery. The necessary adjustment came in 1920, and it was due to the German classical philologist Ferdinand Sommer. Sommer, who began his study of Hittite after having acquired for this purpose the qualifications of an orientalist, insisted that progress in the study of the language could only be achieved by application of strict philological procedure. And indeed, the advance brought about by the intervention of Sommer and other Indo-European linguists was quick: the Indo-European character of Hittite was proved conclusively and accepted by all.[1]

Two additional languages, Palaic and Luwian, which were discovered for the first time in the Boghazköy archives, have proved to belong to the same group as Hittite; in the course of time, this group was given the name of the Anatolian group of languages.[2] The most eastern of the

---

1 It is especially obvious in the system of the noun. The case endings are very close to those of Greek and Latin. In the system of the verb there is a striking similarity to the so-called athematic conjugation in Greek. Thus, the word *esmi*, 'I am', is closely paralleled by the Greek εἰμί and the Sanskrit *asmi*. The conjugation of the group of verbs characterised by the suffix -*nu*- is very similar to that of the -νυ- verbs in Greek, and so on.
2 For a useful assessment of these languages in terms of linguistic geography see now Drews 2001: 254–67.

Bronze Age Anatolian languages is Hittite itself. It is true of course that in the fourteenth–thirteenth centuries BC the Hittite empire spread into large parts of western Anatolia, but there is good reason to suppose that the homeland of the Hittites was in Central Anatolia or perhaps even further to the east. The Palaic language, which is very close to Hittite, seems to have been spoken to the south of the Black Sea, in historic Paphlagonia. The most western of the three Bronze Age Anatolian languages was Luwian. This was the language of the kingdom of Arzawa, placed by scholars along the western coast of Asia Minor. Although the main characteristics of Luwian are identical to those of Hittite and Palaic, there are also some significant differences.[3] Additional discoveries have shown that there is reason to suppose that during the Bronze Age Luwian was spoken over even wider regions of Western Anatolia.

In the last decades of the nineteenth century, hieroglyphic inscriptions in an unknown language began to be discovered on stone monuments in North Syria and Anatolia. The language of these inscriptions was labelled 'Hieroglyphic Hittite'. 'Hieroglyphic Hittite' does not appear in the Boghazköy archives, although it can be seen on the seals excavated on the site, as well as on rock faces and walls. At first, the scarcity of the material and the uniqueness of the script impeded attempts at a full-scale analysis of this language; it was only with the discovery in 1947 of the great bilingual inscription from Karatepe in Cilicia, written in both Phoenician and 'Hieroglyphic Hittite', that a key to the decipherment was found. This brought the study of 'Hieroglyphic Hittite' to the present state, at which it is possible to read the greater part of the inscriptions in this language. One of the most significant results of the decipherment was that it became clear that what had been called 'Hieroglyphic Hittite' was in fact a form of Luwian. Although most of the Hieroglyphic Luwian inscriptions belong to the so-called Neo-Hittite states which emerged in Syria and the Taurus mountains at the beginning of the Iron Age, the location of the more ancient ones strongly suggests that in the Bronze Age Luwian was the dominant language of Cilicia and probably of the whole of Asia Minor. These are the very areas identified by Kretschmer and others as the home of the non-Indo-European Aegean substratum.

---

3 Noun, adjective and pronoun plurals are produced in Luwian by means of the ending -*nzi* (-*es* in Hittite); instead of the genitive, the relation of possession is typically expressed in this language by means of adjectives ending in -*assis* or -*assas*, especially productive in the formation of place-names; while the vocalism of Hittite and Palaic is based on the phonemes *i, e, u, a*, the vocalism of Luwian is based on *i, u, a* only.

Let us not forget, however, that the theory of the Aegean substratum arose on the basis of the study of the languages known to scholars even before the discovery of Hittite. These were the languages of Asia Minor attested on inscriptions of the Classical and Hellenistic periods written in epichoric variants of the Greek alphabet: Lycian, Lydian, Carian, 'Tyrrhenian' (the language of the Lemnos inscription, closely related to Etruscan) and Etruscan itself, which was generally held to be related to the languages of Asia Minor. One of the major results of the decipherment of Hittite and other Bronze Age Anatolian languages has been the growing understanding that the nineteenth-century identification of the languages of Asia Minor as non-Indo-European was in fact erroneous: although the study of many Anatolian languages of the historic period is still in progress, the results obtained so far point firmly towards the affiliation of these languages (with the exception of Phrygian, which is not an Anatolian language proper, see above, p. 31) to the Anatolian group of the Indo-European family of languages.

The language of Asia Minor the study of which has made the most spectacular progress is without doubt Lycian. The decisive identification of Lycian as an Indo-European language was achieved in the 1940s by the Danish linguist Holger Pedersen, while in the 1950s Emmanuel Laroche demonstrated the close relationship between Lycian and Luwian, which allowed the affiliation of Lycian to the Anatolian family of languages. It has also been shown that Lydian too is an Anatolian, that is, an Indo-European, language, although it may be doubted whether it belongs to the same subgroup of the Anatolian languages as Hittite, Palaic, Luwian and Lycian. As far as Carian is concerned, the decipherment of this language has not yet been completed, but the results attained recently by J. D. Ray firmly point towards the Anatolian family of languages.[4] The recently published Carian–Greek bilingual inscription from Kaunos substantiates Ray's reconstruction, thus making it virtually certain that in Carian we have yet another language belonging to the Anatolian group.[5]

The case of Etruscan deserves special attention. It was recognised long ago that Etruscan is, to quote Massimo Pallottino, 'a Mediterranean

---

4 In the system of the noun, the nominative, genitive and accusative case endings are identical to those of the other Anatolian languages; in the system of the verb, there is a striking similarity between the Carian passive participle and the passive participle widespread in Luwian and Lycian; the particle *u-p-j* can be compared to the Luwian demonstrative *apa*, and so on. See further Ray 1990: 65–6, 71.

5 Especially noteworthy is the 'genitival accusative' *ot₂onosn* (='Αθηναῖον), which is closely paralleled in Luwian. Cf. above, n. 3; Frei and Marek 1997: 34–5, 48.

language more or less closely related to the pre-Hellenic languages of the Aegean'.[6] Surprisingly enough, the change in the accepted linguistic affiliation of the languages to which Etruscan is thought to be related has not affected the established view as to its non-Indo-European character. This is even more surprising in view of the fact that it can be shown that many features of Etruscan suggest its Anatolian affinities.[7] In view of this, it might prove useful to revive the theory advanced by Kretschmer in his late publications, according to which there is a need to postulate an additional family of languages related to Indo-European, which would include Etruscan, Tyrrhenian (= Lemnian), Rhetian and 'Pelasgian'.[8]

The association of the Aegean substratum with Anatolian languages is in itself hardly new. Thus, in his assessment of the language situation in the Bronze Age Aegean made in 1926, Carl Darling Buck wrote: 'If one seeks a working hypothesis, and more cannot be expected at present, the one which works best is that the population of the Middle Helladic period, as well as that of the Early Helladic, was of that group, of Anatolian affinities, which left its record in geographical names, etc.'[9] Yet the implications of the Indo-European character of the languages associated with the pre-Hellenic substratum are still realised by only a few. Among contemporary scholars, it was above all Leonard Palmer who formulated these implications in clear and unambiguous terms. In his last book, *The Greek Language* (1980), Palmer pointed out that Kretschmer's original conclusions issued mainly from the comparison of the suffix -*ss*- of Greek place-names with a similar suffix in Lycian, which was not then considered an Indo-European language. 'But', Palmer wrote,

new sources of information have compelled a different answer to thesis 4 ['Lycian is certainly a non-Indo-European language']: Lycian is an IE language belonging to the Anatolian group. For those who accept Kretschmer's analysis and conclusions (and modern scholars are virtually unanimous in doing so) it follows that another group of IE speakers took possession of Greece before the arrival of the Greeks, just as Celts preceded the Anglo-Saxons in the British Isles.[10]

---

6 Pallottino 1955: 65.
7 As in the Anatolian languages, the vocalism of Etruscan is based on the phonemes *i, e, u, a* only, and there is no distinction between the voiceless and the voiced stops. The case system corresponds to that of the Indo-European languages, and there are clear correspondences in the pronoun system. The list of isoglosses, as was shown in Carruba 1977, is very impressive, and so on. Even less than that sufficed to identify Tocharian as a language of the Indo-European family. See further Adrados 1989: 363–83; Woudhuizen 1991: 133–50; Briquel 1994: 329.
8 Kretschmer 1940: 231–79 and 1943: 84–218.
9 Buck 1926: 26.
10 Palmer 1980: 9–10.

Significantly, this conclusion comes close enough to the modified position of Kretschmer himself as expressed in 1925 in his 'Die proto-indogermanische Schicht' and further developed in articles published in the 1940s in *Glotta*.[11] Thus, with the progress of Anatolian studies, when it was shown that the languages spoken in both prehistoric and historic Asia Minor belonged to the Anatolian group, the presence of non-Indo-European speakers in the Eastern Mediterranean, formerly postulated for the entire region, became sharply reduced. As far as the present evidence goes, there are no visible traces of non-Indo-European speakers to the west of the Semitic languages of Syria and to the north of the Egyptian of Africa. Moreover, as Onofrio Carruba has shown in a recent article, Luwian is the only substratum language that can be traced west of a line drawn from the Bosporus in the north to the Gulf of Alexandretta in the south, that is, over the entire territory of Asia Minor.[12] In view of these facts, it is hard to avoid the conclusion that the orthodoxy of the non-Indo-European pre-Hellenic substratum has lost its *raison d'être*.

The significance of the new assessment of the linguistic identity of the Aegean substratum goes far beyond the field of linguistics. The case of matrifocality is the most conspicuous example. All the theories of matriarchy, beginning with Bachofen, proceeded from the evidence supplied by the historic peoples who had been associated with the 'Aegean substratum' – the Lycians, the Lydians, the Carians and so on. Yet, as we have seen, the linguistic evidence testifies to the Indo-European provenance of these peoples. Accordingly, the widespread practice of ascribing all the cases of matrifocality and related phenomena discovered among speakers of the conventional Indo-European languages to the influence of the non-Indo-European Aegean substratum should be revised together with the revision of the linguistic identity of the Aegean substratum itself. It is reasonable to suppose that such a revision will eventually lead to a more complex picture of early Indo-European society, a picture able to embrace both patriarchal and matriarchal Indo-Europeans, both nomadic and sedentary, both warlike and peaceful, and so on (see also below, Chapter 4).[13]

---

11 Kretschmer 1925; 1940; 1943.
12 Carruba 1995: 18. Cf. Drews 1997; Finkelberg 1997a ; Renfrew 1998.
13 Thus, it has already been shown that the old axiom 'the Indo-European peoples = cremation, the non-Indo-European peoples = inhumation', which was once a *sine qua non* of the standard view of Indo-European society, does not stand the test of the evidence at our disposal. See the brilliant analysis of the Italian material by Pallottino 1955: 39; cf. Finkelberg 1997: 14–16; Renfrew 2001: 38.

Let us return now to Greece and Crete. As we have seen, the suffixes
-*nth*- and -*ss*, which a hundred years ago gave rise to the hypothesis of the
non-Indo-European pre-Hellenic substratum, can now be accounted for
as typically Anatolian or, to be more precise, Luwian. And although in
default of a scholarly consensus as to the provenance of the language of
Linear A we cannot be absolutely certain that the same conclusion also
applies to the linguistic situation in Minoan Crete, the even spread of the
suffixes -*ss*- and -*nth*- over Western Asia, Greece and Crete (Maps 1 and 2)
strongly suggests that before the arrival of the Greek-speaking tribes the
whole area in question was linguistically homogeneous.

In 1965, Leonard Palmer advanced the hypothesis that the language of
Linear A should be identified as Luwian. He was not the only one to
maintain that the language of Linear A is a language of the Anatolian
group. Hittite was proposed by Simon Davis, Lycian by myself, and
Luwian again by Edwin Brown. Indeed, it cannot be denied that
Anatolian languages are rapidly gaining in popularity in scholarly publications dealing with Linear A.[14] As far as I can see, this phenomenon
is due partly to the increase in our knowledge of these languages, and
partly to the current assessment of the cultural situation in the Eastern
Mediterranean in the second millennium BC. As the Hittitologist Itamar
Singer put it only recently, 'If indeed Cretan is a Luwian language, its use
in Western Anatolia should not come as a surprise . . . the entire Aegean
basin must be considered to have been a basically homogenous cultural
koinē already in the second millennium BCE.'[15] We have seen that there is
good reason to identify the linguistic substratum in the Eastern Mediterranean as Anatolian or, more precisely, Luwian. If the language of Linear
A is an Anatolian language, this would mean, put as simply as possible,
that the language spoken in Crete in the second millennium BC was part
of the broadly defined Anatolian idiom that spread over the entire
territory of the Eastern Mediterranean.

Although the date of the arrival of the people who preceded the Greeks
in the Aegean is not of direct relevance to the present discussion – it is
enough for our purposes that they were firmly established in the land
prior to the coming of the Greeks – it is an intriguing question, which has

---

14 Palmer 1965: 333–8; Davis 1967; Finkelberg 1990/91; Brown 1992/93; Finkelberg 2001a.
15 Singer 2000: 25. But cf. already Buck 1926: 4–5: 'The strong suspicion that the language of these
    Cretan writings is related to those of Asia Minor is then not based on any internal evidence from
    the writings themselves, but upon indications of cultural relations between the early Cretan
    population and that of Asia Minor, and the evidence of place-names in Crete as well as in other
    parts of the Aegean including the Greek mainland.'

been answered differently by different scholars. It is especially noteworthy that, while the absolute dates of the arrival of the pre-Hellenic population are still open to discussion, this does not affect the fact that there exists a broad consensus according to which the population which the Greeks encountered upon their arrival in Greece must have been speakers of Anatolian.

In 1928, analysis of the Early Bronze Age pottery unearthed in Greece and Crete brought Carl Blegen to the conclusion that the people who spoke the language possessing the suffixes -*nth*- and -*ss*- expanded into Crete and Greece from southwestern Anatolia at the beginning of the Early Bronze Age (ca. 3100–3000 BC). J. Mellaart in 1958 and J. L. Caskey in 1973 posited their arrival at the cultural break between Early Helladic II and Early Helladic III (ca. 2200–2150 BC); both associated the people in question with Luwians.[16] Accepting the argument of the Anatolian provenance of the Aegean substratum, John Coleman recently suggested that 'proto-Anatolians' arrived in Greece ca. 4500–4400 BC with one of the early waves of the Kurgan peoples.[17] Finally, in his attempt to find a uniform archaeological reality that could account for the dispersal of Indo-European languages all over Europe, Colin Renfrew proposed in *Archaeology and Language* (1987) that the arrival of the Indo-Europeans should be associated with the archaeological evidence concerning the spread of new populations in Europe in the course of the so-called Neolithic Revolution. Renfrew suggested that the first farmers of Europe, who settled in Greece and Crete in the course of the seventh millennium BC, were Indo-European speakers from Western Asia, and that the Neolithic Revolution led to the gradual spread of the Indo-European languages all over the European continent.[18] This hypothesis, in that it assumes that the first Indo-European speakers came to Europe from Western Asia, obviously fits in well with the Anatolian affinity of the so-called pre-Hellenic substratum.[19]

16 Haley and Blegen 1928, 149–52; Mellaart 1958; Caskey 1973: 135–40; cf. Drews 1988: 20.
17 Coleman 2000. Cf. Carruba 1995; Finkelberg 1997a.
18 Note, however, that the position of Anatolian within the Indo-European family of languages indicates that even if the first Neolithic farmers of Europe are admitted to be of Indo-European stock, there is no way to see in them, with Renfrew, the direct ancestors of the Greeks, the Celts, the Germans, the Slavs and the other Indo-European speakers inhabiting Europe today. The speakers of Anatolian Indo-European and the speakers of the mainstream Indo-European languages could not have arrived simultaneously for the simple reason that the degree of linguistic divergence between these two groups can only be explained if a long earlier period of separation is taken into account. See further Finkelberg 1997a : 8–13, 16–18.
19 In a paper elaborating on his earlier theory of the coming of Indo-Europeans into Europe, Renfrew suggested that if the inhabitants of Bronze Age Crete did speak an Indo-European

The emerging consensus as to the association of the pre-Hellenic substratum with the Bronze Age Anatolian languages is thus part of the general change of perspective brought forth by the progress in Anatolian studies. It is not only that yet another blank spot on the historical map of the Bronze Age Aegean has been filled in. Little as we still know about the Anatolians, we can now with due caution apply some of this knowledge to the Bronze Age Aegean. It is to be hoped that this broadening of the cultural horizons of Aegean civilisation will eventually lead to a better understanding of both Minoan Crete and Mycenaean Greece.

CONTEXTUALISING THE BRONZE AGE AEGEAN

If it is correct that the pre-Hellenic populations with whom the Mycenaean Greeks mixed were of Anatolian stock, this would lead us not only to Anatolia but also further east, for the simple reason that the Anatolians of Asia, Indo-Europeans though they were, cannot be taken separately from the other civilisations of the ancient Near East. 'Of course none of the civilizations or languages which developed in the region can properly be studied in isolation', Trevor Bryce wrote regarding the Hittite civilisation. 'The Near Eastern world, then as now, was characterised by a high degree of cultural coherence as well as cultural diversity, and by a complex network of political and commercial interrelationships. It is virtually impossible to acquire expertise on a particular Near Eastern civilisation

language brought by the first, Neolithic, inhabitants of the island, this language must have become separated from the Proto-Indo-European unity at such an early stage that in the second millennium BC it would have had very little in common with either the mainstream Indo-European or the Anatolian languages with which it had originally been connected. In that case, Renfrew argued, the position of G. A. Owens, who made this suggestion, should be distinguished from that of scholars such as Palmer 'who relate the Minoan language to the Luwian of the later Bronze Age of western Anatolia, the presence of which in Crete would be the product of more recent population movements'. See Renfrew 1998: 259, cf. Owens 1996: 194. It seems to me, however, that to argue in favour of such an absolute isolation of the Minoan language is not to take into account the continuous distribution of languages over the given territory. That is to say, if the Neolithic farmers who came to Greece and Crete spoke the same language as the population of western Anatolia and if archaeologists are correct in claiming that there was no disruption in their dispersal over the new territory, we have no reason to suppose that these immigrants were culturally or linguistically isolated either from each other or from the territory of their departure. This would mean that if the Neolithic immigrants to Europe did speak an early Anatolian idiom, there could have been no sharp break between their spoken idiom and the neighbouring languages of Western Asia: both groups of languages must have developed side by side so as to create the continuum of Anatolian languages known to us from later periods. The same conclusion would also follow if we adopt an alternative scenario, according to which the speakers of the so-called 'substratum languages' arrived in the Aegean with a wave of migration that considerably postdated the Neolithic.

unless one has an understanding of the broad political and cultural context in which it arose and ran its course.'[20] Archaeological evidence accumulated in recent years strongly suggests that the same would apply to the Bronze Age civilisation of the Aegean.

In everything concerning the international contacts of Aegean civilisation the evidence relating to Minoan Crete is especially illuminating. The discoveries of recent years have shown that what once looked like an insular civilisation totally isolated from the rest of the world was in fact a true maritime power with outposts all over the Aegean, from Samothrace in the north to Thera in the south. Thus, it has been demonstrated beyond doubt that nearby Cythera was in fact a Minoan colony, that is, as Jeremy Rutter puts it, 'a settlement populated largely, perhaps exclusively, by Minoans and their descendants rather than a Cycladic settlement heavily influenced by Minoan art and culture and possibly including a small resident Minoan population'.[21] Moreover, as the recent excavations by Wolf-Dietrich Niemeier have shown, even Miletus in Caria can be safely regarded today as a Cretan colony, which sustained a quite substantial Minoan population during Late Minoan IA–IB (ca. 1600–ca.1450 BC); evidence for connections with Minoan Crete has also been found at other sites along the western coast of Asia Minor.[22]

The case of Thera is especially noteworthy. Although not a Minoan colony in the strict sense of the word, Thera developed a civilisation that offered a synthesis between Minoan influences and the local Cycladic traditions. This can best be seen in the Theran frescoes: proceeding from the specifically Cretan technique of fresco painting, the artists of Thera created a unique and independent style of their own. Thera thus offers a valuable piece of evidence regarding the expansion of Minoan civilisation into places that cannot be considered Minoan in the strict sense of the word. It is in Thera again that an illuminating testimony was found concerning Middle Bronze Age contacts between the Aegean and the Near East.

Two of the three so-called Canaanite container jars discovered at Akrotiri are inscribed with the Linear A signs *77 (= *ka*) and *54 (*re*).[23] As the excavator of Akrotiri, C. G. Doumas, has pointed out, the signs in

---

20 Bryce (1998): 1. See now also Bryce (2002): 257–68.
21 Rutter 1996: Lesson 18. For the archaeological criteria for identifying a colony see esp. Niemeier 1998: 26–30, 47–9.
22 Niemeier 1998: 27–30.
23 See Doumas 1998: 134–5. I am grateful to Judith Weingarten for drawing my attention to this evidence.

question also occur in both Linear B and Old Canaanite script; however, chronological considerations make it impossible to associate the signs on the Thera jars with either of the latter. Since the Akrotiri jars surely belong before the eruption of the Thera volcano in the sixteenth or the seventeenth century BC, they predate both Linear B and Old Canaanite script by several centuries. Accordingly, the suggestion by Doumas that the two Canaanite amphorae in question were originally made in Canaan for export to the Aegean seems the only plausible one, especially if we take into account that so-called Canaanite container jars emerge in excavations at various sites all over the Aegean.[24] This conclusion goes surprisingly well with the evidence supplied by the Tel Haror graffito, a potsherd inscribed with Linear A signs and dated to the end of the seventeenth–beginning of the sixteenth century BC, which was recently uncovered in ancient Canaan (see below). This synchronisation between the Linear A signs inscribed on Canaanite amphorae found in the Aegean and the Aegean graffito found at a Canaanite site effectively demonstrates that already in the Middle Bronze Age the interconnections between the Aegean and the Near East ran deeply enough to involve the art of writing.

At the same time, we can no longer claim unreservedly that the cultural contacts that took place in the Bronze Age proceeded invariably in one direction, from east to west. Archaeological discoveries of recent years, such as wall paintings executed in the characteristically Minoan fresco technique discovered in Tel Kabri in western Galilee and Tell el-Dab'a in the eastern Nile Delta, or Linear A inscriptions found at the Canaanite sites of Tel Haror and Tel Lachish,[25] strongly suggest that, rather than automatically treating the Aegean civilisation as a passive recipient of influences coming from the East, we should also take into account that this civilisation could exert its own influence on its eastern partners. Thus, the fact that the paintings at Tel Kabri and Tell el-Dab'a show the unmistakably Minoan fresco technique (which is also characteristic of the Alalakh frescoes in northern Syria excavated in the 1930s by Sir Leonard Woolley) has led scholars to the conclusion that these frescoes were painted by travelling Minoan artists invited by eastern rulers to decorate their palaces in the characteristic Minoan style which then enjoyed wide international prestige. On the whole, the quantity of Minoan and Mycenaean artefacts and pottery discovered in Anatolia

24 Doumas 1998: 135. On the Canaanite container jars see Cline 1994: 95–7.
25 Minoan fresco paintings: Niemeier 1991: 189–201; Cline 1995: 267–70; Niemeier and Niemeier 1998: 69–96; Linear A inscriptions: Godart 1994; Finkelberg 1998a, and below.

and the Near East has become significant enough to allow a large international conference, 'The Aegean and the Orient in the Second Millennium', to have been held in 1997.[26] All this considered, it would not be an overstatement to say that Minoan Crete can safely be regarded today, to use Niemeier's apt definition, as the 'westernmost member' of the ancient Near East.[27]

The only feature by means of which 'East' and 'West' could be effectively distinguished even at this early stage seems to have been the use in the West of systems of writing other than the cuneiform script adopted everywhere in the East.[28] In the second millennium BC the Eastern Mediterranean, the Aegean included, became the centre and major producer of systems of writing which differed in principle from both cuneiform to the east and Egyptian hieroglyphic to the south of this area. From Hieroglyphic Luwian, which still overlaps with cuneiform writing in Anatolia, through Cypro-Minoan, Cypriot Syllabic and samples of other epichoric scripts in the Levant, to Cretan Hieroglyphic, the script of the Phaistos Disk and the syllabaries of the Aegean, we have a continuum of non-cuneiform scripts the limits of whose dispersal roughly coincide with those of the dispersal of the suffixes -*nth*- and -*ss*-.

The first Aegean syllabary to be discovered was the Classical Cypriot script used for writing Greek down to the third or second century BC. Its decipherment, based on the Phoenician bilingual inscription of Idalium, was initiated in 1870 and effectively completed by 1876.[29] The script has two principal variants, and although most of the inscriptions are Greek, some are written in the so-called Eteocyprian language, which resists translation. The discovery in 1979 of the eleventh-century BC bronze obelos inscribed with the Greek dialect Arcado-Cyprian genitive form of the proper name Opheltas (*o-pe-le-ta-u*) confirmed what scholars thought even before this evidence came to light, namely, that although the earliest Cypriot inscriptions known thus far belonged to the sixth century BC, the syllabary itself should be traced back to the Bronze Age.

Another Cypriot script, first identified in 1896, was used during the Late Bronze Age both in Cyprus itself and in nearby Ugarit. The exact nature of the relationship between this still undeciphered script, which is

---

26 Cline and Harris-Cline 1998, but see already Schachermeyr 1967.
27 Niemeier 1991: 199: 'We have evidence for exchange of information on the equipment of the palaces within the ancient Near East (to which Minoan Crete belonged in a certain sense as westernmost member).'
28 The idea was first suggested to me by Itamar Singer, but see already Evans 1909: 8, 77–80.
29 See Ventris and Chadwick 1973: 60–6; Mitford and Masson 1982: 71–82.

known to us in at least three variants, and the Classical Cypriot syllabary
is still far from clear. Although the definition of this script as Cypriot
Linear is clearly preferable for methodological reasons, it has become
generally known by the name of Cypro-Minoan, given to it by Sir Arthur
Evans.[30]

Evans' excavations at Knossos started in 1900, and almost immediately
led to the discovery of the first tablets in what is known today as the
Linear B script. The epigraphic materials accumulated in subsequent years
as a result of Evans' excavations at Knossos and the Italian excavations at
Phaistos proved rich enough to allow Evans to identify three different
scripts. This led to the following classification:

1. so-called Cretan Hieroglyphic (or Pictographic) Script, dated to ca.
   2000 to ca. 1700 BC (MM IA–MM II); it is attested almost exclusively
   in Crete itself (but recently also in Samothrace) and appears mostly on
   seals;
2. Linear Script of Class A, dated to ca. 1750 to ca. 1450 BC (LM IIIA1–2); it
   is attested mainly in Crete, Southern Greece and the Cyclades, but
   recently also in the northeastern Aegean, Asia Minor and Israel, and
   appears on clay tablets and stone libation tables, as well as on silver,
   bronze and gold objects.[31]
3. Linear Script of Class B, which presumably replaced Linear A
   somewhere about 1400 BC; documents in this script, later shown to
   have been brought to Knossos by Mycenaean settlers and to have been
   a vehicle for recording the Greek language, were unearthed in Crete
   (Knossos, Khania) and mainland Greece (Pylos, Thebes, Tiryns,
   Mycenae); it only appears on clay tablets and on painted inscriptions
   on ceramic vessels such as stirrup jars.

Cypro-Minoan, Classical Cypriot, Cretan Hieroglyphic, Linear A and
Linear B are far from being the only so-called Aegean scripts that
circulated in the Eastern Mediterranean. Two additional Cretan samples
that should be taken into account are the script of the Phaistos Disk

---

30 See Ventris and Chadwick 1973: 61; Dow 1973: 606. On Cypro Minoan scripts in general see
Palaima 1989.
31 Whereas the evidence at older scholars' disposal led them to the conclusion that Cretan
Hieroglyphic and Linear A presented, as Evans 1909: 8, put it, 'successive types of Minoan
writing', and therefore the latter developed directly out of the former, the new evidence makes it
obvious that Hieroglyphic and Linear A are 'virtually contemporary in terms of their appearance'
(Rutter). On the new evidence see Rutter 1996: Lesson 10; Tsipopoulou and Hallager 1996: 43;
Duhoux 1998: 3; Schoep 1999. Cf. John Younger, 'Reading notes: Duhoux: Cretan scripts',
AEGEANET 22 Dec 1998.

(ca. 1800–ca. 1600 BC) and that of the Arkalokhori bronze double axe (ca. 1600 BC).[32] In the Levant, the inscriptions from Byblos, from Balu'ah in Moab, from Deir 'Alla in the Jordan valley, and from Tel Aphek in Canaan each present a unique script with possible Aegean connections.[33] Generally speaking, it looks as though there was a common stock of 'banal' signs all over the Eastern Mediterranean, and that these signs were used in various combinations in different syllabic scripts.[34] Later, some of these signs became part of early alphabets of Asia Minor, such as Carian, Lycian and Lydian. In view of this, it is hard not to agree with Evans that it is 'a remarkable coincidence' that the geographical area which in the Bronze Age gave rise to various linear scripts was exactly the one over which a new system of writing, that of the Phoenician alphabet, spread at the beginning of the Iron Age.[35]

Much of the view of the isolation of Aegean civilisation, which firmly established itself immediately upon Evans' discovery of the 'Palace of Minos' at Knossos, seems to be based on the presumption of the isolation of the linear scripts, formulated at an early stage in the history of Aegean studies as a result of the assessment of the then available evidence. Thus in 1973, in his contribution to the third edition of the *Cambridge Ancient History*, Sterling Dow still could characterise the dispersal of the Linear A script in the following words:

Its distribution was wide but seemingly thin: Linear A has been found at no fewer than a score of sites in Crete, whereas outside Crete only one tablet is known at present (Kea) plus some individual signs on other objects, and of these signs many are potters' marks and the like, which may not be, properly, Linear A at all.[36]

---

32 See further Duhoux 1998: 3–16.
33 Cf. Naveh 1987: 21–2. The inscription from Deir 'Alla is especially illuminating in this respect. While some signs of this inscription recall those of Linear A, others seem typically Cypro-Minoan or even Canaanite. It goes without saying that, contrary to what many are inclined to believe, the sole fact of the coincidence of several signs of the Deir 'Alla inscription with those of Linear A cannot serve as proof of its Linear A provenance. We should look for a script that can serve as the common denominator of all the signs attested, and this is certainly not Linear A (or Linear B for that matter). On the inscription from Deir 'Alla see also Franken 1964: on the tablet from Tel Aphek see now Singer (forthcoming).
34 For further discussion see Finkelberg, 'Linear A from Lachish', AEGEANET 27 Oct 1998; Weingarten, ibid. 28 Oct 1998; Finkelberg, ibid. 29 Oct 1998; Younger, ibid. 30 Oct 1998; Eyma, ibid. 31 Oct 1998; Weingarten, ibid. 3 Nov 1998.
35 Evans 1909: 77; see also 54–61. Evans also suggested that the 'unexpected supersession of cuneiform writing in Canaan could be due to the emergence of the Philistines in this region' (ibid. 80). On the Philistines see below, Chapter 7.
36 Dow 1973: 593; cf. Chadwick 1967: 13.

In subsequent years, however, additional Linear A inscriptions started
to emerge in the Peloponnese (Laconia, Tiryns) and especially the Cyclades (Melos, Thera, Cythera), and the fact that many of these inscriptions
proved to be locally incised gave rise to lively discussion as to the role of
the Cyclades in the distribution of the Minoan script.[37] It seems, however,
that still more recent finds may soon necessitate transferring the focus of
the discussion to areas even more remote from Crete, thus completely
undermining the old view of the cultural isolation of the Minoans.

In 1995, Dimitris Matsas published a Linear A inscription – in fact, one
in a series of five finds inscribed in Cretan Hieroglyphic and Linear A –
unearthed in Samothrace in the northeastern Aegean. The archaeological
context places these finds – two roundels, two noduli and a nodule – as
early as Middle Minoan II – Middle Minoan IIIA (the second half of the
eighteenth century BC), thus making them roughly contemporary with the
earliest known Linear A texts found in Crete.[38] In 1996, Eliezer Oren and
Jean-Pierre Olivier published a Middle Bronze Age III Minoan graffito
discovered at the Canaanite site of Tel Haror in the western Negev.[39] In
1996 again, the discovery by Wolf-Dietrich Niemeier at Miletus in Asia
Minor of a Late Minoan Ib potsherd which bears an inscription containing three Linear A signs was announced in the press; the type of clay used
indicates that the pottery was made locally, and it is clear that the signs
were inscribed before the vessel was fired.[40] In the course of excavation
directed by David Ussishkin, the Canaanite site of Tel Lachish produced a
fragment of a limestone vessel bearing a Minoan inscription, which was
published by Ussishkin, Alexander Uchitel and myself in 1996; the
composition of the stone indicates that the inscription was incised locally
while the archaeological context suggests a surprisingly late date in the
earlier part of the twelfth century BC.[41] Finally, a clay reel inscribed with
signs that seem to represent an epichoric variant of the Linear A script

37 See esp. Renfrew and Brice 1977: 111–19; Hooker 1979: 46–7; Janko 1982b : 97–100; Palaima 1982:
    15–18 and 1988: 269–342; Olivier 1988: 255 (no. 11) and 262–3; Michalidou 1992/93: 18–20.
38 Matsas 1995: 235–47; cf. Matzas 1991: 159–79.
39 Oren et al. 1996: 91–117, esp. 113, 116–17.
40 Scientific American (July 1996): 20; Niemeier 1996: 8/–99.
41 Finkelberg, Uchitel and Ussishkin (1996): 195–207; Eshet (1996): 208. This is not to say that, as
    some are inclined to believe, the Lachish inscription should be associated with one of the groups
    of the Sea Peoples. As we shall see in Chapter 7, the characteristic feature of the new population
    groups which arrived in the Levant at the end of the Bronze Age and settled along the
    Mediterranean coast was the Mycenaean-type pottery of which the characteristic 'Philistine
    pottery' was a later development. Yet no specimens of the 'Philistine pottery' have been unearthed
    in Lachish, which can only mean that, even if the late dating of the Lachish inscription is correct,
    its association with the Philistines, attractive as it may appear, is actually out of the question.

emerged in the course of the excavations of Drama, southeastern Bulgaria, in 1996 and was published by Alexander Fol in 2000; in this case as well, the archaeological context points to Late Helladic IIIB–IIIC.[42]

Thus the discoveries of recent years bear witness to the fact that in the second millennium BC considerable scribal activity involving Linear A script took place not only in Crete itself but also along the entire eastern coast of the Mediterranean. It goes without saying that, as distinct from the Minoan artefacts, which may or may not involve the actual presence of Minoan speakers, the use of the Minoan system of writing may well indicate the presence of such speakers in the places where the locally incised Linear A inscriptions were found. Not only Southern Greece and the Cyclades, which have always been regarded as Crete's natural sphere of influence, but the entire Eastern Mediterranean, from Bulgaria and Samothrace in the north to the Negev in the south, should now be taken into account in this connection. It seems indeed that the cumulative evidence provided by recent discoveries is about to cause a dramatic change in the current picture of the extent to which Minoan civilisation and probably also the Minoan language itself were disseminated.

Although the mainland Mycenaean civilisation developed later and under considerable Minoan influence, it eventually prevailed, and in the Late Bronze Age Crete became a Mycenaean province. The former Minoan colonies turned Mycenaean, and from ca. 1450 BC Mycenaean influence replaced Minoan not only in the Aegean but also in western Anatolia.[43] As the decipherment of Linear B by Michael Ventris has demonstrated, the language of the Mycenaean civilisation was Greek. The Hittite involvement with *Ahhiyawa*, generally believed to represent the Achaean Greek world of the second half of the second millennium BC, naturally comes to mind in this connection.[44] In view of this, it would be hard not to agree with Charles Gates that 'The Aegean basin, its west and east shores and the islands in between, must be considered as a unified region in the Mycenaean period, with the east shore being an integral part of the Mycenaean world, not a thin coastline of transients from the West Aegean.'[45]

The picture thus emerging goes surprisingly well with Martin West's explanation of the subtitle *West Asiatic Elements in Greek Poetry and Myth*

42 Fol 2000. I am grateful to Aren Maeir for drawing my attention to this publication.
43 See esp. Gates 1995: 289–98; Niemeier 1998: 25–41; Mee 1998: 137–48.
44 On recent assessment and bibliography of the '*Ahhiyawa*-problem' see Mee 1998: 142–3; Niemeier 1998: 41–5.
45 Gates 1995: 297.

that he gave to his sweeping demonstration of the all-pervasive character of Near Eastern influences on Greek civilisation. According to West, although Eastern influences on Archaic Greek literature are undeniable, it would be more correct to define those influences as 'Western Asiatic' rather than as 'Near Eastern' in the strict sense of the word. 'This is to signal the fact', he writes,

that I have drawn my comparative material almost wholly from Mesopotamian, Anatolian, Syrian, and biblical sources, and deliberately left Egypt more or less out of the picture. I have occasionally cited Egyptian material, when it demanded to be cited, but in general my view is that the influence of Egypt on Greek poetry and myth was vanishingly small in comparison with that of Western Asia.[46]

One may wonder at the same time whether commercial encounters, usually seen as the principal channel of the transmission of Near Eastern influences to the Bronze Age Aegean, are enough to account for the extent and intensity of the contacts between Aegean civilisation and the East. That is to say, instead of treating each literary, religious and cultural feature shared by the Bronze Age Aegean and the civilisations of Western Asia in terms of external influences, it seems much more economical to assume that they resulted from a systemic affinity.[47] Thus, the palace administration system working with clay seals and inscribed clay tablets, which is generally recognised to have constituted the core of Minoan and, later, Mycenaean civilisation, has proved to be only one in a series of similar systems adopted in the Near East, from Sumer to Ugarit. That the archives of Pylos and Knossos can be compared with profit to those of Nuzi, Alalakh and Ugarit became clear to Ventris and Chadwick already in the course of their decipherment of Linear B. In the first edition of *Documents in Mycenaean Greek* (1956) they wrote:

In spite of some differences in climate and culture, the similarities in the size and organization of the royal palaces and in the purposes for which the tablets were written ensure close parallels, not only in the listed commodities and their amounts, but even on occasion in details of phraseology and layout.[48]

It is significant in this connection that Greek legend saw entire regions in Western Asia as inhabited by descendants of Inachos, that is, the same

46 West 1997: vii. Cf. Webster 1964: 65; S. Morris 1992: 105–16.
47 Cf. Wasserman 2001: 262.
48 Ventris and Chadwick 1973: 106. Cf. Uchitel 1988): 23: 'But when I began my research [of Linear B archives], holding no preconceived opinions on the matter, I found to my own surprise that the most relevant texts for comparative purposes are those from Sumerian economic archives from the 3rd millennium BC, especially some of the texts from the Third Dynasty of Ur, i.e. the last century of the 3rd millennium BC.' See also Weingarten 1990: 63–4 and 1997: 147–66; Niemeier 1991: 189–90; West 1997: 18–19.

people with whom the Greeks presumably mixed upon their arrival in Greece at the end of the third–beginning of the second millennium BC. Consider, for example, the following myth, associated with a side branch of the stemma of Inachos (Fig. 2). In search of Europa, who had been kidnapped by Zeus at Tyre or Sidon, her brothers Kadmos, Kilix and Phoenix dispersed over Greece, Cilicia and Phoenicia respectively, and settled there.[49] Their father Agenor was a descendant of Inachos and brother to Belos who fathered Aigyptos and Danaos: as we have seen, Perseus, Heracles and eventually the kings of Sparta traced their descent to the latter. Europa herself was brought by Zeus to Crete where she gave birth to Minos, Sarpedon and Rhadamanthys. Minos became king of Crete, Sarpedon went to Lycia and ruled there, whereas Rhadamanthys became firmly associated with Euboea. Egypt, Canaan, Cilicia, Lycia, Greece, Crete – these are the geographical horizons addressed by the dispersal of the descendants of Inachos.

Generally speaking, it is immediately obvious that Greek legend felt quite at home in the Eastern Mediterranean. As distinct from the Western Mediterranean, which was invariably envisaged as inhabited by monsters, witches and fabulous peoples, the East was treated as familiar ground across which many heroes of Greek legend performed their exploits. Io crossed the lands of the East and finally arrived in Egypt where she founded a dynasty whose representatives became kings of Argos; Perseus reached Jaffo in Palestine, married the king's daughter Andromeda and took her to Mycenae; Bellerophon went to Lycia where he married the king's daughter and founded a new royal dynasty, and so on.

Thus the evidence of linguistics, of archaeology and of Greek tradition coincide in that they show unequivocally that the proper place of Bronze Age Aegean civilisation is in the cultural context of ancient Western Asia. As we know today, this cultural context included not only Sumerian, Semitic and Hurrian, but also a considerable Anatolian, i.e. Indo-European, element. It follows from this that the cultural interaction between the Aegean and Western Asia must have run much deeper than the loan words, floating motifs and other piecemeal borrowings that would normally result from casual commercial encounters between strangers. The hypothesis that the Mycenaean Greeks became mixed with populations of Western Asia would provide this phenomenon with a proper historical and cultural context. That is to say, if the populations

---

49 Cf. Hdt. 7.91; Schol. Eur. *Phoen.* 6; Apollod. 3.1. For discussion see Frazer 1921 (vol. I): 296–8 (on Apollod. 3.1); West 1985: 83.

with whom the Mycenaean Greeks intermingled were of Anatolian stock, this would mean that their intermarriages and eventual fusion with those populations amounted to their becoming assimilated into the cultural milieu of Western Asia. It is to be expected therefore that the same features would be immanent in both Greek civilisation and the civilisations of Western Asia and that some of them – for example, the Succession Myth which, as told in Hesiod's *Theogony*, is most closely paralleled in the Hittite version of the Hurrian *Song of Kumarbi*[50] – would be taken over by the Greeks as an integral part of their cultural heritage.

50 See esp. West 1966: 20–2 and 1997: 279–80, 589; Bryce 2002: 222–9.

CHAPTER 4

Kingship in Bronze Age Greece and Western Asia

ROYAL SUCCESSION IN HEROIC GREECE

Contrary to appearances, Greek tradition does not make provision for royal succession from father to son.[1] Consider, for example, the story of Pelops, a newcomer from Asia Minor, who became king in Elis in virtue of his marriage to Hippodameia, daughter of the local king Oinomaos. Although Pelops is said to have fathered many sons, it is remarkable that none of these sons succeeded him on the throne. Atreus and Thyestes, the two most prominent sons of Pelops, were exiled by their father for the murder of Chrysippos, Pelops' son by another wife. Yet, according to Pindar, Pelops fathered six sons, and other sources give him even more. All of these sons became kings elsewhere rather than in Elis itself.[2] This compares well with the case of Peleus and Telamon, the sons of Aiakos, king of Aegina, who are also said to have killed their half-brother, Phokos, and because of this were exiled by their father: Peleus became king in Phthia, Telamon in Salamis.[3] It goes without saying that the behaviour of Pelops and Aiakos toward their sons is strikingly at variance with what could be expected of dynastic kings, for it appears that no sons were left to succeed these kings on the throne. The next kings of Elis and Aegina must have been of a different line.

Consider also the case of Oineus and his descendants. The Aetolian entry in the Homeric Catalogue of Ships contains a brief remark to the effect that the reason why the leaders of the Aetolians in the Trojan War were not of Oineus' line was that by that time no sons of this king were

---

1 This point was made almost simultaneously in Atchity and Barber 1987, Finkelberg 1991 and Lyle 1992.
2 Pelops and Hippodameia: Pi. *O.* 1.67–71, 88; the murder of Chrysippos: Hellan. 4 F 157 Jacoby (= Schol. *Il.* 2.105); Thuc. 1.9.2; the sons of Pelops: Pi. *O.* 1.89; Schol. Eur. *Or.* 4. For the discussion see West 1985: 109–10.
3 Pi. *N.* 5.14–15 with Schol.; Diod.Sic. 4.72.6–7; Hyg. *Fab.* 14; Paus. 2.29.2.

left: 'The sons of Oineus of great heart were not there any longer, nor Oineus himself, and golden-haired Meleagros was dead.'[4] The explanation fails to account for the fact that, even after Meleagros' death there still remained such prominent descendants of Oineus as his son Tydeus and Tydeus' son Diomedes. Tydeus, again, had been exiled from Aetolia for murdering a relative; he went to Argos, where he married a daughter of king Adrastos. His son Diomedes, who married another daughter of the same king, succeeded his father-in-law, whereas his grandfather Oineus, left with no direct descendants in Aetolia, was succeeded by his son-in-law Andraimon.[5]

Bellerophon went from Greece to Lycia, where he married the king's daughter and became king. Pelops migrated in the opposite direction and became king of Elis in exactly the same way. Teukros, instead of returning to his native Salamis after the Trojan War, settled in Cyprus, where he became king; his father Telamon was left in Salamis with no male descendants to succeed him. Melampous came from Messenia to Argos, married one of the daughters of the king Proitos and became king; although Proitos had a son of his own, this son, Megapenthes, is said to have been born too late to succeed his father. Xouthos came from Thessaly to Athens, helped king Erechtheus in his war against Euboea, married his daughter and became king. And so on.[6] In many cases the situations described above are given a more or less plausible explanation but, leaving the explanations aside, we are left with a recurrent pattern which comes close to Hecataeus' concise account of Orestheus, son of Deukalion: 'And Orestheus son of Deukalion went to Aetolia to become king (ἐπὶ βασιλείᾳ)'.[7]

Who were the successors of Pelops in Elis, of Aiakos in Aegina, of Telamon in Salamis? Our sources do not supply the answer. The genre of the king-list, widespread in literatures of the ancient Near East, was totally alien to Greek heroic tradition. Instead, this tradition arranged the names of kings according to the genealogical principle. The distinction between the two genres, genealogy and king-list, is not merely conventional: while the king-list is committed to preserving the unity of place, the genealogy

---

4 *Il.* 2.641-2 (athetised by Zenodotus): οὐ γὰρ ἔτ' Οἰνῆος μεγαλήτορος υἱέες ἦσαν, / οὐδ' ἄρ' ἔτ' αὐτὸς ἔην, θάνε δὲ ξανθὸς Μελέαγρος.
5 Tydeus Apollod. 1.76; Diomedes *Il.* 5.412; Andraimon Apollod. 1.64, 78, cf. *Il.* 2.638.
6 Bellerophon: *Il.* 6.155–95; Pelops: above, n. 2; Teukros: Pi. *N.* 4.46–7; Paus. 2.29.4; Melampous: *Od.* 15.225–41; Apollod. 2.28–9, cf. 1.102; Xouthos: Eur. *Ion* 57–64, 289–98; Strab. 8.7.1, p. 383; Paus. 7.1.2.
7 Hecat. 1 F 15 Jacoby.

follows the given line of descent wherever its representatives are found. The genealogy and the king-list would only concur if the king-list followed dynastic succession from father to son. And it goes without saying that, as soon as the king is not succeeded by his son, the identity of his successor cannot be established on the basis of the genealogy.[8]

Yet, although early Greek tradition follows only genealogical sequences, attempts at drawing up something similar to king-lists do emerge from time to time in later sources. Let us consider the perspective of royal succession as preserved in Pausanias' account of the first kings of Attica:

Amphiktyon attained kingship in the following way. They say that the first king of what is now Attica was Aktaios. After Aktaios' death Kekrops, who was married to his daughter, succeeded him on the throne. Kekrops had three daughters - Herse, Aglauros and Pandorsos - and a son Erysichthon. This son did not become king in Athens because he died in his father's lifetime, so that Kekrops was succeeded by Kranaos, the most powerful man among the Athenians. They say that Kranaos also had daughters, one of whom was Atthis, and that the country, previously called Aktaia, was named Attica after her. Although Amphiktyon was married to Kranaos' daughter, he nevertheless rose up against him, and put an end to his reign. Later on he in his turn was thrown out by Erichthonios and his supporters.[9]

It emerges from this account that of the four kings who according to Pausanias succeeded Aktaios on the throne, not even one was son of his predecessor. At the same time, at least two of them, Kekrops and Amphiktyon, are described as their predecessors' sons-in-law. In his account of another early kingdom, that of Megara, Pausanias explicitly states that in the royal succession Nisos–Megareus–Alkathoos the kingship was transmitted from father-in-law to son-in-law.[10]

To be sure, accession to the throne as a result of marriage to the king's daughter is a well-known motif in the Greek Heroic tradition. Not only the first kings of Athens and Megara, but also Pelops, Bellerophon, Melampous, Peleus, Telamon, Teukros, Andraimon, Diomedes and many others achieved kingship by virtue of their marriages to the daughters of their predecessors. This has usually been understood to mean that the

---

8 Cf. the caveat expressed in Henige 1974: 94: 'At the same time it need scarcely be emphasised that an ascendant genealogy which does not claim to be more than that should by no circumstances ever be treated as a king-list.'

9 Paus. 1.2.6; cf. Apollod. 3.180–6.

10 Paus. 1.41.5: διαδέξασθαι δὲ τὴν βασιλείαν γαμβρὸν Νίσου τε Μεγαρέα καὶ αὖθις Ἀλκάθουν Μεγαρέως.

daughter's husband would succeed his father-in-law if the latter had no sons of his own.[11] Sometimes, even if a son is actually attested, he can be disposed of as one who, like Proitos' son Megapenthes, was allegedly born too late or, like Kekrops' son Erysichthon, died too early to succeed his father on the throne. Another example of a similar exegesis, relating to the Megarian king Megareus and his son Timalkos, whose alleged death at the hands of Theseus allowed Megareus' son-in-law Alkathous to succeed him on the throne, is preserved by Pausanias in his account of the early kings of Megara.[12]

Let us examine now the well-attested sequence Tyndareos–Menelaos, which, again, is not based on father-to-son succession:[13] Menelaos succeeded Tyndareos in Sparta by virtue of marriage to his daughter Helen. At the same time, Tyndareos definitely had two sons, Kastor and Polydeukes, who were alive and well when their sister was given in marriage to Menelaos. Yet Helen's brothers not only do not dispute their father's decision to make one of Helen's suitors king of Sparta – as the *Catalogue of Women* clearly shows, they were even envisaged as being actively involved in choosing the man who was supposed to become their father's successor.[14] Thus, although there can be no doubt that Tyndareos had male descendants, the kingship was bestowed on his son-in-law rather than on one of his sons.

At this stage, it is important to emphasise that in so far as the king is succeeded by his son-in-law the queen would be succeeded by her daughter. That is to say, wherever kingship by marriage is practised as a regular pattern of succession, rather than a line of kings, we would have a line of queens that runs from mother to daughter. Thus in Sparta again, while the king Tyndareos was succeeded by his son-in-law Menelaos, Tyndareos' wife Leda was succeeded by her daughter Helen. Characteristically, in most versions Orestes succeeds Menelaos on the throne by virtue of his marriage to Hermione, the daughter of Menelaos and Helen.[15] It seems, then, that the mother-to-daughter succession in heroic

---

11 That is, in accordance with the *epikleros* pattern, on which see below, p. 94.
12 Paus. 1.41.5, quoted above, p. 14.
13 Cf. Atchity and Barber 1987: 16–17; Finkelberg 1991: 305–6.
14 Hes. frr. 197.3–4; 198.7–8; 199.1–3 M-W.
15 Already in Pi. *P.* 11.31–2; *N.* 11.34–5. According to Pausanias, Orestes became king of Sparta because the Spartans preferred him to Nikostratos and Megapenthes, Menelaos' sons by a slave-girl. However, in the *Catalogue of Women* Nikostratos is presented as son of Menelaos and Helen; this version is followed in Apollodorus; see Hes. fr. 175 M-W; Paus. 2.18.6; Apollod. 3.133; cf. West 1985: 119 and n. 203. The alleged illegal birth of Nikostratos looks as far-fetched as the late birth of Megapenthes and the early death of Erysichthon and Timalkos.

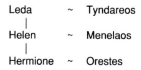

Figure 3. Succession in the female line in Sparta (after Finkelberg 1991).

Sparta should be expanded so as to include not only Leda and her daughter Helen but the latter's daughter Hermione as well (Fig. 3).

Each single case, taken alone, proves nothing. But the evidence is cumulative, and the persistence with which the same basic situation recurs over and over again suggests that, as far as heroic Greece is concerned, kingship by marriage was envisaged as a standard pattern of royal succession. Still more so when we are fortunate enough to possess a document that can only be properly understood by application of this pattern. I mean the situation in Ithaca as described in the *Odyssey*.[16]

It was recognised long ago that the social background of the Ithaca situation is difficult in more than one respect. To recapitulate the standard analysis by M. I. Finley, it is far from clear why the king's son Telemachos not only cannot automatically assume the position of his missing and presumably dead father, but is even ready to entertain the possibility that the future king of Ithaca is to be found somewhere among the local nobles who are wooing his mother.[17] Indeed, not only the suitors but also Telemachos himself state explicitly on more than one occasion that Odysseus' son is not considered the next king of Ithaca: Telemachos' real concern is not so much with the kingship as with his household, *oikos*, which is being destroyed by the suitors.[18] The position of Odysseus' father Laertes is still more puzzling:

> Why did he not sit on the throne of Ithaca? . . . Nor is there a hint that Odysseus had usurped his father's position . . . Yet, so far was the ex-king from authority that all the while the suitors were threatening to destroy the very substance of his son and grandson, Laertes could do no more than withdraw in isolation to his farm, and there to grieve and lament.[19]

Finally, there is every reason to wonder why those who wish to occupy Odysseus' position insistently connect this with marriage of one of them

---

16 Cf. Finkelberg 1991: 306–7.
18 *Od.* 1.394–5, 400–2; 20.334–7.

17 Finley 1979: 84–5.
19 Finley 1979: 86–7.

to the king's wife Penelope. To quote Finley again, 'the Penelope situation had become so muddled in the long prehistory of the *Odyssey* that the actual social and legal situation is no longer recoverable.'[20]

Finley's analysis, as indeed many other analyses of the social situation in Ithaca, proceeds from the presumption that Odysseus' legitimate successor on the throne of Ithaca is his son Telemachos, that the king who preceded Odysseus was his father Laertes and that accession to the throne by one of the suitors can hardly have anything to do with the former king's wife Penelope. The trouble, however, is that neither Telemachos, nor Laertes, nor the suitors, nor Penelope behave in accordance with this presumption. The behaviour of the *Odyssey* characters and indeed the entire situation reflected in this poem only become consistent when approached on the assumption of matrimonial accession to the throne.

If the dynastic succession is transmitted through the female line, the king's son's ascending the throne would amount to incestuous marriage to his mother or sister. Compare, indeed, the case of Oedipus, which is perhaps the most conspicuous example of the father-to-son succession in the Greek heroic tradition. This would be enough to disqualify Odysseus' son Telemachos as his father's successor on the throne of Ithaca. The only person who would count in such a situation is one who has the prospect of marrying the queen. As a matter of fact, this conclusion comes close enough to that arrived at by many *Odyssey* scholars. Thus, Finley, though rejecting solutions based on matriarchy or matrilinear descent, nevertheless admits that the prerogative of bestowing the kingship 'mysteriously belongs to Penelope':

> Along with his [Odysseus'] rule, his successor was also to take his wife, his widow as many thought. On this point they were terribly insistent, and it may be suggested that their reasoning was this: that by Penelope's receiving the suitor of her choice into the bed of Odysseus, some shadow of legitimacy, however dim and fictitious, would be thrown over the next king.[21]

Yet comparison of Penelope's case with that of Klytaimestra, whose receiving the man of her choice into the bed of Agamemnon (who, according to some versions, himself became king of Mycenae upon murdering Klytaimestra's first husband Tantalos) made a king of Aigisthos, shows clearly enough that it was not merely a shadow of legitimacy but this very

---

20 Finley 1979: 90.   21 Finley 1979: 91, 90.

legitimacy itself that marriage with the queen was to bestow on the future king of Ithaca.[22]

In the course of time the institution of kingship by marriage, which can be shown to underlie many episodes of Greek legend, was reinterpreted in the light of later ideas of succession and blurred by a host of stock motifs, such as those of the exiled prince, the sonless king and the like.[23] However, neither the story of Helen's marriage nor that of Penelope and her suitors, both of them the pivotal points of the Trojan tradition, lent themselves to such restructuring. It is these two cases that highlight the cumulative evidence supplied by Greek legend as to the nature of royal succession in Bronze Age Greece. To provide the practice described with a viable historical parallel, we should turn to the documents of ancient Western Asia.

INTRODUCING THE HITTIE TAWANANNA

It was noticed long ago that in historic times in Asia Minor there still existed 'a marriage custom, according to which inheritance and kingship was transmitted through the female line, which often led to the practice of incest within royal families'.[24] As with other so-called 'Asianic' customs, it was unequivocally identified as distinctly non-Indo-European. The greater was the astonishment when, with the discovery of the Hittite royal archives, the same characteristics were found to have existed in the Hittite monarchy. It is not surprising, therefore, that they were ascribed to the non-Indo-European Khattian substratum of the Hittites. Compare, for example, the assessment of the status of the Hittite queen made by O. R. Gurney in 1973:

> It is generally agreed that the peculiar position of the Hittite queen, whose title, *tawanannash*, was inherited only on the death of her predecessor and was retained for life, can only be explained as a survival of a system of matrilinear succession which must once have prevailed among the ancient Khattians. It has been suggested that the king (*labarnash*) was originally merely 'the queen's

---

22 The Klytaimestra situation compares well with that in Argos, where the queen Aigialeia and her new spouse Kometes son of Sthenelos are said to have expelled the former king Diomedes on his return from Troy, and in Crete, whence the former king Idomeneus was expelled in exactly the same way. See Apollod. *Epit.* 6. 9–10. On Klytaimestra and Tantalos see Eur. *IA* 1148–56; Apollod. *Epit.* 2. 16; Paus. 2.18.2; 2.22.4.

23 On similar African practices of transferring present succession patterns into the past see Henige 1974: 55–9.

24 Ramsay 1928: 238.

consort': the Indo-European immigrants would have achieved kingship by marrying the local 'matriarch', as did so many heroes of Greek legend who succeeded to thrones in Anatolia by marrying the daughter of the local king and, having done so, sought to establish their own patriarchal system.[25]

As we have seen, heroes of Greek legend succeeded to thrones by marrying the daughter of the local king not only in Anatolia but also in Greece itself. Nevertheless, the case of the Hittite queen is worth dwelling upon, in that it offers us the unique opportunity to confront the material of Greek legend with written sources belonging to the Bronze Age. As we shall see, these sources not only supply the traditional material dealt with thus far with historical substance but also suggest a broader cultural context against which the Bronze Age Aegean should be considered.

It is generally recognised that the peculiar feature of the Hittite monarchy as it emerges from the records relating to the so-called Old Hittite Kingdom (1750–1500 BC) is the independent position of the queen. To quote T. R. Bryce: 'As a general rule, it seems that the woman who held this position was the wife of the reigning king, that she held important powers in her own right, perhaps as chief priestess of the Hittite realm, and that if she outlived her husband she retained her status and authority until her own death', while J. G. Macqueen wrote as early as 1959:

The position of queen among the Hittites is unusual both for the important part she played in matters of cult and state, and for the fact, so often commented upon, that she continued to reign after the death of her husband. Not until after her death could the new king's wife assume the style of 'queen'. Of these facts there can be only one explanation. The queen must originally have reigned in her own right.[26]

As Hittite tradition has it, Hittite history began with the legendary King Labarna (or Tabarna). However, the earliest Hittite texts, which can be dated to the reign of the founder of the Old Hittite Kingdom Hattusili I (ca. 1650 BC) and that of his successor Mursili I, contain not a single reference to the events of the reign of Labarna. The name itself occurs

---

25 Gurney 1973b: 667. Cf. above, p. 51.
26 Bryce 1983: 56; Macqueen 1959: 181; see now also Bryce 2002: 21: 'the reigning queen and chief consort of the king, high priestess of the Hittite realm and sometimes a politically powerful figure in her own right, who retained her status until the end of her life even if she outlived her husband'. See also Goetze 1957a: 93; Gurney 1954: 51–4, 82 and 1973b: 667. According to Bin-Nun 1975 (see esp. p. 102) and Sürenhagen 1998, Tawananna should not be considered the king's wife, but the extant evidence can hardly support such an interpretation, cf. Macqueen 1986: 76; Gurney 1973a: 237 ('the whole of Hittite usage demands that we should recognise Labarna and Tawananna as wedded king and queen'); Bryce 1983: 56–7, 1998: 96 and 2002: 21 (quoted above).

quite frequently, but it appears to be used mainly as a title and is found applied to Hattusili I himself, to his sister's son whom he had adopted and proclaimed his heir but later disinherited, and once to his predecessor whom he styles elsewhere as 'son of my grandfather' (see the Appendix). In later periods, the title was also used to designate the Hittite kings in general, especially in so far as their activities in matters of ceremony and ritual were concerned; in this specific context, it was often linked with the queen's title, Tawananna.

In a bilingual Hittite–Akkadian text (the so-called *Annals of Hattusili*), which was discovered in 1957, Hattusili I applies to himself the title 'the brother's son of Tawananna':[27]

HITTITE
    [Thus Tabar]na Hattusili, Great
    [King, King of Hattu]sa, man
    of Kussar: in the Land of
    Hattusa [he ruled as king,]
    the brother's son of Tawananna.
AKKADIAN
    Great King Tabarna exercised
    kingship in Hattusa, the
    [brother's son] of Taw[ananna.

It is hard not to agree with Gurney that Hattusili's self-identification as 'the brother's son of Tawananna' (i.e. Tawananna's brother's son) is problematic in more than one respect:

It is, however, characteristic of a matrilinear society that kingship and authority in general are exercised, not by the husband, but by the brother of the 'matriarch'. Succession passes in the female line, and so in effect a ruler is succeeded by his sister's son: the husband is outside the family. Consequently, if Tawananna represents the ancient 'matriarch', Labarna should have been her brother and his successor should have been her son. Is it possible that some such ideas lie behind the enigmatical phrase 'brother's son of Tawananna' used by Hattusili I to describe his filiation? As it stands, the phrase gives just the reverse of the sense required by this hypothesis.[28]

As far as I can see, the main difficulty concerning the interpretation of the expression lies in the fact that, since Tawananna is generally believed to have been the wife of Labarna and since brother–sister marriage was strictly prohibited in Hittite society, the father of the reigning king could

---

27 *Annals* I, 1–3 (KBo X1 + KBo X2); ed. Imparati and Saporetti 1965. The English translations of
    Hittite texts are by O. R. Gurney unless otherwise stated.
28 Gurney 1973b: 667; for further discussion see Bryce 1998: 97; Sürenhagen 1998.

not have been the king who reigned before him. However, if we assume that what is dealt with here is a case of dynastic succession transmitted from mother to daughter, this difficulty ceases to exist. As we saw in the preceding section, one of the characteristic features of matrilinear succession is that it automatically precludes the father–son accession to the throne.

Let us now try to analyse the expression 'the brother's son of Tawananna' as it stands.[29] The expression clearly implies that, apart from Hattusili himself, three persons should be taken into account: Tawananna, Tawananna's husband and Tawananna's brother. Since we have to accept the limitations imposed by the prohibition of brother–sister marriage among the Hittites, we can say with certainty that Tawananna's brother could not have been the reigning king, Labarna. And since it is reasonable to assume that Tawananna had a husband who was, at the same time, the reigning king, we have to postulate yet another person, Tawananna's husband Labarna. The relationships between Hattusili's antecedents would, therefore, be as follows:[30]

```
           ┌─────────────┐
Labarna-Tawananna   Tawananna's brother
```

It seems to follow from this scheme that what we have here is a case of royal succession involving two lines – that of Labarna and that of Tawananna's brother – whose male representatives assume the throne in turn. On the assumption that Labarna cannot be succeeded by his son, the question as to who will be his immediate successor on the throne is of course of crucial importance. Let us assume that the Labarna and the Tawananna dealt with in this scheme are the first king and queen of the dynasty. In so far as Tawananna II would be the daughter of Tawananna I, Labarna II cannot be the son of Labarna I and Tawananna I (again, because brother-sister marriage was prohibited). As far as I can see, the two most plausible candidates to succeed Labarna I would be Tawananna I's brother's son and Tawanannas I's brother himself.

It is true of course that the position of the son of Tawananna's brother would agree well with the formula 'Tawananna's brother's son' which was the starting-point of this discussion. His marriage to Tawananna's

---

29 Cf. Finkelberg 1997b.
30 For a similar reconstruction see Bryce 1983: 57. Sürenhagen 1998 also suggests that Labarna was succeeded by his sister's son, but he takes Labarna and Tawananna as brother and sister rather than husband and wife.

daughter would be an instance of cross-cousin marriage of the 'father's sister's daughter' type.[31] Yet, when considered dynastically this kind of marriage would imply that it is only the members of one line, that of Tawananna's brother, who would have a right to the throne whereas the members of Labarna's line would be excluded from royal succession. Surely, this does not look like an especially promising dynastic principle. As distinct from this, the marriage of Tawananna I's brother to his sister's daughter would render him Labarna II and would enable the son of Labarna I and Tawananna I to become Labarna III by marrying his niece, the daughter of Labarna II and Tawananna II. In that case, Labarna IV would be the son of Labarna II and Tawananna II, having ascended the throne by marrying the daughter of Labarna III and Tawananna III, and so on (see Fig. 4). This kind of marriage, viz. to a woman who is both mother's brother's daughter and sister's daughter, guarantees that male members of both ruling clans would have access to the throne. It is none other than a particular case of alternate succession, a system of succession attested also for other traditional societies; when more than two lines are involved, this system of succession is also called rotational.[32]

If a king marries the daughter of his predecessor who is also his sister's daughter, the male representatives of both ruling clans would have access to the throne and the term 'the brother's son of Tawananna' would be equally applicable to each reigning king (see Fig. 4). This seems to agree with the spirit of Hattusili's inscription, because the formula 'the brother's son of Tawananna' that Hattusili applies to himself in both the Hittite and the Akkadian version looks like a dynastic title indicative of the legitimacy of his accession to the throne rather than an *ad hoc* identification of his relationship to the other members of the Hittite royal house.[33]

---

31 This line of interpretation is adopted e.g. in Sürenhagen 1998: 75–94.

32 Cf. Henige 1974: 8: 'Rotational and promotional systems, which allow various segments of a society to participate in the ruling office, are common in Africa.' On alternate succession see esp. Lyle 1990: 119–33 and 1997: 67–9; see also below, pp. 79–87. Note also that the kind of marriage described above would conform to the special relationship between nephew and maternal uncle as suggested for the Proto-Indo-European kinship system. See Gamkrelidze and Ivanov 1995: 674–5; for Archaic and Classical Greece and early Byzantium see Bremer 1983 (with bibliography); for the medieval examples, see Pembroke 1965: 244–7.

33 Bryce 1983: 57–8, also regards Hattusili's predecessor as 'his uncle by marriage, husband of the Tawananna referred to in the *Annals*, and son-in-law of Hattusili's grandfather, referred to in the *Testament*', and holds that the title in question somehow gives legitimation to Hattusili's succession, but in his opinion 'this particular form of regnal succession is unique amongst the Hittite kings, and may well have been due to a unique set of circumstances which resulted in Hattusili's succession'. Sürenhagen 1998: 86–7, unequivocally interprets the title as giving legitimation to accession to the throne. See also Puhvel 1989: 353; Bryce 1998: 97.

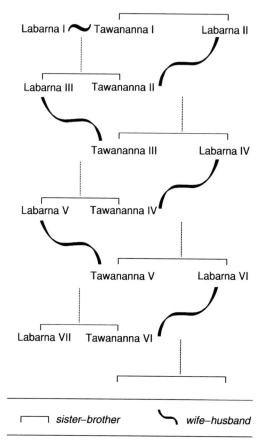

Figure 4. Royal succession in the Old Hittite Kingdom (after Finkelberg 1997b).

Let us turn now to the actual chain of succession in the Hittite royal house as it comes to light in our sources. According to the so-called *Testament of Hattusili*, Hattusili proclaimed his sister's son as his heir, but then disinherited him and adopted as heir a boy named Mursili; the latter is styled his son in the so-called *Telipinu Edict*, written about a hundred years later, and his grandson in another relatively late text (see further the Appendix).[34] As we learn from the *Telipinu Edict*, after coming

34 The Aleppo treaty (KBo I 6). On the *Telipinu Edict* see below.

of age Mursili led a highly successful campaign against Babylon, destroyed the city and defeated all the lands of the Hurrians. Shortly after returning to his capital Hattusa, he was assassinated as a result of conspiracy and his brother-in-law Hantili ascended the throne. Hantili was succeeded by his son-in-law Zidanta, who was soon assassinated by his 'son' (presumably, his legitimate heir, see the Appendix) Ammuna, who became king in his stead. After unspecified bloodshed that followed the death of Ammuna, a certain Huzziya became king. Telipinu was married to Huzziya's eldest sister Istapariya, and when Huzziya was found to be plotting the death of his sister and brother-in-law, Telipinu drove him and his five brothers into exile and assumed the throne or, to use his own words, 'ascended the throne of his father'.[35]

Whatever the exact details of the dynastic struggle described in the *Telipinu Edict*, it cannot be denied that its underlying pattern is that of perpetual confrontation between kings' sons on the one hand and kings' sons-in-law on the other: either the former try to get rid of the latter in order to accelerate their accession to the throne or the latter try to dispose of the former in order to ensure the stability of their reign.[36] This corroborates our earlier suggestion that what is found here is in fact a system of alternate succession in which only the members of two clans are allowed to participate. At the same time, the situation is further complicated by the fact that not all of the king's sons are necessarily also sons of his queen. It may be suggested indeed that, although a really smooth succession could only be guaranteed if the heir was the son of both a Labarna and a Tawananna, the title 'the brother's son of Tawananna' applied to both categories of sons, and it is reasonable to suppose that among the king's sons who participated in the dynastic struggle there were those who were not sons of a Tawananna.

With his accession to the throne, Telipinu laid down a law of succession. I quote:[37]

Let a prince, a son, of the first rank, become king. If there is no prince of the first rank, let one who is a son of the second rank become king. If, however, there is no prince, (no) son, let them take a husband for her who is a daughter of the first rank, and let him become king.

35 According to Goetze 1957b: 56, by 'father' Telipinu really means 'father-in-law'.
36 Cf. Dovgyalo 1963: 76–8.
37 *Telepinu Edict* II, 36–9 (2Bo TU, 23A = KBo III 1); ed. Hoffmann 1984.

It is usually held that this law of succession announces the establishment of the patrilinear succession dear to the heart of the Indo-European invaders.[38] Leaving aside the question of whether matrilinear succession should necessarily be considered a non-Indo-European practice (above, p. 51), it seems highly implausible that Telipinu, who himself became king as a result of his marriage to the sister of his predecessor and who was succeeded by his son-in-law Alluwamna,[39] could have issued a decree that would make both his own and his successor's accession to the throne illegitimate. This being the case, I would suggest a different line of interpretation for the *Telipinu Edict.*

It is generally assumed that the 'rank' of a king's son depends on whether the mother was the queen or a secondary wife.[40] This would mean that the 'son of the first rank' is a 'brother's son of Tawananna' who is also the son of Tawananna and 'the son of the second rank' a 'brother's son of Tawananna' who is however not Tawananna's son.[41] This interpretation concurs with the accepted one in that the distinction between the two categories of sons is seen as that between the sons by the primary wife and those by a secondary wife of the king: one of the latter can become king only when no sons of the primary wife are available. Yet the current conclusion that the succession implied here is necessarily a patrilinear one is unwarranted. Consider again the third possibility specified by Telipinu: 'If, however, there is no prince, (no) son, let them take a husband for her who is a daughter of the first rank, and let him become king.' A 'daughter of the first rank' is of course one who belongs to the dynastic matriliny which supplied the Tawanannas. No provision for 'a daughter of the second rank' is made in the female line. The reason is clear: while the queen's husband can be one who does not fully belong to the line of Tawananna, the queen herself cannot. That is to say, whereas Telipinu's law of succession regulates the order of accession to the throne among the male members of the royal family, it does not touch the principle of matrilinear succession itself. Whether he was a son of the first rank or a son of the second rank or even a total stranger (see further

---

38 See e.g. Macqueen 1959; Dovgyalo 1963; Gurney 1973b: 667; Bryce 1983: 152–3 and 1998: 114–16; Sürenhagen 1998: 94.
39 See Goetze 1957b: 57, cf. Gurney 1973b: 663; Bryce 1998: 119 and n. 53.
40 Gurney 1973b: 666; Bryce 1983: 153; 1998: 115 and 2002: 27–9. For a detailed discussion see Dovgyalo 1963: 73–4.
41 Cf. Bryce 2002: 29: 'If she [Tawananna] had no sons the succession passed to a son of the second rank – presumably the offspring of the so-called *esertu* wife, a woman inferior in status to the chief wife though still of free birth.'

the Appendix), the Hittite king had to fulfil one essential condition: he had to be the husband of Tawananna.

It is worth mentioning in this connection that the title 'the brother's son of Tawananna', which, as we have seen, was probably used for designating the legitimate successor to the throne in the Old Hittite Kingdom, compares well with 'Shilkhakha's sister's son', a royal title which was regularly applied to the rulers of ancient Elam. Shilkhakha was the second king in the dynasty of Eparti (ca. 1850 BC), and his sister attained the status of an ancestral mother of the dynasty: 'Of the later Eparti kings only those were considered truly entitled to the throne who were descended from Shilkhakha's sister, who also appears in the sources as "gracious mother" (*amma hastuk*). It is clear that there was in ancient Elam, embedded in the fratriarchal succession to the throne, a legitimating right in the female line.'[42] If we take into account that Shilkhakha was succeeded on the throne by his sister's son Attakhushu, this will give us a further reason to conclude that succession in the female line applied not only to the Old Hittite Kingdom but also to ancient Elam.[43] With this in mind, let us turn again to heroic Greece.

A LINE OF QUEENS AND ROTATIONAL SUCCESSION

As early as 1905 Sir James Frazer pointed out in his *Lectures on the Early History of the Kingship* that the succession of the first Latin kings was in the female line, that is, through marriage with the king's daughter or widow; he also adduced several episodes from Greek legend, including some of those discussed above.[44] Frazer, as well as other scholars afterwards, took this evidence to mean that in both Greece and Rome kingship by marriage amounted to matrilinear reckoning of descent or, to put it in his own words, that we have here 'a state of society where

---

42 Hinz 1973: 261. The relationships within the founding triad of the Eparti dynasty, viz. Eparti (the first king), Shilkhakha (the second king) and Shilkhakha's sister, come very close to those between Tawananna's husband (Labarna I), Tawananna's brother (Labarna II) and Tawananna herself as outlined above.

43 Eparti is usually taken as father of Shilkhakha who, however, is not regarded as being married to his own sister. This creates difficulties as regards the status of both Shilkhakha's sister and Shilkhakha's successor, cf. Hinz 1973: 261: 'On his succession to the throne about 1830 BC Shilkhakha installed his "sister's son" Attakhushu as prince of Susa, doubtless because he had no son of his own. The sources do not say who Attakhushu's father was: whether he was Shilkhakha's brother or someone else who had married the sister.' However, comparison with the Hittite scheme of succession allows us to suggest that Eparti was married to Shilkhakha's sister, that he was succeeded by Shilkhakha and that the latter was succeeded by Eparti's son Attakhushu.

44 Frazer 1905: 238–41. Cf. also Frazer 1922: 152–8.

nobility is reckoned only through women, in other words, where descent through the mother is everything and descent through the father is nothing'.[45] However, examination of the evidence involved shows that, as far as the Greek sources are concerned at least, the interpretation proposed by Frazer is unwarranted.

The simple and undeniable fact is that reckoning of descent in the Greek genealogies is strictly patrilinear. The Greeks, from Homer to later genealogists, were perfectly able to trace a person's agnatic descent up to Deukalion himself or to another legendary forefather. Thus, Glaukos' genealogy as given in the *Iliad* comprises six generations (Aiolos - Sisyphos - Glaukos - Bellerophon - Hippolochos - Glaukos); Aineias' eight (Zeus–Dardanos–Erichthonios–Tros–Assarakos–Kapus–Anchises–Aineias) and Kodros' genealogy adduced by Hellanicus comprises twelve generations (Deukalion–Hellen–Aiolos–Salmoneus–Tyro–Neleus–Periklymenos–Boros–Penthilos–Andropompos–Melanthos–Kodros).[46] Nothing even remotely similar to this can be found in the female line. Any attempt to trace a sufficiently long line of matrilinear descent is doomed to failure, obviously because Greek heroic tradition, our main source, shows a lack of interest in genealogies reckoned through women.[47] Considering that, as we have seen, we have good reason to believe that in Bronze Age Greece kingship by marriage was a generally accepted practice, this fact seems to indicate that patrilinear reckoning of descent and kingship by marriage were not mutually exclusive after all. Accordingly, determining the relationship between the two is our next task.

Greek tradition is unanimous in that the Aiolid Melampous came from Messenia to Argos, where he cured the daughters of the king Proitos of their madness, married one of them, Iphianassa, and thus became king.[48] According to some, Melampous' marriage was accompanied by a dynastic arrangement stipulating that not only Melampous himself but also his brother Bias would receive a share in the kingship. As a result, the Argive kingdom was divided into three parts, of which two went to the descendants of Melampous and Bias and one to the representatives of the local

45 Frazer 1905: 234.
46 Glaukos: *Il.* 6.152–5, 195–206; Aineias: *Il.* 20.215–40; Kodros: Hellan. 4 F 125 Jacoby. On Kodros' genealogy see also Fig. 1 and below, pp. 94–5.
47 Both the *Catalogue of Women* as reconstructed by Merkelbach and West and West's subsequent analysis of the structure of this poem demonstrate beyond doubt that the entries dealing with women are subordinated to the overall patrilinear arrangement of the genealogical material, see Merkelbach and West 1967 and West 1985: 31–50, 173–82.
48 Pherec. 3 F 114 Jacoby, cf. *Od.* 15.238–41.

dynasty, descendants of Proitos' son Megapenthes.[49] Yet a closer examination of this arrangement shows that the tradition of the triple kingship of
Argos should not be taken as meaning that at any given moment there
were three kings jointly ruling over Argos.

To begin with, Bias' marriage to a daughter of Proitos, which was
supposed to be part of the arrangement, is hard to reconcile with his
marriage to Neleus' daughter Pero, which is one of the principal Greek
traditions as regards the ancient heroines.[50] In the *Catalogue of Women*,
it is already as the husband of Pero that Bias goes to Argos, presumably
only to receive a share in Proitos' kingdom, whereas the *Odyssey* definitely implies that Bias remained in Pylos and that Melampous went to
Argos alone.[51] This finds a further corroboration in the fact that, while
the descendants of Bias and Pero are well known to Greek tradition,
there is no trace of Bias' children by a daughter of Proitos. As to
Megapenthes, we saw above (pp. 66–8)that the entire issue of his late birth
most probably purported to account for the disturbing fact that a son of
Proitos did not succeed his father in Argos. It seems to follow from this
that of the three persons – Melampous, Bias, Megapenthes – who presumably became kings of Argos upon the agreement between Melampous
and Proitos, only Melampous himself can be seriously considered as king
of Argos.

In the next generation, Melampous' sons Antiphates and Mantios are
hardly more than mere names, and there is no trace of such kings in
Greek tradition.[52] As distinct from this, Talaos, presumably son of Bias
and Pero, is explicitly referred to by Pindar as the ruler of Argos.[53]
However, placing Talaos a generation after Melampous is difficult
for chronological reasons. Indeed, if we try to synchronise the line of
Melampous with that of his brother Bias, we shall find that the four-
generation sequence Melampous–Antiphates–Oïkles–Amphiaraos is
answered by a three-generation sequence Bias–Talaos–Adrastos, which is
hardly possible because Amphiaraos and Adrastos must belong in the
same generation, that of the Seven against Thebes. Note that not only
Adrastos but also other sons of Talaos (Aristomachos, Hippomedon,
Mekisteus, Parthenopaios, Pronax) are referred to in various sources as

49 Hdt. 9.34; Diod.Sic. 4.68; Apollod. 1.102; 2.28–9; Paus. 2.18.4.
50 *Od.* 11.281–97; 15.226–39; Pherec. 3 F 33 Jacoby.
51 Hes. fr. 37.5–15 M-W, cf. West 1985: 79 n. 109; *Od.* 15.235–9.
52 *Od.* 15.242–55, cf. Hes. fr. 136 M-W; Pherec. 3 FF 115–16 Jacoby. For a discussion of Melampous'
    descendants see West 1985: 79–81.
53 Pi. *N.* 9.13–15.

participating in that expedition. Significantly, such an early authority on Greek genealogies as Pherecydes of Athens does not include Talaos in his list of the children of Bias and Pero; the first mention of Talaos as son of Bias and Pero is as late as Apollonius Rhodius.[54] In view of this, it seems reasonable to take Talaos as grandson rather than as son of Bias and Pero. This would leave us with Megapenthes' son Anaxagoras as the only candidate to succeed Melampous, and indeed Anaxagoras was known not only as king of Argos but also as the founder of a clan.[55]

Accordingly, the representatives of the next generation must have been Oïkles (Melampous' line), Talaos (Bias' line) and Hipponoos (Megapenthes' line). Of these three, Oïkles, though famous enough, was at home in Arcadia rather than in Argos, whereas Hipponoos is reported to have been king of Olenos in Achaia.[56] This would entail that Melampous not only ruled alone but was succeeded by a single king who was neither his own son nor the son of his brother Bias but Megapenthes' son Anaxagoras and that the latter was succeeded by Talaos, a representative of the line of Bias. The triple kingship of Argos should, therefore, be understood as rotational or circulating succession, a widespread system of succession which Henige defines as follows:

An individual may become ruler because he is chosen to represent the lineage whose turn it is to succeed in a system where there are several eligible lineages. Such a ruler will be genetically unrelated to his predecessor.[57]

As far as the case under discussion is concerned, this would mean that only the lineages of Melampous, Bias and Megapenthes had the right to sit on the throne of Argos in turn. This should help us to decide who was originally considered to be the Argive king in the generation of the Seven.

This generation was represented by Amphiaraos (Melampous' line), Adrastos (Bias' line) and Kapaneus (Megapenthes' line). If the Argive kingship was indeed based on the principle of rotational succession, the next in turn was Melampous' descendant Amphiaraos. Yet it was Bias' descendant Adrastos who is usually seen as king of Argos in the generation of the Theban War.[58] Note, however, that Adrastos was at home also in

---

54 Ap. Rhod. 1.118–20. The children of Bias and Pero mentioned by Pherecydes are Perialkes, Aretos and Alphesiboia, see Pherec. 3 F 33.37 Jacoby.
55 Oἱ Ἀναξαγορίδαι Paus. 2.18.5; 2.30.10. On Anaxagoras' genealogical position see West 1985: 177; cf. also ibid. 81 and n. 111.
56 Oïkles: Apollod. 3.87; Paus. 8.36.6; Hipponoos: Diod.Sic. 4.35.1–2; Apollod. 1.74.
57 Henige 1974: 131. See also above, n. 32.
58 See, however, Pi. *N.* 9.13–14, where Adrastos and his brothers are seen as having been expelled from Argos by Amphiaraos: φεῦγε γὰρ Ἀμφιαρῆ ποτε θρασυμήδεα καὶ δεινὰν στάσιν / πατρίων οἴκων ἀπό τ' Ἄργεος· ἀρχοὶ δ' οὐκ ἔτ' ἔσαν Ταλαοῦ παῖδες, βιασθέντες λύᾳ.

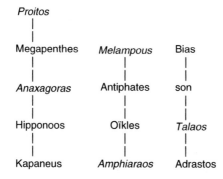

Figure 5. Kings of Argos (after Finkelberg 1991).

Sicyon and it is only as the Sicyonian king that he is known to the composer of the Catalogue of Ships.[59] Note also that Sicyon and not Argos was the place that had Adrastos' *heroon* and cult.[60]

As distinct from this, no other kingdom is attested for Amphiaraos, whereas the fact that his sons appear as Helen's Argive suitors in the *Catalogue of Women* strongly suggests that their father was envisaged as the ruler of Argos.[61] It seems, then, that Amphiaraos' original position was misinterpreted in the later tradition that, naturally enough, was inclined to believe that Talaos' successor on the throne must have been his son Adrastos rather than his son-in-law Amphiaraos.[62] Accordingly, the Argive 'king-list' from Proitos to the generation of the Theban War can be represented as shown in Figure 5 (the names of the actual kings of Argos are italicised).

Interestingly, the above analysis renders illegitimate the kingship of Diomedes, reported for the next generation, because Diomedes belonged to none of the three lineages whose representatives sat in turn on the throne of Argos (though in some sources he is connected through the female line with the lineage of Megapenthes). In the Homeric Catalogue of Ships, where the triple kingship of Argos is already represented as simultaneous, the Argive forces are led by Sthenelos (Megapenthes' line),

---

59 *Il.* 2.572: καὶ Σικυῶν', ὅθ' ἄρ' Ἄδρηστος πρῶτ' ἐμβασίλευεν.   60 Hdt. 5.67.

61 Hes. fr. 197.6–7 M-W.

62 In a similar manner, Agamemnon is sometimes represented as king of Amyclae, of which his son Orestes was generally believed to be king, and the latter as king of Mycenae. Adrastos' kingship at Argos was rejected on independent grounds by Nilsson 1932: 113–14, see esp. p. 114: 'Adrastos was not king of the city of Argos, though he is genealogically annexed to the kingly house of Argos'. Cf. also above, n. 23.

Euryalos (Bias' line), but above all by Diomedes, who in fact occupies the place of the descendants of Melampous.[63] It is noteworthy that the illegitimacy of Diomedes' rule was recognised by Pausanias, in whose opinion the kingship of Argos really belonged to Kapaneus' son Sthenelos. Pausanias' conclusion fits in well with the order of succession as reconstructed above: according to this order, the legitimate successor of Amphiaraos was indeed the representative of Megapenthes' line in the next generation, that is, Kapaneus' son Sthenelos.[64]

Let us turn now to the female line of the royal house of Argos. Here, the sequence of kings Proitos–Melampous is answered by the sequence of queens Stheneboia[65]–Iphianassa, a clear-cut case of mother-to-daughter succession. Unfortunately, we have a lacuna in the following generation, because the name of Anaxagoras' wife is not known to us. But the queen in the generation after this was surely Talaos' wife Lysimache, and her daughter Eriphyle, the sinister protagonist of the Theban saga, was the wife of Amphiaraos who, as we saw, must have originally been seen as Talaos' successor on the throne of Argos. The fact that both the Stheneboia–Iphianassa and the Lysimache–Eriphyle sequence present mother-to-daughter succession strongly suggests that Anaxagoras' queen was the daughter of Iphianassa and Melampous and the mother of Lysimache (Fig. 6).

A comparison of the male and the female line of the kings of Argos shows that, as in the case of alternate succession in the Hittite monarchy, rotation between the ruling clans was designed to ensure succession in the male line under the conditions of kingship by marriage. Its ultimate purpose was obviously to guarantee that only the eligible patrilinear lineages would have access to the throne. That this would be a correct interpretation of the triple kingship of Argos is corroborated by the fact that similar arrangements can be shown to have been relevant to other kingdoms of heroic Greece as well.

---

63 *Il.* 2.563–6. Euryalos is son of Adrastos' brother Mekisteus, Adrastos himself having been rendered childless after the death of his son Aigialeus in the expedition of the Epigoni. This is apparently why Homer emphasises that Euryalos is a descendant of Talaos from whom Adrastos also descends, see *Il.* 2.566, 23.678: Μηκιστέος υἱὸς Ταλαϊονίδαο ἄνακτος.

64 Paus. 2.30.10. The tradition according to which Kometes son of Sthenelos married Diomedes' wife Aigialeia in the time of the Trojan War and expelled Diomedes from Argos upon his return from Troy (above, n. 22), may be significant in this connection. However that may be, as far as Homer is concerned, the rule formulated by Henige for rotational succession systems in Africa seems to be applicable, see Henige 1974: 33: 'In rotational succession systems rulers representing extinct lineages will often be forgotten when their legitimizing functions are no longer required.'

65 Or Antheia, see *Il.* 6.160.

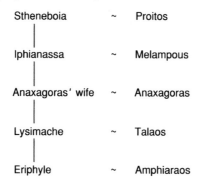

Figure 6. Queens of Argos (after Finkelberg 1991).

Amyklas, the son of Lakedaimon and Sparta, is credited by Apollodorus with the line of descendants Amyklas–Kynortas–Perieres–Oibalos–Tyndareos. The line is problematic in that it makes us postulate with no good reason the existence of two persons named Perieres, Perieres son of Kynortas and Perieres son of Aiolos, the latter attested as early as the *Catalogue of Women*; in addition, Apollodorus occasionally takes Perieres as father of Tyndareos.[66] Only Perieres son of Aiolos is known to Pausanias, and, as distinct from Apollodorus, he is consistent in representing Oibalos as Tyndareos' father.[67] It seems that Apollodorus' confusion as regards Perieres' genealogical position resulted from the contamination of Amyklas' genealogy, viz. Amyklas–Kynortas–Oibalos–Tyndareos, with the king-list of Amyclae which featured Perieres as Tyndareos' predecessor on the throne. That is to say, Perieres the Aiolid, who succeeded Kynortas and was followed by Tyndareos, was erroneously taken by Apollodorus as son of the former and father of the latter.[68] Considering that, according to Pherecydes, Amyklas was succeeded on the throne by his son-in-law Argeios son of Pelops,[69] there seems reason to suggest that originally the succession of the rulers of Amyclae was represented as follows: Amyklas–Argeios the Pelopid–Perieres the Aiolid–

---

66 Apollod. 1.87; 3.117; 3.123 (with Frazer's Loeb commentary *ad loc.*); Hes. fr. 10.3 M-W.
67 Paus. 2.21.7; 3.1.3–4; 4.2.2, cf. 4.2.4. Tyndareos appears as son of Oibalos already in the *Catalogue of Women*, see Hes. fr. 199.8 M-W.
68 That Amyklas' genealogy as given by Apollodorus resulted from a contamination and that the correct stemma is Kynortas–Oibalos–Tyndareos was argued on independent grounds in West 1985: 67 n. 86. Cf. also above, nn. 8 and 23.
69 Pherec. 3 F 132 Jacoby: Ἀργεῖος δὲ ὁ Πέλοπος ἔρχεται παρ᾽ Ἀμύκλαν εἰς᾽ Ἀμύκλας, καὶ γαμεῖ τοῦ Ἀμύκλα θυγατέρα Ἡγησάνδραν (= Schol. *Od.* 4.22), cf. also Schol. Eur. *Or.* 4.

Tyndareos the Amyklaid. If this reconstruction is correct, the kingship
of Amyclae was, as in the case of Argos, based on rotational succession
between three patrilinear lineages – those of Amyklas, of Pelops and
of Aiolos – and the marriage of Menelaos the Pelopid to Tyndareos'
daughter Helen fully conformed to this arrangement.

The rulers of Bronze Age Thebes are usually regarded as descendants of
Kadmos. Yet, the tradition has also preserved the names of Theban kings,
such as Pentheus or Kreon, who were not of Kadmos' line. Both are
descendants of Echion, one of the earth-born Spartoi, who became
Kadmos' son-in-law by marrying his daughter Agaue. Since the descendants of both Kadmos and Echion emerge in our sources as kings of Thebes
and since the 'earth-born' nature of Echion suggests a local origin of his
clan, it seems reasonable to suppose that, as in the case of Argos, in
Thebes too we have a dynastic arrangement which led to alternate
succession between the local lineage and the lineage of the newcomer
Kadmos.[70] There is little evidence as to the female line of the royal house
of Thebes, but it seems significant that queen Iokaste, marriage to whom
made the newcomer Oedipus king of Thebes, was both widow of Laios,
who belonged to the line of Kadmos, and sister of Kreon, who was a
descendant of Echion.

There are two conflicting traditions as regards the royal dynasty of
Mycenae. On the one hand, Mycenae was generally believed to have been
founded by Perseus, a prince of the royal house of Tiryns, and at least one
Perseid, Perseus' grandson Eurystheus, is unanimously reported as the
king of Mycenae. On the other hand, Mycenae is firmly associated with
the Pelopids Atreus, Thyestes and Agamemnon, and Homer's account of
the holders of the royal sceptre of this city totally ignores the Perseids.[71]
This discrepancy led M. L. West to the conclusion that one of the two
traditions as to the kings of Mycenae, namely, the one that connects it
with the Pelopids, is not authentic.[72] Yet the examples of Argos, Amyclae
and Thebes strongly suggest that we are dealing with alternate succession

70 In his account of Boeotia, Pausanias gives the succession of the kings of Thebes during and after
   the Trojan War as alternating between the descendants of Polyneikes' son Thersandros and those
   of Peneleos, the leader of the Boeotians in the Trojan War, see Paus. 9.5.14–16, cf. *Il.* 2.494.
   Nothing is known of Peneleos' origin, but he was certainly not descended from Kadmos. It may
   be significant in this connection that Leitos, the other non-Kadmeian leader of the Boeotians in
   the Trojan War (*Il.* 2.494), is given the epithet γηγενής, 'earth-born', in Eur. *Iph.A.* 259.
71 *Il.* 2.104–8 Ἑρμείας δὲ ἄναξ δῶκεν Πέλοπι πληξίππῳ, / αὐτὰρ ὁ αὖτε Πέλοψ δῶκ' Ἀτρέϊ,
   ποιμένι λαῶν· / Ἀτρεὺς δὲ θνῄσκων ἔλιπεν πολύαρνι Θυέστῃ, / αὐτὰρ ὁ αὖτε Θυέστ'
   Ἀγαμέμνονι λεῖπε φορῆναι / πολλῇσιν νήσοισι καὶ Ἄργεϊ παντὶ ἀνάσσειν.
72 West 1985: 157–9; cf. J. Hall 1995: 580.

between two clans, the Perseids and the Pelopids, the purpose of which was to secure their royal position at Mycenae.

Had the descent been only reckoned in the female line, anyone would have done as the queen's husband and, accordingly, the king. However, we saw that it was only the representatives of several patrilinear lineages, not a few of them belonging to the stemma of Aiolos, who became in turn kings of Argos, of Amyclae, of Thebes, of Mycenae. This seems to entail that, although the royal succession was transmitted in the female line, the question who would be the next king was decided on the basis of patrilinearly reckoned descent. The king, then, was simultaneously a member of two nomenclatures: that of descent (the 'genealogy'), which was reckoned from father to son, and that of local rulers (the 'king-list'), which could only be reckoned on the basis of the mother-to-daughter succession. Yet, as the absence of matrilinear genealogies and king-lists clearly shows, it was only the agnatically reckoned descent that eventually counted.

Considering that, under the conditions of kingship by marriage, only the king-lists could preserve unity of place, the fact that Bronze Age nobles did not care to keep such lists unambiguously indicates that they identified themselves in tribal rather than in local terms. That is to say, they saw themselves as the 'Aiolids', the 'Perseids', the 'Pelopids', rather than as the 'Thebans', the 'Mycenaeans' or the 'Amycleans'. There is reason to suppose that this lack of local identity, embedded as it was in early genealogical thinking, was directly responsible for the commonly acknowledged fragmentation of the legendary history of Greece. That is to say, when the descendants of Kadmos, who in historic times were found in Thera, Cyrene and Akragas, traced their genealogy, they naturally did not count those kings of Thebes who were not of their line; as the descent group of Echion either did not survive into the historic period or exerted no influence on Greek tradition, the Kadmeian part of early Theban history was the only one to be preserved. For the Heraclidae, the early history of Mycenae was the history of Perseus and his descendants Eurystheus and Heracles; for the Pelopids, it was inextricably connected with the houses of Atreus and Thyestes. Since in the course of time the Perseids became associated with the Dorians and the Pelopids with the Aeolians of Asia Minor,[73] it should come as no surprise that the Mycenae

---

73 In so far as the founders of the Aeolian colonies in Asia Minor claimed to be descendants of Orestes' son Penthilos, see Str. 9.2.3, p. 401; 9.2.5, p. 403; 13.1.3, p. 582; Paus. 2.18.6; 3.2.1; cf. 7.6.1–2. Note that the formation stage of Homeric tradition is firmly associated with these Aeolian colonies.

of the Dorian and the Mycenae of the Aeolian tradition in fact exist in two different dimensions. Given the character of royal succession in heroic Greece, the true local perspective, if it ever existed, could only have been found in the matrilinear genealogies of queens.

It seems that the position of the queen can be satisfactorily accounted for if we assume that she was the priestess of the goddess of the land. The importance of the mother-goddess in the Eastern Mediterranean is too well known to be dwelt upon here:

As far back as our records reach, they stress the supreme importance in Asia Minor of a female deity . . . She is one of the typical mother-goddess figures of the Eastern Mediterranean and Western Asia, and as the mother of all things she is the queen of all things. A male deity becomes her son, or, if he is her husband, assumes a subordinate position. She is Mother Earth, and all being and fertility proceed from her.[74]

The Goddess stood at the centre of the cult, where she was represented by her priestess, whereas her male consort had his human counterpart in the figure of the 'king-priest'. The king thus owed his kingly position to his being a human incarnation of the divine consort of the Goddess, a role that he could play only by virtue of his marriage to her priestess. And, as the matrilinear succession of queens unequivocally shows, the priestess was bound to hand down her position to her daughter or to another woman of her matriliny.

We have thus to envisage a line of queens going back to time immemorial, in fact to all those local nymphs and eponyms of cities whose names open the greater part of Greek genealogies. Priestesses of Hera of Argos, whose succession was one of the systems used in Greek chronology, might well represent such a dynasty. Unfortunately, almost nothing has been preserved of Hellanicus' *Priestesses*, which dealt with the subject, but Felix Jacoby's reconstruction brings out the names of Io, the Danaid Hypermestra, Perseus' grandmother Eurydike, Eurystheus' daughter Admete and so on; statues of all of them could be seen in the Argive Heraion even at the time of Pausanias.[75] It may well be that the

---

74 Macqueen 1959: 177. The same seems also be true of early Ireland where, as Herbert 1992: 264, argues: 'women were not sovereigns, but the sovereignty itself was conceived of as female. The mythic model of royal rule which the Celtic world shared with many other ancient cultures was that of the *hieros gamos* or sacred marriage. According to this model, successful and prosperous government of society was the outcome of union between female and male elements, between the goddess of the land and its sovereign.'

75 Hellan. 4 FF 74–84 Jacoby; Thuc. 2.2.1, 4.133; Paus. 2.17.3 and 7.

Mycenaean Potnia, 'Mistress', referred to on Linear B tablets at both Knossos and Pylos, was just such a figure.[76]

The terms 'matriarchy' and 'mother-right', once lavishly used in works on ancient society, have gradually given way to a much more restrained and sceptical attitude. This is not to say, however, that the facts that inspired the once so popular 'matriarchal' literature have ceased to exist. However, it is strongly felt today that the real situation was much more complex than the pioneers of the matriarchal theory were ready to admit. We saw above that kingship by marriage did not involve matrilinear reckoning of descent. The same seems to be true of the relation of this institution to so-called matriarchy in so far as the latter is understood to the effect that societies that practised kingship by marriage were actually ruled by women. It is true of course that in the specific situation produced in Ithaca the person who was to choose the next ruler was the queen herself, but the situation of Penelope, as well as that of other wives who had been left at home for the years of the Trojan War, was rather an exception than the rule. The standard situation was that of the daughter who, like Helen, was being given in marriage by her male relatives. It was therefore these male relatives, and above all the bride's father, who decided who would be the husband of his daughter and therefore the next king. That is to say, although one could become king only through marriage with the royal heiress, the institution of kingship by marriage was practised in a society that was politically controlled by men.

We have seen that not a few of those who became kings by marrying a representative of the local matriliny were descendants of Aiolos, that is, belonged to the descent group that most likely stood for the Mycenaean Greeks. This obviously implies that their offspring were of a mixed, Hellenic and indigenous, descent. Does this mean that the original line of descent of those who intermarried with other descent groups ceased to exist? To examine this question, we have to broaden the scope of our inquiry by turning to sources that lie beyond the realm of legend.

---

76 See *po-ti-ni-ja*, 'for the Mistress', KN 172; *da-phu-ri-to-jo po-ti-ni-ja*, 'for the mistress of the Labyrinth', KN 205; cf. *a-ta-na po-ti-ni-ja*, 'for Mistress Athena', KN 208; *po-]ti-ni-ja i-qe-ja* 'for the Mistress of Horses', PY 312, etc., in Ventris and Chadwick 1973: Glossary, s.v. According to the current view, the Mycenaean Potnia should be interpreted as exclusively a divine figure, but cf. John Younger's AEGEANET posting on 9 April 1997: '. . . the female Potnia has, in my opinion, been wrongly identified *only* as a goddess (she may have been, but I'm pretty sure she was a human too and the head of another type of administration, a religious one . . . (Younger's italics.) Cf. Dickinson 1994: 291. On Potnia see also below, pp. 157–8.

CHAPTER 5

Marriage and Identity

ENDOGAMY AND EXOGAMY

With one or two notable exceptions, the institution of kingship ceased to exist in most of the Greek states as early as the Dark Age. Even in Sparta, such principal features of the kingship as the lack of alternate succession between the two royal houses, the lack of mobility, the strict endogamy and, above all, the father-to-son accession to the throne show clearly enough that what we have here is a form of kingship essentially different from that practised in the Bronze Age.[1] It is obvious that kingship by marriage should have come to an end together with the abolition of kingship as such. However, in so far as we have good reason to suggest that the main function of the queen was religious rather than political, the abolition of kingship does not necessarily demand that the 'queenship' should be abolished as well. If the political power of the king ensued from his being the consort of the queen who was the priestess of the local goddess, the king's loss of political status could not deprive the queen of her priestly prerogative. The priestess was bound to perform her functions along the same lines under any regime, monarchic or otherwise. That is to say, so long as the priestess transmitted her position to her daughter or another member of her matriliny, her matrilinear dynasty continued to exist, though the political consequences it once entailed were no longer relevant. Some striking examples of matrilinear sequence that can be shown to have existed in priestly families up to the Hellenistic period appear to favour this conclusion.[2]

1 On the kingship in historic Sparta see also below, pp. 100, 146–7.
2 See Broadbent 1968: 18–23, where she reconstructs the genealogy of a family of Epidaurian nobles: the unifying element in the genealogy is a direct female descent line for the women of the family, which is likely to have been preserved for eight successive generations from the third century BC; Broadbent suggests that the women of the family, who bear the names Chariko and Laphanta in alternate generations, were priestesses of the local female deities Damia and Auxesia.

As far as our evidence goes, the only form of rule in which elements of kingship by marriage were present even in the historic period was tyranny.[3] It is indeed tyranny that allows us to observe facts that may throw additional light on the Bronze Age institution of kingship. In 1954 Louis Gernet published his 'Marriages of tyrants', a study of a marriage arrangement in the family of the tyrants of Syracuse.[4] The tyranny of Dionysius the Elder over Syracuse was established in the final years of the fifth century BC. After becoming the single ruler, Dionysius took two wives, Aristomache of Syracuse and Doris of Locri, both daughters of persons of high rank, marrying both on the same day.[5] Dionysius' son by his Locrian wife, Dionysius the Younger, was destined to succeed his father on the throne. Dionysius also had two daughters by his Syracusan wife, one of whom he married to the younger Dionysius, whereas the second daughter was given in marriage to the tyrant's own brother. When Dionysius' brother died, his widow was married to Dion, Dionysius' brother-in-law.

In commenting on this arrangement, Gernet remarks that 'while tyrants by definition represent a kind of thinking that is agnatic in terms of succession, and a type of dynasty that owes nothing to any person, the arrangements in question do presuppose a dualistic form of thinking', and accounts for this dualism as due to 'the role of the female line of succession and, willy-nilly, the importance of women'. He continues:

We have already seen how Dionysius made use of the ideas in connection with the line of his Syracusan wife. The sons did not count, but one gets the impression that he needed to neutralize the female line in some way: the daughters are married off to Dionysius' son and brother . . . the issue of this line, all of whom were designated to provide wives for the 'males', allowed the family of Dionysius to continue to be self-sufficient. From one end to the other, the lineage of Dionysius' Syracusan wife (its purpose was not to produce princes) appears to have been an effective means of providing princesses.[6]

Gernet does not discuss the status of Dionysius' Locrian wife, but it seems obvious enough that in so far as the purpose of the lineage of his Syracusan wife was to produce princesses, that of his other wife was to produce princes. It thus appears that Dionysius acted on the assumption that only he who descended from the lineage of his Locrian wife and married into the lineage of his Syracusan wife could be qualified as his legitimate successor on the throne of Syracuse.

3 But see now also Geiger 2002, on Hellenistic monarchies.
4 English translation in Gernet 1981: 289–302.
5 Plut. *Dion* 3.3.5 styles Aristomache 'the native' (ἡ ἐπιχώριος) and Doris 'the stranger' (ἡ ξένη).
6 Gernet 1981: 296.

After discussing several other examples of peculiar marriage arrangements in the families of Greek tyrants, Gernet concludes his brief but
fascinating study by remarking that marriage to an indigenous woman is
equivalent to acquiring sovereignty over the land: 'the woman a man
marries confers the kingship on him'.[7] He also suggests that the marriage
arrangements practised by the tyrants must somehow be connected with
Bronze Age marriage practices as they come to light in Greek heroic
tradition.[8]

At the same time, while the institution of kingship by marriage can
account for the position of Dionysius' Syracusan wife, it does not explain
the need for the second female line. Yet it is this line and not the one that
gave him the sovereignty that was meant to provide Dionysius with an
heir and successor to the throne of Syracuse. A piece of evidence supplied
by Polybius seems to throw light on the issue. In Book 12 of his *History*,
Polybius discusses the marriage customs of the Epizephyrian Locrians,
one of the Greek tribes who colonised Magna Graecia:

First of all [they say] that the Locrians derive everything that relates to high birth
(πάντα τὰ διὰ προγόνων ἔνδοξα) not from men but from women. Thus only
those are considered noble (εὐγενεῖς) among them who are said to be of 'the
hundred families'. These are the hundred families that had been held in great
esteem by the Locrians even before they left the mother-country . . . Some
women belonging to these families left with the settlers, and their descendants
are still considered the nobility and called 'of the hundred families'.[9]

This passage has often been taken as testifying to matrilinear reckoning
of descent among the Epizephyrian Locrians;[10] however, this would
amount to claiming that, for example, Pericles' citizenship law (451/450
BC), according to which only those who were of Athenian descent on both
their father's and their mother's side qualified as Athenian citizens,
testifies to matrilinear reckoning of descent among fifth-century Athenians.
Aristotle's remark in the *Politics* that a citizen is normally defined as 'one
born of citizen parents on both sides rather than on one side only, be it
the father's or the mother's', and that some carry this requirement still
further back 'to the ancestors in the second or the third generation or even

---

7 Gernet 1981: 300.   8 Gernet 1981: 292.   9 Polyb. 12.5.6; cf. Arist. fr. 541.
10 Some commentators follow Polybius in accepting Aristotle's interpretation of the Locrian custom
to the effect that, as in the case of the Spartan Partheniai (see below), the consorts of the Locrian
noblewomen were not of citizen status. This interpretation was rejected by Timaeus against
whom Polybius' argument is directed; see e.g. Vidal-Naquet 1981: 193–5; Sourvinou-Inwood 1974:
188–93; 197–8. My interpretation of the episode agrees with the mainstream approach as found
e.g. in Dunbabin 1948: 36–7, Graham 1964: 115–16, and Walbank 1967: 331, who find Timaeus'
version much more well founded than that of Aristotle.

further' points in the same direction.[11] I would suggest in view of this that Herodotus' account of the Ionian colonisation of Asia Minor provides the marriage customs of the Epizephyrian Locrians with a more appropriate historic context. Herodotus states unequivocally that in so far as the Greek settlers did not bring women with them but took Carian wives, their descendants could not pass for genuine Ionians:

Even those who set off from the prytaneum of Athens and therefore consider themselves the most genuine Ionians of all brought no women with them to the settlement but took Carian brides whose fathers they had killed. For this reason these women established a custom, which they took an oath to observe themselves and which they also handed over to their daughters, that they should never take their meals with their husbands nor call them by their names, because they made them their wives after having killed their fathers, husbands and sons.[12]

Centuries after the colonisation of Ionia, the daughters of Greek fathers continued to preserve the identity of their remote ancestors and to count their descent from the indigenous population of the land. Even more significant, the descendants of the males who entered these exogamous marriages were not seen as continuing the descent line of their fathers. Would the situation have been different if the colonists had brought with them to Ionia women of their own descent and their children had been the descendants of both? Several well-known historic examples suggest that this would have been the case. In Corinth, the ancient ruling clan of the Bacchiadae retained its identity for centuries by practicing strict endogamy among the two hundred families that made up the group,[13] and the same was true of the kings of Sparta. The main if not the only requirement of both kings and queens of Sparta was that they should belong to the clan of the Heraclidae. 'Did not you notice', we read in *Alcibiades I*, 'how great are the means at the disposal of the Spartan kings, whose wives are publicly watched over by the ephors, lest the king come to power begotten by some other person than one of the Heraclidae?'[14]

---

11 Arist. *Pol.* 1275b 22–5. For a detailed discussion of Pericles' citizenship law see Patterson 1981; cf. also Isaac 2004: 116–21.

12 Hdt. 1.146.2–3. Cf. Paus. 7.2.5 on the foundation of Miletus: 'When the Ionians prevailed over the previous inhabitants of Miletus, they killed all the males (except for those who ran away when the city was conquered) and married their wives and daughters.'

13 Cf. Hdt. 5.92b ἐδίδοσαν δὲ καὶ ἤγοντο ἐξ ἀλλήλων.

14 Pl. *Alcib. I* 121b. Cf. also Plut. *Agis* 11. 2, referring to some ancient law which forbade a Heraclid to have children by an alien woman. For the discussion see Ogden 1996: 226–7, 252–62. It is not out of the question that what T. J. Cornell calls the 'closing' of the patriciate in early Rome, a process that directly resulted from the Twelve Tables prohibition on intermarriage of the patricians, should be accounted for along similar lines. Cf. Cornell 1995: 250: 'Both Cicero and Livy report the rule in similar fashion – that there should be no right of legitimate marriage between *plebs* and

That is to say, rather than indicating matrilinear reckoning of descent, maternal descent acted as the crucial factor in preserving the clan or, in the case of fifth-century Athens, even the civic identity of the offspring. To quote what Cynthia Patterson wrote about Pericles' citizenship law: 'Athenian fathers married their daughters to Athenian husbands in order to produce more Athenian sons. The woman (wife and daughter) was the vital yet "invisible" link.'[15] When taken against this background, the case of the Locrian colonists starts to look like yet another instance of strict endogamy practised within a given population group the principal aim of which was to preserve the group's identity.

Let us consider now the twelve-generation genealogy of Kodros, the Neleid king of Athens, as given by Hellanicus in the fifth century BC (Fig. 1):

Deukalion and Pyrrha . . . gave birth to Hellen; Hellen and Othreis gave birth to Xouthos, Aiolos, Xenopatra; Aiolos and Iphis daughter of Peneios, to Salmoneus; Salmoneus and Alkidike, to Tyro; Tyro and Poseidon, to Neleus; Neleus and Chloris, to Periklymenos; Periklymenos and Peisidike, to Boros; Boros and Lysidike, to Penthilos; Penthilos and Anchiroe, to Andropompos; *Andropompos and Henioche daughter of Armenios son of Zeuxippos son of Eumelos son of Admetos, gave birth to Melanthos*: upon the Return of the Children of Heracles, the latter moved from Messenia to Athens, and he begat Kodros.[16]

Notwithstanding the strictly agnatic reckoning of Kodros' descent, two women were made prominent in this genealogy – Tyro daughter of Salmoneus and mother of Neleus, and Henioche wife of Andropompos and mother of Melanthos. At first sight, Tyro looks like an intruder on the patrilinear scheme: she is represented as continuing the line of her father Salmoneus, and her son Neleus is represented as her successor. Note, however, that Tyro's position fits in perfectly well with the so-called *epikleros* pattern, well known to us from the historic period: in the absence of sons, the father's line would be continued by his daughter, whose sons would count as male descendants of their maternal grandfather.[17] As distinct from this, the introduction of Henioche's genealogy side by side with that of her husband Andropompos does not affect the strictly agnatic reckoning of the descent of their son Melanthos. Why then is she the only woman in the entire sequence for whom a detailed genealogy is provided?

---

patres – which almost certainly reflects the wording of the original law. Here *patres* obviously means not senators, but the whole patrician order, including both sexes.' Cf. also ibid. 252–6.
15 Patterson 1981: 161.
16 Hellan. 4 F 125 Jacoby (my italics).
17 On the *epikleros* pattern see esp. Gernet 1921. On Tyro see also below, p. 101.

In view of the above discussion, the following explanation seems to suggest itself. Since Henioche's son Melanthos was regarded as the founder of the new ruling dynasty in sub-Mycenaean Athens, it was important to emphasise that he was of the same aristocratic descent on both the paternal and the maternal side. Indeed, Hellanicus' scheme unequivocally demonstrates that Henioche descended from Admetos whose father was Pheres son of Kretheus the brother of Salmoneus the Aiolid, from whom her husband also descended (see Fig. 1).[18] Just as with the kings of Sparta and the Locrian and Corinthian nobles, both father and mother of the new ruler of Athens belonged to the same descent group. The importance ascribed to this fact in Hellanicus' genealogy strongly suggests that Melanthos' pure Aiolid descent acted as one of the qualifications making him a suitable candidate for kingship.[19]

We may suppose in the light of this that Dionysius' Syracusan wife was considered exogamous in the same sense as the Ionian women in Herodotus. Greek though she might well have been by any other standard, on her mother's side she ultimately belonged to the indigenous matriliny, and this was the only thing that eventually counted. By the same token, Dionysius' marriage to his Locrian wife, who was to become the mother of his heir, must have been considered endogamous in exactly the same sense as were the marriages of the Spartan kings, the Epizephyrian Locrians, the Bacchiadae, the parents of the Athenian king Melanthos or of the fifth-century Athenians. This allows us to suggest that, as distinct from his Syracusan wife, who was a representative of the local matriliny, Dionysius' Locrian wife belonged to the descent group of Greek immigrants on both the paternal and the maternal side, perhaps even being descended from one of the 'hundred families' mentioned by Polybius, and that this qualification would have been enough to make her son a suitable candidate for becoming the ruler of the city. This would explain why Dionysius' marriage to the Syracusan bride was meant to bestow on him sovereignty over the land whereas his marriage to the Locrian bride was to give him the legitimate male descendant who was to continue his line.

18 On the circumstances of the ascendance of the Neleid dynasty of Pylos to the throne of Athens see esp. Paus. 2.18.7; 9.5.8; Str. 9.1.7, p. 393; cf. 14.1.3, p. 633.
19 Compare to this the ancient Athenian rule, refereed to in Arist. F 412, that the nine archons should be Athenians on both sides for three generations (ἑκατέρωθεν ἐκ τριγονίας). Similarly, the priests and priestesses of Athenian cults had to be Athenians on both sides, see the discussion in Patterson 1981: 114. Cf. Ogden 1996: 323 and above, n. 14.

Let us return for a moment to some of the examples of kingship by marriage belonging to the Heroic Age as discussed in Chapter 4. Pelops' sons by Hippodameia were exiled by their father for the murder of their stepbrother Chrysippos, Pelops' son by another wife.[20] Peleus and Telamon, the sons of Aiakos king of Aegina, were exiled because they killed their stepbrother Phokos, Aiakos' son by another wife.[21] Meleagros and Tydeus were sons of Oineus king of Aetolia, but by two different wives; the same is true of Ajax and Teukros, the two sons of Telamon king of Salamis – with the difference, however, that Telamon's exogamous son Teukros, born of a captive Trojan princess, was universally referred to in Greek tradition as Telamon's 'bastard', _nothos_; the relationship between Hippolytos, Theseus' son by the Amazon, and Demophon and Akamas, his two 'legitimate' sons by Phaedra, seems to have been of exactly the same nature.[22] In other cases, general confusion exists as to who exactly was so-and-so's wife and accordingly the mother of his sons. The very fact that there are cases in which we have two alternative candidates for this position strongly suggests that it was the bigamous practices of Bronze Age rulers that created confusion in the later tradition.

This is not to say that the marriage arrangements practised in Bronze Age Greece were altogether identical to those introduced by Dionysius the Elder in fifth-century Syracuse. In Greece of the fifth century BC, the extravagant marriage of the tyrant of Syracuse was clearly an isolated event with no broader social context. The situation in Bronze Age Greece must have been different. Rather than marrying his own half-sister, the Bronze Age prince would go to the neighbouring kingdom to become king there, and his sister would be given in marriage to the representative of that kingdom's royal line. As a result, the royal families involved in the rotational succession both preserved their clan identity and guaranteed the status of king to their male descendants. It goes without saying that, as

---

20 Schol. _Il._ 2.105; Hellan. 4 F 42; Thuc. 1. 9.   21 Paus. 2.29.9–10.

22 Actually, Theseus' marriage to Phaedra was his second attempt to secure himself a daughter of Minos as a bride: the first was his aborted marriage to Ariadne. Hippolytos, Theseus' son by the Amazon, is unanimously styled in Greek tradition as Theseus' 'bastard', whereas Phaedra's sons Demophon and Akamas are generally regarded as his legitimate heirs. This seems to indicate that while the Amazons, usually treated as a Thracian tribe, were envisaged as indigenous to Attica, Theseus and his clan were seen as ultimately of Cretan descent. The conclusion may have some corroboration in the fact that Theseus is usually credited with conquering Athens from the Amazons and that even the Areopagus was habitually regarded as the traditional abode of these 'daughters of Ares': see Aesch. _Eum._ 688; Plut. _Thes._ 27–8; Paus. 1.2.1; 1.2.15; 2.41.7. As distinct from this, Theseus never sought to win sovereignty over Crete, whose relationship with Athens in Greek legend does in fact evoke that between the mother-city and a colony.

distinct from the case of Dionysius, this system made it impossible to keep a direct line of royal succession from father to son, and we saw indeed that no such lines of succession are observable for Bronze Age Greece.

The above seems to indicate that in approaching Bronze Age dynastic marriages we should look for deeper structures than the ones implied by a simple monogamous arrangement. In fact, we have to make provision for the four following positions: (a) the daughters of the endogamous wife; (b) the daughters of the exogamous wife; (c) the sons of the endogamous wife; (d) the sons of the exogamous wife.[23] Let us try to define the genealogical function of each of the categories in question.

It seems clear enough that, although the endogamous wife's manifest function was to produce legitimate male heirs, her daughters (line a) are nevertheless indispensable for the simple reason that it is only by their means that their husband's clan identity can be preserved. That is to say, only marriage to a woman of one's own lineage could give her husband legitimate male descendants fit to continue his line.

The daughters of the exogamous wife (line b) are also indispensable because only marriage to a woman belonging to the indigenous matriliny could guarantee her husband the sovereignty over the land.

The sons of the endogamous wife (line c) are again indispensable because it is these legitimate heirs who guarantee the continuation of their father's line of descent. Indeed, the manner in which the genealogies are structured shows that this was the most important category of progeny to which both female lines were subordinate, in that they were meant to supply the mothers (line a) and the wives (line b) for this category of sons.

The same, however, cannot be said of the sons of the exogamous wife (line d), the one, let us recall, whose function was to provide daughters rather than sons. The genealogical structure intended to perpetuate the father's lineage on the one hand and to maintain sovereignty on the other seems to make no provision for this category of progeny, i.e. for the so-called illegitimate sons, or *nothoi*. The sons of the exogamous line were

---

23 The significance of distinguishing between two female lines was first made clear to me thanks to Emily Lyle's paper 'Modelling Early Indo-European royal succession with some insights from the Asante', read at the University of Edinburgh in October 1997. According to Lyle, the genealogical reckoning of the Asante makes provision for two female lines, of which one supplies the males who are qualified for kingship and the other supplies the females marriage with whom actually makes one a king. To put it in Lyle's own terms, the two female lines were meant to produce 'mothers of kings' on the one hand and 'mothers of queens' on the other.

driven out of their father's line of succession and had to establish their status by other means.[24]

As distinct from their half-brothers whose function was to preserve their father's lineage, rather more often than not the princes born to exogamous wives became founders of new descent groups. Let us take for example the case of the sons of the Athenian king Kodros, who were generally held to be founders of the Ionian colonies in Asia Minor. Pausanias writes about them: '. . . the sons of Kodros were appointed as the rulers of Ionians although they were not related at all to the clan of Ion: on the side of Kodros and Melanthos they were Messenians from Pylos, and Athenians on their mother's side'. The sons of Kodros issued from the marriage of the Neleid king of Athens to a woman of the local Athenian matriliny, and therefore belonged to neither of their parents' descent groups. They formed a new clan, which led the Ionians to their new settlements in Asia Minor.[25] This compares well with the case of Hegesistratus, born of the sixth-century Athenian tyrant Pisistratus and his Argive wife Timonassa. In spite of his mother's high rank, Hegesistratus was generally regarded as Pisistratus' 'bastard', *nothos*, and considered an Argive rather than an Athenian; he was eventually made the single ruler of Sigeum.[26]

It speaks volumes for the situation in Greece in the second millennium BC that actually all the cases of kingship by marriage dealt with in Greek legend concern newcomers to the land who obtained sovereignty by marrying indigenous females. In principle, however, we should also ask how this form of kingship was practised by homogenous population groups, for example, among the indigenous population or in the descent groups not practicing exogamy. Since it was only women of the local

---

24 It seems that similar rules applied in the Inca society of the Cuzco valley, where the terms *churi*, 'son', and *concha*, 'sister's son', designated the king's endogamous and exogamous sons, respectively; under the form of *huacca concha*, 'poor nephew', or 'orphan nephew', the latter was applied to the children of the Inca king by non-Inca women. In colonial society, the term *concha* served to designate free but landless peasants. See Zuidema 1990: 21.

25 Paus. 7.2.3; cf. Hdt. 1.147.

26 Cf. Gernet 1981: 291–2; Ogden 1996: 45–6. As Ogden 1996: 18–19, 47–58, has shown, the emergence, side by side with the old clan identity, of the new civic identity of the citizens of the polis could well produce a clash of interests between the marriage practices of the clan and those of the polis. Note that, to preserve one's own clan identity, it will suffice to marry a woman of one's own clan whether or not she also possesses citizen status in one's city-state. Yet from the city-state point of view the descendants of such marriages, legitimate though they were by the normal standards, would not automatically count as full citizens for the simple reason that their mother was not of citizen status. This is how the *metroxenoi*, 'born of an alien mother', a category of *nothoi* which could not emerge under the conditions of Bronze Age marriage, came into existence.

matriliny who could bestow sovereignty on their consorts, it is reasonable to suppose that in the homogenous population groups sovereignty could well be obtained by means of monogamous marriages with women of one's own descent. That is to say, one and the same woman would both bestow sovereignty on her consort and bring him legitimate male descendants fit to become kings.

The simplest case would obviously be brother-sister marriage as apparently practised by the pharaohs of Egypt.[27] It is easy to see how in such a case one and the same woman would guarantee the ruler both sovereignty over the land and continuation of his line. Yet, as far as our evidence goes, most societies of the ancient world preferred to avoid this form of marriage. That is to say, if most homogenous population groups still preferred the bigamous solution, this was mainly due to the fact that under the conditions of kingship by marriage they had to practise rotational succession in order to avoid incest.

But even in the case of strictly endogamous descent groups the brother-sister marriage was perhaps the simplest but by no means the only form of marriage available. Thus, a marriage involving no incest could also be achieved if all the males of a given descent group are eligible to marry the women of their own matriliny. Frazer's comments on examples of elective kingship in Africa that he collected can apply to such cases:

> It has often been asked whether the Roman monarchy was hereditary or elective. The question implies an opposition between the two modes of succession which by no means necessarily exists. As a matter of fact in many African tribes at the present day the succession to the kingdom or chieftainship is determined by a combination of the hereditary and the elective principle; that is, the kings or chiefs are chosen by the people or a body of electors from among the members of the royal family.[28]

The famous episode in the story of Heracles to the effect that the first male in a given generation to be born in the clan of Perseus would reign over Mycenae also seems to suggest a non-hereditary kingship to which only the males of the ruling clan could be admitted.[29] In cases like these, one and the same woman, in that she both belonged to the local matriliny

---

27 Cf., however, Troy's 1986: 104–5, caveat to the effect that the kinship terminology, including 'brother' and 'sister', was used in ancient Egypt so extensively as to cover all the collateral (neither parent nor child) relationships by blood or marriage, including that between husband and wife. On a similar use of kinship terminology in the Old Hittite Kingdom see the Appendix.

28 Frazer 1905: 254. On similar discussions concerning the Hittite monarchy see Bryce 1998: 91–3, 114–16 and below, p. 180. On Roman kingship see now also Cornell 1995: 119–50, esp. 141: 'The most obvious peculiarity about the Roman kingship is that it was not hereditary.'

29 Apollod. 2.4.5; cf. *Il.* 19.95–133.

and was of the same descent as her husband, could both bestow sovereignty on the ruler and provide him with legitimate heirs.

Note again that strict clan endogamy as practised by the Bacchiadae of Corinth or the Heraclidae of Sparta would amount to recognition of the fact that all men and women of the given lineage are equally eligible as potential kings and queens. In situations such as this it becomes much less relevant whether the form of succession adopted is matrilinear or patrilinear. Indeed, if all the women of the clan are equally eligible in virtue of their belonging to the clan matriliny, it does not matter whether or not the succession of queens proceeds from mother to daughter. In view of this, it may be suggested that the endogamous marriage arrangement among the members of a homogenous group could well have been one of the factors that prompted the transition from matrilinear to patrilinear succession which took place in Sparta and probably also in other Dorian states.[30]

FROM INTERMARRIAGES TO ETHNIC FUSION

At an earlier stage of this discussion (see p. 89), I raised the question whether intermarriages between heterogeneous descent groups led to the complete dissolution of the groups involved. It seems that we are now in aposition to give a qualified answer to this question. As the above discussion has shown, side by side with the mixed progeny who were the natural outcome of exogamous marriages, people participating in such marriages also kept producing endogamous descendants who were meant to sustain their line. We have also seen that, as distinct from the exogamous daughters, whose function was to sustain the local matriliny, there was no institutionalised solution for the exogamous sons. This is not yet to say that the male offspring issuing from exogamous marriages were necessarily envisaged as unwelcome. To see that this was far from being the case, we should also consider the exogamous marriages of females.

A peculiar form of 'marriage arrangement', which is rehearsed over and over again in Greek legend, was to have a woman of noble descent give birth to sons who were considered to have no mortal father at all. Io bore Epaphos to Zeus; Europe bore Minos, Radamanthys and Sarpedon to

---

30 Note that the Heraclidae themselves were not Dorians but descendants of Inachos and that the Bacchiadae were also a Heraclid clan. This could well mean that, in accord with the Dorian charter myth of the Return of the Heraclidae, their women counted as belonging to the indigenous matriliny. On Dorians and Heraclidae see J. Hall 1997: 56–65; on the Dorian charter myth see Malkin 1994: 33–45; on the Dorian kings see below, pp. 146–8.

Zeus; Tyro bore Neleus and Pelias to Poseidon; Danae bore Perseus to Zeus; Alkmene bore Heracles to Zeus; Aithra bore Theseus to Poseidon – this list can be continued to include almost all the prominent heroes of Greek legend. Although children of such unions were not considered to have been begotten by a mortal father, they nevertheless counted as illegitimate sons, or *nothoi*. In other words, the union with a god was also regarded as a form of exogamy. The case of Tyro, especially, reveals the deeper meanings implied in this kind of 'marriage arrangement'. Let us, then, take a closer look at it.

When still unmarried, Tyro daughter of Salmoneus was impregnated by Poseidon and gave birth to two sons, Neleus and Pelias. Later she was given in marriage to her own uncle Kretheus, her father's brother, and gave birth to Aison, Pheres and Amythaon. The struggle for sovereignty between the legitimate Aison and the illegitimate Pelias and their respective offspring provides genealogical background for the Argonautic saga. Note now that the case of Tyro offers an elegant genealogical solution, not dissimilar to that of the Hittite Tawananna, in that it allows for one and the same woman to function as the mother of both exogamous and endogamous progeny.[31] The case of Alkmene, who bore the exogamous Heracles to Zeus and the endogamous Iphicles to her cousin and legitimate husband Amphitryon, obviously also belongs to this category. Before being officially married, the prospective endogamous wife, that is, the woman of the same descent as her future husband, was engaged in religiously sanctioned sexual intercourse which was meant to give birth to exogamous progeny, a practice that was habitually interpreted as the union of a mortal woman and god.[32]

The purpose of female exogamy will become clearer if we consider that the same rules that regulated the identity of individuals were also at work in establishing broader identities of entire population groups. Take for example the case of the Argonauts. The leader of the Argonauts Jason and his companions passed in Greek tradition under the collective name of 'Minyans', i.e. those born to the daughters of Minyas, the eponym of a tribe which was envisaged in Greek legend as inhabiting the historic

---

31 Each Tawananna functioned as an exogamous queen whenever she bestowed kingship on her consort (her maternal uncle) and as an endogamous queen whenever she gave birth to the son who was to become king in the alternate generation. On Tawananna see above, Chapter 4.

32 Intercourse with a stranger before marriage is strongly reminiscent of the so-called sacred prostitution, which seems to have been rather common in the ancient world, cf. Herodotus' description of sacred prostitution at Babylon (1.199), with Asheri's commentary *ad locum*, in Asheri 1988: 380; cf. Str. 16.1.20, p. 745. Cf. also below, pp. 165–6, on the Anthesteria festival.

district of Boeotian Orchomenos in Central Greece. This is neatly reflected in the following verses by Apollonius Rhodius:

These therefore were the comrades who joined the son of Aison. All their chiefs used to be called Minyans by those who dwelt around, for most of the bravest claimed that they were of the blood of the daughters of Minyas: thus Jason himself was born of Alkimede the daughter of Klymene who was a daughter of Minyas.[33]

The 'Virgins' Sons', or 'Partheniai', of Sparta, born by Spartan maidens out of wedlock in order to keep up the population during the absence of the men in the First Messenian War and later sent out to found Tarentum in Italy (end of the eighth century BC), would provide this myth with a proper historic background.[34]

Conspicuous in that they were identified through their lack of pure descent, the exogamous sons of females seem to have been destined to enhance the communities of their origin in the case of insufficient increase in population and to be instrumental in their expansion when depopulation was no longer a problem.[35] Colonisation was their most manifest function. In this respect, they did not differ essentially from the exogamous sons of males (see above on the sons of Kodros). The Minyans went to the easternmost shores of the Black Sea; the sons of Kodros founded the first Ionian colonies in Asia Minor; the Partheniai were generally believed to have founded Tarentum in Italy, and so on. Nevertheless, judging by such collective names as 'Minyans' or 'Partheniai', the children of the religiously sanctioned exogamous unions of females were special in that they were regarded as a population group *sui generis*. In Greek tradition, the sons born of such unions - those, as Plato ironically called them,

---

33 Ap. Rhod. 1.228–33. Cf. Pi. *P.* 4. 69; Hdt. 4. 145–50.
34 See Huxley 1962: 115 n. 214, quoting Hom. *Il.* 16.189, Hesychius and Suda s.v.: 'A παρθένιος is the child of an unmarried woman, who is therefore still considered a παρθένος.' Cf. Ogden 1996: 18, 21–5. On the Partheniai of Sparta see Antiochos 555 F 13 Jacoby (= Str. 6.3.2, pp. 278–9); Ephoros 70 F 216 Jacoby (= Str. 6.3.3, pp. 279–80); Arist. *Pol.* 5 1306b 27. The fathers of the Partheniai are alternately referred to as perioikoi, helots, slaves, or sometimes even as citizens of Sparta. See further Huxley 1962: 37; Asheri 1977: 42; Vidal-Naquet 1981: 194–7. For other historic parallels see Asheri 1977.
35 On the problem of *oligandria* and the peculiar marriage solutions it involved even in historic times see Asheri 1977. The foundational myth of the Samnites as preserved in Str. 5.4.12, p. 250, also seems to be relevant. The Sabines vowed to dedicate to Mars all the male infants born during a certain year. When grown up, these 'sons of Mars' were sent away to found a colony (εἰς ἀποικίαν), with a bull leading the way; they arrived in the land of the Opici, sacrificed the bull to Mars and settled in the place. The myth reflects the widespread Italic custom of the so-called sacred spring (*ver sacrum*), which apparently served as an institutionalised response to overpopulation. Cf. Cornell 1995: 305 (with bibliography).

'bastards (*nothoi*) of gods either by the Nymphs or by some other women' – were styled ἡμίθεοι, 'demigods', and treated as a special category of mortals who formed the Race of Heroes. It is symptomatic in this connection that the greatest of the heroes, Heracles, became the divine patron of the *nothoi* in historic Athens.[36]

As the above discussion shows, the exogamous sons of females, who of necessity were of mixed descent, were certainly produced on purpose. One of the most famous foundation myths of Greek tradition allows us to take this argument several steps further.

Among the descendants of Inachos there were two brothers, Danaos and Aigyptos, who were believed to belong to the ruling house of Egypt. Danaos fathered fifty daughters and Aigyptos fifty sons. The sons of Aigyptos sought to marry their cousins against their will, and in order to avoid the marriage the fifty Danaids and their father fled to the Peloponnese, the land of their ancestors. They were followed there by their suitors, who eventually forced Danaos to surrender the girls. However, on the wedding night the Danaids, instructed by their father, slaughtered their cousins. All but one: Hypermestra fell in love with her bridegroom Lynkeus and spared his life. Eventually, Lynkeus and Hypermestra founded the royal dynasty of Argos, whereas the other Danaids were given in marriage to the winners of a race contest and, together with their native husbands, founded new settlements all over the Peloponnese.[37]

As a result of the exogamous marriages of the daughters of Danaos, a new population group emerged whose identity was established through their settler mothers rather than through their native fathers: the 'Danaoi', or 'the descendants of the daughters of Danaos', was one of the names given to the Bronze Age population of the Peloponnese in the epic tradition. Only the offspring of the endogamous marriage between the cousins Lynkeus and Hypermestra preserved the pure clan identity of their ancestors and transmitted it to their offspring, who formed the

---

36 Pl. *Ap.* 27d 8–9. The Athenian *nothoi* were enrolled at Cynosarges, the place of the gymnasium of Heracles, see Plut. *Them.* 1; Dem. 23.213; cf. Ar. *Birds* 1660–6. For a discussion see Humphreys 1974; Patterson 1981: 128 n. 115; Ogden 1996: 55–8, 199–203.

37 The race for the daughters of Danaos: Pi. *P.* 9.195–206; Paus. 3.12.2; Apollod. 2.21. According to Paus. 3.22.11, Side in Lacedaemon was named after Danaos' daughter; Amymone the Danaid discovered the springs of Lerna and the local river was named after her (Paus. 2.37.1, cf. Apollod. 2.12; Hes. fr. 128 M-W); Achaios' sons Archandros and Architeles came to Argos from Phthiotis and married Skaia and Automate, daughters of Danaos; Archandros gave his son the name of Settler (Μετανάστης; Paus. 7.1.7). Cf. also Paus. 4.30.2; 4.35.2; 7.22.5; 10.35.1.

nobility of the land. Not only Perseus and Heracles but also the kings of Sparta were counted among the descendants of this couple.[38]

The myth of the daughters of Danaos clearly implies that giving the settler women to indigenous males was meant to lead to the emergence of a mixed population group that would form a link, as it were, between the newcomers and the indigenous population. This practice would correspond to what the anthropologists Ronald Cohen and John Middleton describe as downward asymmetry in intermarriage, occurring 'when women from a higher-ranked or dominant group marry individuals from lower-ranked or subordinate groups in the area':

In general, the greater the tendency for intergroup relations to be based on ties of patron–client relations, then the greater the tendency for such relations to be solidified by marriage ties in which the superior provides a wife for the subordinate. In such situations and within such families there is a correlated tendency for the customs of the dominant group or person to spread into that of the subordinate through the aegis of mothers who have come from the dominant group.[39]

This practice is rarer than upward asymmetry (see below) and can co-occur with it.

But why were Lynkeus and Hypermestra the only couple who nevertheless concluded an endogamous marriage? The myth of the daughters of Danaos shows that, exactly as in the case of the marriages of individuals, rather than being mutually exclusive, the principles of endogamy and exogamy acted as mutually complementary and their combination as vital for the survival of a given population group. The function of the aristocratic minority issuing from the endogamous marriages was, to borrow a term coined by the anthropologist Mary Helms, to be 'living ancestors',[40] that is, to bestow on the rest of the population the inherited clan identity of which they were the only authentic bearers; the function of the majority who sprang from the mixed marriages was to furnish the inherited identity

---

38 The distinction was apparently kept in the religious sphere as well: while the name of Hypermestra appears on Hellanicus' list of the priestesses of Hera of Argos, the rest of the Danaids were generally believed to have brought the cult of Demeter to Greece. See also below, p. 105.

39 Cohen and Middleton 1970: 21–2. This compares well with the case of the Graikoi, a northern Hellenic tribe that gave the Hellenes their Roman designation 'Greeks'. Aristotle actually held the two peoples to be identical, saying that the Graikoi changed their name to Hellenes, and this is repeated in other sources. Alcman in the seventh and Sophocles in the fifth century BC styled the *Graikes* as 'the mothers of the Hellenes'. According to the interpretation proposed by Martin West, this 'suggests a myth that men of the Hellenes married women of the Graikoi': Arist. *Meteor.* 352b1–2; Alcman fr. 155 Page; Soph. fr. 518; Apollod. 1.7.3; West 1985: 54.

40 Helms 1998: 6 and passim.

with live bearers. That is to say, the endogamous marriages were indispensable in that only in virtue of such marriages could the identity of the given population group be preserved, and the exogamous marriages were indispensable in that only by their means could the increase and the very survival of the population group in question be guaranteed.

The above throws light on the important role played by women in colonisation. Messene the daughter of Triopas is said to have arrived in Messenia from Argos with the joined forces of Argos and Lakedaimon; together with her local husband Polykaon the son of Lelex she founded Andania, the new royal capital of Messenia. Manto, the daughter of Tiresias, led a migration from Thebes to Asia Minor, where she founded Kolophon together with her Cretan husband Rhakios. Kyrene, the daughter of Hypseus king of the Lapiths, was carried by Apollo to Libya, where the city of Cyrene was named after her, and so on.[41] Characteristically, migrations of women of noble birth involved not only the foundation of new cities but also the introduction of new cults. The Danaids brought with them the mysteries of Demeter; Messene was credited with establishing the mysteries of Demeter in her new city of Andania; Manto founded a shrine of Apollo at Klaros, and so on.[42] The story of the foundation of Massalia by the Phocaeans of Asia Minor seems to point in the same direction. The colonists were instructed by an oracle to take with them a 'leader' (ἡγεμών) from the Ephesian Artemis; this leader was a woman called Aristarcha (a cult epithet of the goddess), one of the most prominent women of Ephesus (τῶν ἐντίμων σφόδρα γυναικῶν); she became the priestess of Artemis in the new settlement.[43]

It seems obvious from the aforesaid that in the case of a marriage arrangement between newcomers and the indigenous population the concrete form taken by such an arrangement would directly depend on whether or not the newcomers had brought with them women of their own descent. If they had not, these newcomers, just like Herodotus' Ionians, would only be able to enter exogamous marriages with women of alien descent.[44] This would correspond to the widespread practice of upward asymmetry in intermarriage, which is usually accompanied by a

---

41 Messene: Paus. 4.1.1–2, cf. 4.3.9; 4.27.6; 4.31.11; Manto: Paus. 7.3.1; 9.33.1–2 and below, Chapter 7; Kyrene: Pi. *P.* 9.5–70 (see esp. l. 54, where Kyrene is called ἀρχέπολις), cf. Hes. fr. 215 M-W.
42 The Danaids: Hdt. 2.171; Messene: Paus. 4.1.5 and 9; 4.2.6; 4.26.8; Manto: Diod.Sic. 4.66.5–6; Apollod. 3.85; Paus. 7.3.1; 9.10.2–3.
43 Str. 4.1.4, p. 179. See the excellent discussion of this episode in Malkin 1987: 69–72.
44 As in other cases, this probably did not affect their kings. Thus, according to Pherecydes as quoted by Strabo 14.1.3, p. 633, of the sons of Kodros who became the founders of Ionian colonies in Asia Minor, only the descendants of the legitimate Androklos, founder of Ephesus, were

considerable degree of cultural assimilation into the domestic group.[45] As a result, these exogamous settlers would not be able to sustain their former identity. As Jack Goody put it,

If the incoming group is more than just a handful, and at the same time heterosexual in composition, then it can operate as a breeding unit; such an endogamous group can retain its language and other aspects of culture even under adverse conditions. But if the group consists only of males, which would tend to be the case in situations of conquest, trade, or hunting, then there is always the problem of the 'mother tongue', or, more significantly, the language of peers; women are generally less the explorers of new social territory than the consolidators of the old.[46]

In so far indeed as women of one's own descent were regarded as instrumental in preserving the identity of a given group, it was essential that, as in the case of the Epizephyrian Locrians, at least some of the potential endogamous wives of the settlers should participate in the foundation of the colony and thus allow the founders to operate as a breeding unit.

We saw that only the descendants of women brought to Italy from the mother country were considered the nobility among the Epizephyrian Locrians. This seems to entail that, similar to the case of the Greek settlers of Ionia, the rest of the population of the colony descended from the marriages of the male colonists to the native women.[47] Now in so far as the clan identity is transmitted through the mother as well as through the father, it follows that under no circumstances could children born of the Locrian colonists by native women pass as Locrians or indeed as Greeks. This, however, is not what actually happened in Locri, which seems to indicate that there were Locrians in the narrow and Locrians in the broad sense of the word. The former sprang from the endogamous marriages with the females brought from the mother country and formed the nobility of the land. The latter sprang from exogamous marriages with the indigenous women: it was they who constituted the 'people'.[48]

<hr>

entitled to be called kings and to enjoy certain royal privileges even in later times; significantly, it was at Ephesus that the royal seat of the Ionians was established.
45 Cohen and Middleton 1970: 21.
46 Goody 1970: 121.
47 Cf. Dougherty 1993: 67: 'Although Greek sources are notoriously reticent about intermarriage between the Greek colonists and the native women, there seems to be little doubt that it did take place.' On intermarriages in Greek colonies see also Coldstream 1993; J. Hall 2002: 100–3; cf. West 1997: 618–21.
48 In Athens of the historic period only some 20 per cent of the citizen population were united in the clans, *genē*; this concerned first and foremost the nobles, *eupatridai*. See Parker 1996: 56–66;

It follows from the above discussion that when dealing with heroic Greece we have to take into account three categories of identity: the aristocratic minority of the Greek-speaking settlers, the aristocratic minority of indigenous population groups,[49] and the majority, which presented a mixture of Greek tribes and the indigenous population. There is thus reason to conclude that the majority of those who inhabited Greece by the end of the second millennium BC were of mixed descent and that they were led by a multi-ethnic aristocracy. Since they are often identified in our sources by the collective name 'Achaeans', we may suppose that this was probably the designation of the cultural and political identity which resulted from the process of ethnic and cultural fusion that took place on the territory of Greece in the course of the second millennium BC.

Consider now the following. Whatever the provenance of the language of Linear A, we can actually be certain that it is not Greek.[50] Characteristically, however, with the exception of several Linear A inscriptions discovered in Cythera and the southern Peloponnese, the main bulk of the Bronze Age inscriptions found on the territory of Greece is written in Linear B in the so-called Mycenaean dialect of the Greek language. The Linear B archives uncovered at Knossos, Pylos and Thebes unambiguously testify that by the Late Helladic the presence of the Greek element had become substantial enough to turn Greek into the dominant idiom in the administrative centres of Mycenaean Greece. This seems to indicate that in the course of the second millennium BC the descendants of the population groups that inhabited Greece before the emergence of the Greek tribes became heavily Hellenised. The so-called Neo-Hittite states which flourished in Syria and Anatolia at the beginning of the first millennium BC and which included both the old Anatolian element and the new Semitic one provide a useful parallel. J. D. Hawkins describes this phenomenon, which he calls 'the gradual fusion of the two cultures', as follows:

---

cf. Patterson 1981: 113–14; Ogden 1996: 51. However, even those who did not belong to the *gene* were nevertheless recognised as genuine Athenians.

49 This category ought to be postulated in view of the fact that, in so far as the dispersion of the Hellenes over the Peloponnese was not accompanied by violence, it is reasonable to assume that, rather than being destroyed as in the case of a conquest, the indigenous aristocracy continued to preserve its clan identity exactly as the Greek aristocracy did. The case of the Heraclidae, who even in historic times persisted as a distinct aristocratic group notwithstanding their belonging to a non-Hellenic stemma of the descendants of Inachos, corroborates this suggestion.

50 See further Finkelberg 2001: 85–7.

At least by 1000 BC, a new and intrusive population group appeared in the area, namely the Arameans. Their penetration of Syria and foundation of their own states must have exerted pressure on the already settled Anatolian peoples, yet our sources do not suggest any fissures of the land along ethnic faults.[51]

Yet, the inscriptions testify to the fact that after three hundred years of such peaceful coexistence the whole area had nevertheless gone Semitic.[52]

Should the spread of the Greek language over Bronze Age Greece be accounted for along similar lines? Unfortunately, the Linear B tablets give no indication whatsoever as regards either the extent to which the Greek language was dispersed over Greece or the duration of its presence there. For all we know, the Mycenaean cities could have been no more than isolated colonies which formed a short episode in the history of the region. In order to arrive at a more reliable picture of the language situation in Greece in the second millennium BC, we must turn to dialect geography.

51 Hawkins 1982: 373.   52 Hawkins 1982: 378.

CHAPTER 6

The spread of the Greek language

APPROACHING THE GREEK DIALECTS

'The question of the interrelationship of the Greek dialects', Carl Darling Buck wrote in 1907, 'has an unceasing attraction, not only to the grammarian, but to every student of Greek history. For it always has held and will continue to hold the first place in any discussion of early Greek tribal relations.'[1] The reason is obvious: the way in which the Greek dialects are distributed in the historic period shows beyond doubt that this situation could not have been the original one. Even a casual look at the dialect map of historic Greece makes it clear that something went wrong (Map 3). Of the so-called Aeolic dialects, Boeotian and Thessalian are found in Greece but Lesbian in Asia Minor only; Attic-Ionic and Arcado-Cyprian, as is indicated by their names, are also split by the Aegean; Doric is wedged in between Arcadian on the one hand and Attic on the other, and Doric and Northwest Greek between Arcadian and the Aeolic dialects. 'Migration would certainly give rise to the dialect geography we observe.'[2] Since the normal state of a long-settled area is that of continuous distribution of the dialects of the language spread over the area in question, and since the Greek dialects in their historic positions show no signs of such distribution, it is hard to avoid the conclusion that the historic Greek dialects are no more than fragments of a whole which had ceased to exist before the political map of Greece as we know it was shaped. The question, however, is what the terms are in which this whole should be approached.

The major problem of Greek dialectology has always been that of classification. The entire history of the study of the Greek dialects bears witness to the fact that a clear-cut classification can only be achieved by emphasising one set of linguistic features in a given dialect at the expense

---

1 Buck 1907: 241.   2 Hainsworth 1982: 858. Cf. Drews 1993a: 223; Finkelberg 1994: 4–5.

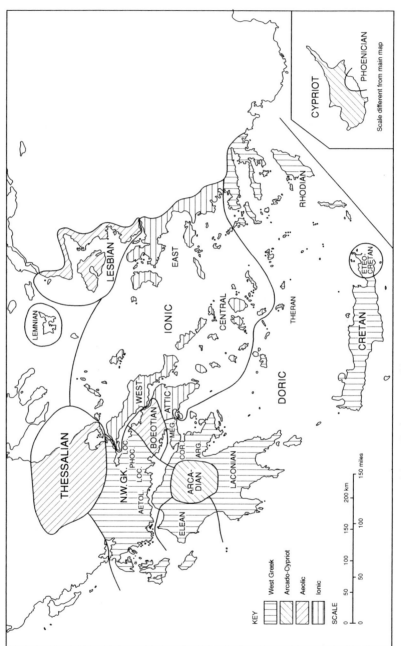

Map 3. Dialect map of historic Greece (after Hainsworth 1982).

KEY

West Greek
Arcado-Cypriot
Aeolic
Ionic

SCALE

0   50   100   150   200 km
0   50   100   150 miles

THESSALIAN

LEMNIAN

LESBIAN

EAST

IONIC

N.W. GK.

AETOL. LOC.

PHOC.

WEST LOC.

BOEOTIAN

MEG.

ATTIC

COR.

ARG.

ARCA-
DIAN

ELEAN

LACONIAN

CENTRAL

THERAN

DORIC

RHODIAN

CRETAN

ETEO-
CRETAN

CYPRIOT

PHOENICIAN

Scale different from main map

of others. Thus, the older classification of Arcado-Cyprian together with Aeolic was only made possible as a result of dismissing as late admixtures such important characteristics linking Arcado-Cyprian with Attic-Ionic as the modal and conditional conjunctions ἄν and εἰ (κε and αἰ in Aeolic), the athematic infinitives in -ναι (-μεν/-μεναι in Aeolic) and the adjectives of the type of τόσος (τόσσος/τόττος in Aeolic). By the same token, the currently adopted classification of Arcado-Cyprian with Attic-Ionic, introduced by W. Porzig and E. Risch in the 1950s, was made possible by suppressing features shared by Arcado-Cyprian and Aeolic, such as o for α with liquids and in other cases, the prepositions ἀπύ and πεδά, the modal particle κε (Cyprian only) and the athematic inflection of contract verbs.[3]

Again, according to the traditional classification Lesbian was seen as 'pure' Aeolic and both Thessalian and Boeotian as 'mixed' dialects which had undergone a considerable West Greek influence. Today, the situation is different: according to the classification introduced by Porzig and Risch, it is Boeotian and especially (East) Thessalian that should be seen as representing the 'pure' Aeolic, whereas Lesbian should be regarded as a 'mixed' dialect strongly influenced by the Ionic of Asia Minor.[4] However, to claim this is to ignore the fact that a number of features shared by Lesbian and Ionic, such as conjunctions of the type ὅτε/ὅτα, the nominative plural οἱ/αἱ of the article, ἱερός, Ἄρτεμις (in contrast to the Boeotian and West Greek ὅκα, τοί/ταί, ἱαρός, Ἄρταμις) are also found in mainland Thessalian and therefore cannot be due to Ionic influence in Asia Minor. Thus, not only Lesbian but also Thessalian should be recognised as 'mixed', and considering that West Greek admixtures in Boeotian are assumed in all classifications, no dialect seems to remain to represent the 'pure' Aeolic.

To a great degree, the same applies to the other dialects as well. Attic-Ionic has features in common with both Arcado-Cyprian and Lesbian, and Arcado-Cyprian with both Attic-Ionic and Aeolic; of the Aeolic dialects, Lesbian shares a number of features with Attic-Ionic and Cyprian, and

---

3 Porzig 1954, Risch 1955; see also Chadwick 1956. Although the great merit of Risch's method was the introduction of criteria that allowed for the isolation of late linguistic features, no feature shared by Arcado-Cyprian and Aeolic has been shown to belong to this category. In his general table of the dialectal features Risch 1955: 75, simply put some linguistic features shared by Arcado-Cyprian and Aeolic (o for α with liquids, the athematic inflection of contract verbs) into a separate category of features 'whose dating is still open' and ignored the others (o for α as in ὄν = ἀνά, ἀπύ for ἀπό, πεδά for μετά). For criticism of the Porzig–Risch classification see Adrados 1956: 240–8; Ruijgh 1961: 206–16 and 1996: 116–19; Palmer 1962: 88–94; Cowgill 1966: 80; García-Ramón 1975: 18–19.
4 See Porzig 1954: 149–55; Risch 1955: 70–1; Chadwick 1956: 46–7.

both Boeotian and Thessalian with West Greek; moreover, some features are common to both Doric and Attic-Ionic. In view of this, it seems reasonable to ask whether being 'impure', 'infected' or 'mixed' should not be recognised as typical of a Greek dialect and whether in trying to force the dialects into the Procrustean bed of a clear-cut classification we are doing justice to the evidence at our disposal.

Generally speaking, the lack of clear-cut demarcation lines between dialects is a linguistic fact that is well known to every student of the subject. The question, however, is how this general truth should be translated into terms of classification. If we proceed from 'pure' models of dialects, we shall come to classify the dialects that do not correspond to these models as 'mixed' or 'impure', even if this means admitting that all the material we possess calls for such a description. If, on the other hand, we recognise that the 'pure' models of the dialects, convenient as they may be for the purpose of classification, are nothing more than scholarly conventions, it will be hard to avoid the conclusion that, rather than clear-cut boundaries between the dialects, we have gradual changes which, taken together, form a dialect continuum.[5] The first approach is characteristic of the comparative method; the second is adopted in dialect geography. The great merit of the latter is that it has been developed as a result of the empirical study of living languages:

> In a country like France, Italy, or Germany . . . every village or, at most, every group of two or three villages, has its own local dialect . . . The difference from place to place is small, but, as one travels in any one direction, the differences accumulate, until speakers, say from opposite ends of the country, cannot understand each other, although there is no sharp line of linguistic demarcation between the places they live.[6]

Rather often than not, dialect continua cross national frontiers, defying conventional distinctions between standard languages. To take several well-known examples, the rural dialects of French, Italian, Catalan, Spanish and Portuguese form part of the West Romance dialect continuum which spreads from Portugal to the centre of Belgium; the West Germanic continuum includes all dialects of German, Dutch and Flemish; the Scandinavian dialect continuum comprises dialects of Norwegian, Swedish and Danish; the North Slavic dialect continuum includes Russian,

---

5 Cf. Chambers and Trudgill 1998: 12: '. . . traditional work in dialectology has not always been very successful in handling linguistic phenomena such as variability, gradience and fuzziness that result from the fact that such continua exist.'

6 Bloomfield 1935: 51. Cf. also Bloomfield 1935: 42–56, 297–345; Hockett 1958: 471–84; Albright and Lambdin 1970: 124; Crossland 1971: 832, 864; Chambers and Trudgill 1998: 5–7.

Ukrainian, Polish, Czech and Slovak; and the South Slavic continuum includes Slovenian, Serbian, Croatian, Macedonian and Bulgarian. 'Given that we have dialect continua, then the way we divide up and label particular bits of a continuum may often be, from a purely linguistic point of view, arbitrary . . . dialect continua admit of more-or-less but not either-or judgments.'[7]

Dialect geography of languages that have developed under settled conditions naturally proceeds from the map, and the charts drawn in this kind of dialect geography are normally the result of empirical observation. This is why dialect geography is sometimes thought to be of limited application in the reconstruction of past history.[8] Indeed, in the case of languages whose original map of dispersal was blurred by migration or foreign invasion, a mechanical application of the technique of dialect geography is both profitless and misleading, and the best proof of this is the low informative value of the extant dialect charts of historic Greek dialects.[9] This is not to say that dialect geography cannot be employed with profit for the purpose of reconstruction. However, in this specific case it is more correct to reverse the procedure: one should first draw up a coherent scheme of purely linguistic relations between the attested dialects and only then transfer this scheme to the map. If this is feasible, that is, if the presumed fragments can be arranged so as to form a whole, this would amount to a reconstruction of the respective positions of the Greek dialects within a dialect continuum. This in turn might throw light on the original geography of Greek settlement and perhaps even on the sociolinguistic processes which led to the disintegration of the continuum.

A group of dialects can be said to form a continuum when it can be shown that the actual relations between them are of the type *ab, bc, cd, de,* that is to say, when each intermediate component, rather than presenting a unique and irreducible idiom, is characterised by a unique combination of linguistic features which can also be found in the other dialects, so that the only irreducible components would be those at the opposite extremes of the continuum (*a* in *ab* and *e* in *de*). The simplest way to test this kind of relationship would be to place each dialect among several others and distribute the relevant linguistic features among the dialects in question. If, as a result of such distribution, dialect B proves to be reducible to dialect A on the one hand and dialect C on the other, then it should be placed between them, the next step being to take dialect C and analyse it

7 Chambers and Trudgill 1998: 7. 8 See e.g. Hockett 1958: 483.
9 Cf. Chadwick 1956: 41.

in the same way, until we eventually arrive at a dialect which cannot be reduced to other dialects, that is, at the end of the continuum.

I shall apply this kind of analysis to all the attested historic dialects, namely, (Attic-)Ionic, Arcado-Cyprian, Lesbian, Thessalian, Boeotian, Northwest Greek, Doric, Cretan and Pamphylian, taking into account their distinctive features as established in scholarly research. It is true that Cretan and Pamphylian are usually regarded as 'mixed' dialects containing a considerable 'Achaean', that is, prehistoric, element.[10] The question, however, is whether the features by which the 'mixed' character of Cretan and Pamphylian is determined are in themselves consistent, that is, whether they make sense in terms of the dialect continuum, and this is exactly what I am going to check. The position of Mycenaean, the only attested prehistoric dialect, will be assessed separately. The artificial character of the so-called Homeric dialect makes it irrelevant for the present investigation.

While the subsequent list of twenty-one isoglosses has much in common with the list of twenty isoglosses introduced by Risch in 1955, it differs from Risch's list in the following respects.

First, I have restored two categories of isoglosses underrepresented in Risch's list (see above, with nn. 3 and 4). These are (1) the isoglosses shared by Arcado-Cyprian and Aeolic, namely, o for α as in ὄν = ἀνά, υ for o as ἀπύ for ἀπό and dat. pl. -αις/-οις as against -αισι/-οισι (the latter does not enclose Lesbian) (see below, nos. 2, 5 and 10) and (2) those shared by Ionic and Thessalian, namely, ἱερός in contrast to ἱαρός and Ἄρτεμις in contrast to Ἄρταμις (below, nos. 3 and 4).

Second, I have abstained from multiplying the isoglosses that enclose the same dialect area. This concerns first of all -μες in contrast to -μεν in first person plural of the verb (Risch no. 17). The dialect area enclosed by this isogloss (Northwest Greek and Doric) is identical to that enclosed by the future in -σέω in contrast to -σω, which I have taken into consideration (no. 18 below).[11] As distinct from this, the distribution of ἱερός/ἷρος

---

10 On Pamphylian see Meillet 1908: 413–25; Luije 1959. 7–20; Brixhe 1976. On Cretan see Hajnal 1987: 58–84 and 1988: 62–87; Duhoux 1988: 57–72.

11 The same holds good of other isoglosses, as for example -ων, -οντος in the active perfect participle, ἴα = μία and ρε = ρι: they are only relevant to the so-called Aeolic group of dialects (Lesbian, Thessalian, Boeotian) and their dialect area is identical to that enclosed by such other isoglosses on our list as πε- from *kʷe- and the dative plural in -εσσι (below, nos. 8 and 11). The isogloss εἴκοσι (from *ε-Ϝίκοσι) in contrast to Ϝίκατι, ἴκατι, whose dispersion is identical to that of -σι from -τι as in δίδωσι (see no. 7 below), also belongs to this category. These and similar isoglosses are absent from Risch's list as well.

: ἱαρός and Ἄρτεμις : Ἄρταμις, isomorphic though it is in the majority of dialects, is significant for determining the position of Pamphylian and Cretan, both of which have ἱαρός but Ἄρτεμις ('Αρτι- in Pamphylian); this seems to be sufficient reason for retaining both of them. Similar considerations have led to my retaining the dat. pl. -εσσι as against -σι, also absent from Risch's list; although its area of distribution is close to that of πε- as against *$k^w e$, they are not fully identical (see below, nos. 8 and 11).

Third, I have temporarily excluded from consideration the features we can be certain were contemporary with the processes that led to the fragmentation of the dialect map of Bronze Age Greece, and therefore could not have been part of the original continuum. These are the Attic-Ionic α > η change (Risch no. 13) and the distinctions produced by the first and the second compensatory lengthening, which brought about simplification of the intervocalic groups consisting of *s* with liquids and nasals (Risch nos. 9 and 14); these, together with the spread of the preposition πεδά as distinct from μετά, will be discussed in Chapter 7.

The above considerations have led to the following list of isoglosses; whether the distinctions produced by them are due to innovation or issue from different choices from the repertoire of inherited features is not relevant as far as their patterns of distribution coincide.[12] The order of presentation is as in C. D. Buck's standard manual; Buck's paragraphs and the available numbers on Risch's list are added after each item for the reader's convenience.[13]

1. o for α before or after liquids: ρο/ορ in Arc.-Cypr., Lesb., Thess., Boeot., in contrast to ρα/αρ in Ionic, NW Greek, Doric, Cretan, Pamph. (Buck 5; Risch no. 19);
2. o for α in other cases as in ὄν = ἀνά in Arc.-Cypr., Lesb., Thess., in contrast to Ionic, Boeot., NW Greek, Doric, Cretan, Pamph. (Buck 6);

---

12 Thus, for example, there is little room for doubt that the distinctions between -αις/-οις : -αισι/-οισι and ποτί : προτί (nos. 10, 17) issue from different choices from the repertoire of inherited features: Proto-Greek inherited both *proti (= Vedic prati) and *poti (= Aves. paiti) from Proto-Indo-European, whereas -οισι and -οις continue the IE locative and the instrumental, respectively. While it is generally true that an agreement of this sort has a much higher degree of chance occurrence than what one might call a positive innovation, the fact that their spheres of distribution (Ionic, Lesbian, Pamphylian and Cretan) coincide both with each other and with that of the innovation ἐνς (no. 16; also in Doric) shows that what is dealt with are genuine isoglosses.
13 All the references are to Buck 1955 and Risch 1955.

3. ἱερός or ἱρός or ἷρος in Ionic, Arc.-Cypr., Lesb., Thess., in contrast to ἱαρός in Boeot., NW Greek, Doric, Cretan, Pamph. (Buck 13.1);[14]

4. Ἄρτεμις in Ionic, Arc.-Cypr., Lesb., Thess., Cretan, Pamph., in contrast to Ἄρταμις in Boeot., NW Greek, Doric (Buck 13.2);

5. ν for o as in ἀπύ = ἀπό in Arc.-Cypr., Lesb., Thess., Pamph., in contrast to Ionic, Boeot., NW Greek, Doric, Cretan (Buck 22);

6. the vocalism *o* in the verb 'to wish' (βούλομαι, βόλομαι, βόλλομαι) in Ionic, Arc.-Cypr., Lesb., Cretan, Pamph., in contrast to *e* (βέλλομαι, βείλομαι, δείλομαι/δήλομαι) in Thess., Boeot., NW Greek, Doric (Buck 49.3; Risch no. 8);

7. -σι from -τι as in δίδωσι in Ionic, Arc.-Cypr., Lesb., in contrast to δίδωτι in Thess., Boeot., NW Greek, Doric, Cretan, Pamph. (Buck 61; Risch no. 1);

8. πε- from *$k^w e$ in Cypr., Lesb., Thess., Boeot., in contrast to τε-/τζε- from *$k^w e$ in Ionic, Arc., NW Greek, Doric, Pamph.,[15] Cretan (Buck 68.2; Risch no.10);

9. τόσος and the like from *τοτψος and the like in Ionic, Arc.-Cypr., in contrast to τόσσος/τόττος in Lesb., Thess., Boeot., NW Greek, Doric, Cretan (uncertain in Pamph., see n. 36) (Buck 82; Risch no. 3);

10. -αισι/-οισι as dat. pl. in the α- and o- stems in Ionic, Lesb., Pamph., Cretan, in contrast to -αις/-οις in Arc.-Cypr., Thess., Boeot., NW Greek, Doric (Buck 104.7, 106.4);

11. -εσσι as dat. pl. of consonant stems in Lesb., Thess., Boeot., Pamph., in contrast to -σι in Ionic, Arc.-Cypr., NW Greek, Doric, Cretan (Buck 107.3);[16]

12. οἱ/αἱ as nom. pl. of the article in Ionic, Arc.-Cypr., Lesb., Thess., Cretan, in contrast to τοί/ταί in Boeot., NW Greek, Doric (not attested in Pamph.) (Buck 122; Risch no. 11);

13. the conjunction ὅτε/ὅτα and the like in Ionic, Arc.-Cypr., Lesb., Thess., in contrast to ὅκα and the like in Boeot., NW Greek, Doric, Cretan, Pamph. (Buck 132.11; Risch no. 7);

---

14 It is possible that Arcado-Cyprian and Attic ἱερός derive from *ἱsero- and Lesbian ἱρος and Ionic ἱρός from *ἱsro-. This, however, does not change the fact that both are opposed to ἱαρός. Cf. Lejeune 1972: 239 and n. 2.

15 See Pamphylian πέδε = πέντε. On the treatment of the labiovelars in Pamphylian see esp. Brixhe 1976: 91–2.

16 Several Northwest dialects, such as Delphian, Locrian and Elean, occasionally show the dative plural in -εσσι, cf. Buck 1955: 89; this phenomenon is usually accounted for as due to the influence of an Aeolic dialectal substratum, see below, pp. 127–8.

14. the conjunction εἰ in Ionic, Arc.-Cypr., in contrast to αἰ in Lesb., Thess., Boeot., NW Greek, Doric, Cretan, Pamph. (Buck 134.1; Risch no. 5);

15. the modal particle ἄν in Ionic, Arc., in contrast to κε/κα in Cypr., Lesb., Thess., Boeot., NW Greek, Doric, Cretan (not attested in Pamph.) (Buck 134.2; Risch no. 6);

16. the preposition εἰς, ἐ(ν)ς, ἰς (from ἐν + ς and from ἐνς < *ἰνς) in Ionic, Lesb., Doric, Pamph., Cretan, in contrast to ἐν, ἰν with the accusative in Arc.-Cypr., Thess., Boeot., NW Greek (Buck 135.4; Risch no. 12);

17. the preposition πρός (from προτί) in Ionic, Lesb., Pamph. (περτ'), Cretan (πορτί), in contrast to πός, ποτί in Arc.-Cypr., Thess., Boeot., NW Greek, Doric (Buck 135.6; Risch no. 2);[17]

18. the future in -σέω in NW Greek, Doric, Cretan, in contrast to -σω in the rest (not attested in Pamph.) (Buck 141; Risch no. 20);

19. the aorist in -σ(σ)α of the verbs in -ζω in Ionic, Lesb., in contrast to -ξα in Arc.-Cypr., Thess., Boeot., NW Greek, Doric (Buck 142; Risch no. 16);[18]

20. the infinitive in -ναι of athematic verbs in Ionic, Arc.-Cypr., Pamph., in contrast to -μεν/-μεναι in Lesb., Thess., Boeot., NW Greek, Doric, Cretan (Buck 154; Risch no. 4);

21. the athematic inflection of contract verbs in Arc.-Cypr., Lesb., Thess., Pamph., in contrast to Ionic, Boeot., NW Greek, Doric, Cretan (Buck 157; Risch no. 18).

In what follows, I proceed from the assumption that, to the degree that the dialect features under discussion can be shown to be innovatory, they should be accounted for as due to the diffusion of a given innovation over the territory of Greek settlement rather than as independent developments issuing sporadically from the same kind of systemic pressure (the so-called 'trivial' innovations). Although systemic pressure can cause two or more different dialects to attempt to solve the same inherent problem,

---

17 The evidence connecting this form with Doric, consisting of a quotation in Apollonius Dyscolus and restoration of this form in Alcman and in a West Argolic inscription, is inconclusive; see Bartonek 1972: 156.

18 Actually, the isogloss embraces both the aorist and the future of the verbs of this group. Note also that the actual opposition is between the dialects that never use -ξα and those that use either -ξα alone or both -ξα and -σ(σ)α/-ττα: Argolic, Arcadian and Boeotian belong to the latter group. There is no conclusive evidence as to the treatment of the aorist of the verbs in -ζω in Pamphylian, see Brixhe 1976: 116; as far as Cretan is concerned, this dialect probably preserves traces of an earlier use of the aorist in -σα, see Thumb–Kieckers 1932: 148, 166, cf. Hajnal 1987: 77–8.

more often than not their means of coping with the problem would be different. Thus, while the replacement of the athematic ending by the thematic one in the dative plural of consonant stems in Aeolic on the one hand and in Northwest Greek on the other was prompted by the same causes, it led to -εσσι in the former and -οις in the latter case.[19] Only when no other explanation is available of the emergence of the same feature in two or more dialects are we entitled to resort to assessing this feature in terms of 'trivial' innovations.

THE DIALECT CONTINUUM OF ANCIENT GREEK

Since we have already seen that Arcado-Cyprian lends itself to being classified with Attic-Ionic on the one hand and with the so-called Aeolic dialects (Thessalian, Boeotian, Lesbian) on the other, it will be convenient to begin our procedure by placing Arcado-Cyprian between Ionic and Thessalian:

Ionic, Arcado-Cyprian, Thessalian. Of the twenty-one isoglosses on the list, Arcado-Cyprian shares six with Ionic to the exclusion of Thessalian, eight with Thessalian to the exclusion of Ionic and five with both Ionic and Thessalian.[20] The two remaining isoglosses, πε- from $*k^we$- in contrast to τε- and the modal particle ἄν in contrast to κε (nos. 8 and 15) are distributed in such a way that Arcadian goes with Ionic and Cyprian with Thessalian. Arcado-Cyprian thus can be reduced to Ionic on the one hand and Thessalian on the other. That is to say, the three dialects form a continuum:

Thessalian ⟷ Arc.-Cypr. ⟷ Ionic

The same can be shown to be true of the position of Thessalian when placed between Arcado-Cyprian and Boeotian:

Arcado-Cyprian, Thessalian, Boeotian. Of the twenty-one isoglosses on the list, Thessalian shares seven with Arcado-Cyprian to the exclusion of

---

19 For examples from other languages see Hoenigwald 1966: 11.
20 With Ionic: the vocalism *o* in the verb 'to wish' (Arc.-Cypr. βόλομαι, Ion. βούλομαι, Thess. βέλλομαι), -σι from -τι, τόσος from *τότψος, -σι in dat. pl. of consonant stems, εἰ instead of αἰ and the athematic infinitives in -ναι (nos. 6, 7, 9, 11, 14, 20); with Thessalian: o for α with liquids and in other cases, υ from o, -αις/-οις in dat. pl. of α- and o- stems, the prepositions ἰν/ἐν + acc. and πός/ποτί, the aorist in -ξα of verbs in -ζω and the athematic inflection of contract verbs (nos. 1, 2, 5, 10, 16, 17, 19, 21); with both: ἱερός, Ἄρτεμις, οἱ/αἱ as nom. pl. of the article, τ instead of κ in temporal conjunctions of the type of ὅτε and the future in -σω (nos. 3, 4, 12, 13, 18).

Boeotian, eight with Boeotian to the exclusion of Arcado-Cyprian and six with both Arcado-Cyprian and Boeotian.[21] There is no isogloss in Thessalian that cannot be reduced to either Arcado-Cyprian or Boeotian or both. Thus,

Boeotian ⟷ Thessalian ⟷ Arc.-Cypr. ⟷ Ionic

Thessalian, Boeotian, Northwest Greek. Of the twenty-one isoglosses on the list, Boeotian shares four with Thessalian to the exclusion of Northwest Greek, seven with Northwest Greek to the exclusion of Thessalian and ten with both Thessalian and Northwest Greek.[22] There is therefore no feature in Boeotian that is not shared with either Thessalian or Northwest Greek or both. In other words, when placed between Thessalian and Northwest Greek Boeotian proves to be a bridge-dialect between the two. Thus,

NW Greek ⟷ Boeotian ⟷ Thessalian ⟷ Arc.-Cypr. ⟷ Ionic

The same would be true of Northwest Greek when placed between Boeotian and Doric:

Boeotian, Northwest Greek, Doric. Of the twenty-one isoglosses on the list, Northwest Greek shares one with Boeotian to the exclusion of Doric, four with Doric to the exclusion of Boeotian and sixteen with both Boeotian and Doric.[23] There is thus no feature in Northwest Greek that is not shared with either Boeotian or Doric or both. In other words, when

21 With Arcado-Cyprian: o for α as in ὄν = ἀνά, ἱερός, Ἄρτεμις, υ for o as in ἀπύ, οἱ/αἱ as nom. pl. of the article, ὅτε and the like and the athematic inflection of contract verbs (nos. 2, 3, 4, 5, 12, 13, 21); with Boeotian: the vocalism *e* in the verb 'to wish', -τι unchanged to -σι, πε- from *$k^w e$- (also in Cypr.), τόσσος/τόττος and the like, -εσσι in dat. pl. of consonant stems, αἱ, κε/κα, the athematic infinitive in -μεν, as well as some other specifically 'Aeolic' features (nos. 6, 7, 8, 9, 11, 14, 15, 20); with both: o for a before and after liquids, -αις/-οις in dat. pl. of the α- and o- stems, the prepositions ἐν/ἰν and ποτί/πός, the future in -σω and -ξα in the aorist of the verbs in -ζω (nos. 1, 10, 16, 17, 18, 19).

22 With Thessalian: o for α with liquids, πε- from *$k^w e$-, -εσσι in the dat. pl. of consonant stems and the future in -σέω (nos. 1, 8, 11, 18); with Northwest Greek: α unchanged to o as in ἀνά, ἱαρός, Ἄρταμις, o unchanged to υ as in ἀπό, τοί/ταί as nom. pl. of the article, ὅκα and the like as against ὅτε/ὅτα and the like and -έω unchanged to -ῃμι in contract verbs (nos. 2, 3, 4, 5, 12, 13, 21); with both: the vocalism *e* in the verb 'to wish' (Thess. βέλλομαι, Boeot. βείλομαι, West Greek δείλομαι/δήλομαι), -τι unchanged to -σι, τόσσος/τόττος in contrast to τόσος, -αις/-οις in the dat. pl. of α- and o- stems, the conditional conjunction αἱ, the modal particle κε/κα, ἐν with the accusative, ποτί in contrast to πρός, -ξα in the aorist of verbs in -ζω and the athematic infinitives in -μεν (nos. 6, 7, 9, 10, 14, 15, 16, 17, 19, 20).

23 With Boeotian: the preposition ἐν with the accusative in contrast to the Doric ἐ(ν)ς (no. 16); with Doric: α unchanged to o with liquids, τε- from *$k^w e$, -σι unchanged to -εσσι and the future in -σέω (nos. 1, 8, 11, 18); the rest with both.

placed between Boeotian and Doric, Northwest Greek proves to be a bridge-dialect between the two. Thus,

Doric ⟷ NW Greek ⟷ Boeotian ⟷ Thessalian ⟷ Arc.-Cypr. ⟷ Ionic

There are a number of features which Doric and West Greek in general share with Ionic. Most of these, such as ρα/αρ as against ρο/ορ, ἀνά as against ὀν, ἀπό as against ἀπύ, -σι as against -εσσι in dat. pl. of consonant stems can be consistently accounted for as common retentions. In principle, this explanation goes well with the fact that Ionic and West Greek are generally presumed to have occupied peripheral positions on the original map of the dispersal of the Greek dialects: in cases like this, overlapping is usually due to the fact that the peripheral dialects fail to participate in the developments taking place in the central area.[24] Yet, one Doric–Ionic isogloss does not fit into this picture. The preposition ἐνς > εἰς is obviously an innovation, which in some dialects replaced the earlier ἐν with the accusative. Only Ionic, Lesbian, Doric, Cretan and Pamphylian share the innovation in question (Ionic, Lesb. εἰς, Doric ἐνς, Pamph. and Cretan ἐνς > *ἰνς > ἰς), whereas Arcado-Cyprian, Thessalian, Boeotian and Northwest Greek preserve the inherited form (ἰν in Arc.-Cypr.).[25] This seems to indicate that the isolation of Doric was in fact not as complete as is usually supposed.

Some considerations of a more general character corroborate this conclusion. We saw that West Greek remained untouched by most of the processes that affected the other dialects. At the same time, it is possessed of all the features that are characteristic of the Greek language and that distinguish it from any other Indo-European language, however

24 Thus, according to Thumb, '. . . die dorischen und nordwestgriechischen Dialekte einmal an der einen äusseren Seite, das Arkadische und Aiolische in der Mitte und das Ionisch-Attische an der anderen äusseren Seite des griechischen Sprachgebiets gesprochen worden sind', whereas in Meillet's opinion, '. . . l'ionien-attique, d'une part, le groupe occidental, de l'autre, représent deux termes extrêmes. L'arcado-cypriote et l'éolien sont intermédiaires.' See Thumb–Kieckers 1932: 63; Meillet 1930: 106. This traditional explanation of the cases of coincidence between Attic-Ionic and West Greek was challenged by Risch, in whose opinion the features common to West Greek and Attic-Ionic should be regarded as common innovations, and by Chadwick, who sought to explain them away by assuming a Doric influence on Attic-Ionic in the period of the great migrations. See Risch 1955: 71–2, 74; Chadwick 1956: 43–4. That the first view is untenable in that it forces us to postulate an innovatory character for a number of inherited linguistic features has been demonstrated by Adrados 1956: 247–8; for criticism of the second view see Ruijgh 1958: 106 n. 4 and 1996: 119; Coleman 1963: 104–5; Cowgill 1966: 92–3. See also Palmer 1962: 89–90.

25 Cf. Duhoux 1988: 58–60. It is true that side by side with ἐν + acc. Boeotian also has ἔττε < ἔστε, cf. ἔντε in Locrian, Delphian (hέντε) and the Northwest Greek *koinē*. This, however, should be accounted for as due to Attic influence on historic Boeotian, cf. Delph. εἴστε. See further Finkelberg 1994: 27 n. 49.

close to Greek it may be. These are the devoicing of the Indo-European voiced aspirates, loss of the final stops, change of final *m* to *n*, aspiration of initial prevocalic and intervocalic sigma, etc. Thus Macedonian, for example, does not share with Greek at least one of the features identifying the unique idiom of the latter, namely, the devoicing of the IE voiced aspirates.[26] When could West Greek, permanently isolated as it was from the other dialects, have had the opportunity to develop these features? To account for the Greekness of West Greek we are bound to postulate a period of common development, whether or not the ἐνς : ἐν distinction is available.

Taking into account that the preposition ἐνς > εἰς is also found in Cretan, a West Greek dialect which has features in common with Attic-Ionic, we can try to place Doric between Northwest Greek on the one hand and Cretan on the other.

Northwest Greek, Doric, Cretan. Of the twenty isoglosses of those on our list that are attested for Cretan, Doric shares five with Northwest Greek to the exclusion of Cretan, one with Cretan to the exclusion of Northwest Greek and fourteen with both Northwest Greek and Cretan.[27] Thus,

Cretan ⟷ Doric ⟷ NW Greek ⟷ Boeotian ⟷ Thessalian ⟷ Arc.-Cypr. ⟷ Ionic

Since the isoglosses that Cretan does not share with Doric point in the direction of Ionic, we can proceed by placing Cretan between Doric on the one hand and Ionic on the other:

Doric, Cretan, Ionic. Of the twenty isoglosses attested for Cretan, it shares eight with Doric to the exclusion of Ionic, five with Ionic to the exclusion of Doric and seven with both Doric and Ionic.[28] That is to say,

---

26 See Mac. ἀβροῦτες : Gr. ὀφρύες, 'eyebrows'; Mac. δαλάγχα : Gr. θάλασσα, 'sea'; Mac. κεβαλή : Gr. κεφαλή, 'head'; Mac. Βερενίκη : Gr. Φερένικος. On the unique idiom of Greek see Thumb–Kieckers 1932: 1–10; Meillet 1930: 16–51; Duhoux 1983: 34–5; Morpurgo Davies 1988: 79. On Macedonian see Thumb–Kieckers 1932: 9–10; Crossland 1982: 843–7; J. Hall 2001: 161–2 (with bibliography) and 2002: 154–5, 165.

27 With Northwest Greek: Ἄρταμις in contrast to Ἄρτεμις, vocalism *e* in the verb 'to wish', dat. pl. in -αις/-οις, τοί/ται as the form of the article, the preposition πός, ποτί (nos. 4, 6, 10, 12, 17); with Cretan: the preposition εἰς, ἐ(ν)ς (no. 16); the rest with both. Note that there is no conclusive evidence as to Cretan treatment of the aorist in -σ(σ)α of the verbs in -ζω (above, n. 18).

28 With Doric: ἱαρός, -τι unchanged to -σι, τόσσος/τόττος, the conjunctions ὄκα and αἰ, the modal particle κα, the future in -σέω and the infinitive in -μεν of athematic verbs (3, 7, 9, 13, 14, 15, 18, 20); with Ionic: Ἄρτεμις, the vocalism *o* in the verb 'to wish', dat. pl. in -αισι/-οισι, οἱ/αἱ as nom. pl. of the article and the preposition πρός/προτί (4, 6, 10, 12, 17); with both: o for α

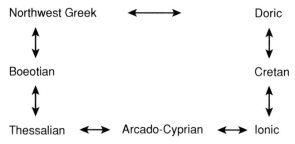

Figure 7. The position of Cretan.

there is not even one isogloss in Cretan that is not shared with either Doric or Ionic or both. This allows us to see in Cretan a bridge-dialect between Doric and Ionic. The latter seems to indicate that the dialect continuum should assume a circular shape rather than the linear one with which we have been working thus far (Fig. 7).

Let us turn now to Lesbian and Pamphylian, the two dialects that have not yet been placed within the dialect continuum. Since we have already seen that Lesbian lends itself to being classified with both Attic-Ionic and Thessalian, we can try to place it between these two dialects:

Ionic, Lesbian, Thessalian. Of the twenty-one isoglosses on the list, Lesbian shares six with Ionic to the exclusion of Thessalian, nine with Thessalian to the exclusion of Ionic and five with both Ionic and Thessalian.[29] The remaining isogloss, viz. the Lesbian infinitive ending of athematic verbs -μεναι (no. 20), obviously relates to both the Ionic -ναι and the Thessalian -μεν.[30] In view of this, we have reason to conclude that Lesbian is reducible to Ionic on the one hand and Thessalian on the other.

with liquids and other cases, ἀπό in contrast to ἀπύ, τε- from *$k^w e$-, -σι as dat. pl. of consonant stems, the preposition εἰς, ἐ(ν)ς and -έω as against -ημι in contract verbs (nos. 1, 2, 5, 8, 11, 16, 21).

29 With Ionic: the vocalism *o* in the verb 'to wish' (Lesb. βόλομαι, Ion. βούλομαι, Thess. βέλλομαι), -σι from -τι as in δίδωσι, αισι/-οισι in dat. pl. of α and o stems, the prepositions εἰς and πρός and the aorist in -σ(σ)α of the verbs in -ζω (nos. 6, 7, 10, 16, 17, 19); with Thessalian: o for α with liquids, υ from o as in ἀπύ, πε- from *$k^w e$-, τόσσος from *τότψος, -εσσι in dat. pl. of consonant stems, the conditional conjunction αἰ, the modal particle κε and the athematic inflection of contract verbs (nos. 1, 2, 5, 8, 9, 11, 14, 15, 21); with both: ἱερος as against ἱαρός (Lesb. ἱρος, see above, n. 14), Ἄρτεμις, οἱ/αἱ as nom. pl. of the article, τ in temporal conjunctions of the ὅτε type and the future in -σω (nos. 3, 4, 12, 13, 18).

30 Whether or not we take -μεναι as a hybrid of -μεν and -ναι or as their common prototype (both opinions circulate in the scholarly literature), this would amount to the same conclusion regarding the intermediary position of this form.

Figure 8. The position of Lesbian (1).

As we saw, the same can be said of Arcado-Cyprian. Since Thessalian in its turn can be reduced to Lesbian on the one hand and Boeotian on the other,[31] we have to conclude that Lesbian should be placed between Ionic and Thessalian in a position parallel to that of Arcado-Cyprian (Fig. 8).

It is characteristic of Lesbian that Ionic and Thessalian are not the only two dialects to which it can be reduced. If we proceed from the position of Lesbian as regards Arcado-Cyprian, we shall see that while some of its isoglosses are shared with Arcado-Cyprian, others point in the direction of Pamphylian. This seems to justify placing Lesbian between these two dialects as well (see below, however, on the status of Pamphylian).

Arcado-Cyprian, Lesbian, Pamphylian. Of the sixteen isoglosses on our list that are attested for Pamphylian, Lesbian shares five with Arcado-Cyprian to the exclusion of Pamphylian, five with Pamphylian to the exclusion of Arcado-Cyprian and five with both Arcado-Cyprian and Pamphylian.[32] The remaining isogloss, viz. the Lesbian infinitive ending of athematic verbs -μεναι (no. 20), which stands apart from Arcado-Cyprian and Pamphylian -ναι, has already been treated above as a compromise solution between the Ionic -ναι and the Thessalian -μεν,

31 With Lesbian: o for α as in ὄν = ἀνά, ἱερός as against ἰαρός, Ἄρτεμις as against Ἄρταμις, υ from o as in ἀπύ, οἱ/αἱ as nom. pl. of the article, τ as against κ in temporal conjunctions as in ὅτε/ὅτα and the athematic inflection of contract verbs (nos. 2, 3, 4, 5, 12, 13, 21); with Boeotian: the vocalism *e* in the verb 'to wish' (Thess. βέλλομαι, Boeot. βείλομαι, Lesb. βόλλομαι), -τι unchanged to -σι, -αις/-οις in the dat. pl. of α- and o- stems, ἐν with the accusative, ποτί as against πρός, -ξα in the aorist of verbs in -ζω and -μεν as the athematic infinitive ending (nos. 6, 7, 10, 16, 17, 19, 20); with both: o for α with liquids, πε- from *kʷe-, τόσσους/τόττυς, -εσσι in dat. pl. of consonant stems, the conjunction αἰ, the particle κε/κα and the future in -σω (nos. 1, 8, 9, 11, 14, 15, 18).
32 With Arcado-Cyprian: o for α with liquids and in other cases, ἱερός as against ἰαρός (Lesb. ἴρος, see above, n. 14), -σι from -τι and the conjunction ὅτε/ὅτα (nos. 1, 2, 3, 7, 13); with Pamphylian: dat. pl. in -αισι/-οισι, -εσσι as dat. pl. of consonant stems, the conjunction εἰ and the prepositions εἰς, ἰς and πρός (nos. 10, 11, 14, 16, 17); with both: Ἄρτεμις, υ from o, vocalism *o* in the verb 'to wish', τε- from *kʷe (Arcadian only) and athematic inflection of contract verbs (nos. 4, 5, 6, 8, 21).

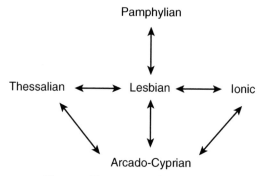

Figure 9. The position of Lesbian (2).

another pair of dialects to which Lesbian can be reduced. This crisscross relationship of Lesbian to the other dialects is indicative of the central position of this dialect within the dialect continuum (see Fig. 9).

Pamphylian is another dialect reducible to more than two idioms. As far as I can see, the dialects to which Pamphylian can be reduced are Cretan, Ionic and Lesbian and/or Thessalian.

Cretan, Pamphylian, Ionic. Pamphylian shares four isoglosses with Cretan to the exclusion of Ionic, one with Ionic to the exclusion of Cretan and eight with both Cretan and Ionic; this accounts for thirteen out of the sixteen isoglosses attested for Pamphylian.[33] The isoglosses that do not allow us to reduce Pamphylian to Cretan and Ionic alone are υ for ο, -εσσι as dat. pl. of consonant stems and the athematic inflection of contract verbs (nos. 5, 11, 21), absent from both Cretan and Ionic.[34] These isoglosses are found in Lesbian and Thessalian, and it can be shown that Pamphylian can further be reduced to Cretan on the one hand and Lesbian/Thessalian on the other.

Cretan, Pamphylian, Lesbian/ Thessalian. Pamphylian shares six isoglosses with Cretan to the exclusion of Lesbian, three with Lesbian to the exclusion of Cretan and six with both Cretan and Lesbian.[35] The

---

33 With Cretan: ἰαρός, -τι unchanged to -σι and the conjunctions ὅτε/ὅτα and εἰς (nos. 3, 7, 13, 14); with Ionic: the infinitive in -ναι (no. 20); with both: α unchanged to ο, Ἄρτεμις, βούλομαι, τε- from *k^we-, dat. pl. in -αισι/-οισι, ἐνς > εἰς/ἰς and πρός/πορτί/περτ' from προτί (nos. 1, 2, 4, 6, 8, 10, 16, 17).
34 For discussion of the latter feature see Brixhe 1976: 118–19.
35 With Cretan vs. Lesbian: α unchanged to ο, ἰαρός, -τι unchanged to -σι, τε- from *k^we, and ὅκα (nos. 1, 2, 3, 7, 8, 13); with Lesbian vs. Cretan: υ from ο, -εσσι and the athematic inflection of contract verbs (nos. 5, 11, 21); with both: Ἄρτεμις, βούλομαι, -αισι/-οισι, the conjunction αἰ, ἐνς > εἰς/ἰς and πρός/πορτί/περτ' (nos. 4, 6, 10, 14, 16, 17).

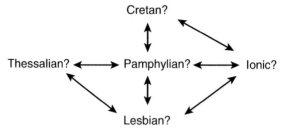

Figure 10. The position of Pamphylian.

isogloss that does not allow us to reduce Pamphylian to Cretan on the one hand and Lesbian on the other is the infinitive in -ναι (no. 20), found in Ionic to which Pamphylian can also be reduced (see above).[36] Finally, Pamphylian can alternately be reduced to Cretan and Thessalian, in that it shares nine isoglosses with Cretan to the exclusion of Thessalian, three with Thessalian to the exclusion of Cretan (the same ones as shared with Lesbian) and three with both Cretan and Thessalian. This would account for fifteen out of the sixteen isoglosses attested for Pamphylian.[37] The isogloss that does not allow us to reduce Pamphylian to Cretan and Thessalian is the same infinitive in -ναι that precludes this dialect from being reduced to Cretan and Lesbian; as we saw, this isogloss is found in Ionic.

As in the case of Lesbian, the crisscross relationship of Pamphylian to the other dialects must be indicative of the central position of this dialect within the dialect continuum. At the same time, since of the twenty-one isoglosses on the list only sixteen are attested for Pamphylian, and since we cannot be certain as to the way in which the rest of the isoglosses would have been distributed, any restoration of the position of Pamphylian within the dialect continuum can only remain tentative. Considering that Ionic remains connected to Pamphylian in either combination, we can suggest the relationships expressed in Fig. 10.

36 Since Pamph. ὄσα, which ostensibly points in the direction of similar Ionic forms (see under no. 9) can be consistently accounted for as due to the lack of gemination in the Pamphylian inscriptions (see Brixhe 1976: 78–9), we cannot be certain as to the Pamphylian treatment of this isogloss.

37 With Cretan: α unchanged to o, ἱαρός, βούλομαι, τε- from *$k^{w}e$-, -αισι/-οισι, ὄκα, ἑνς > ἱς and πορτί/περτ' from προτί (nos. 1, 2, 3, 6, 8, 10, 13, 16, 17); with Thessalian: the same as with Lesbian; with both: Ἄρτεμις, -τι unchanged to -σι and the conjunction αἰ (nos. 4, 7, 14).

Let us consider now the position of *Mycenaean*. If we try to place Mycenaean within the dialect continuum we shall see that its position will virtually concur with that of Arcado-Cyprian. Namely, like Arcado-Cyprian, Mycenaean can be reduced to Ionic on the one hand and Thessalian on the other: its -σι from -τι (*di-do-si* etc.) and ὅτε instead of ὅκα (*o-te*) go with Ionic (if Thess. ὅτ᾽ stands for ὅτα, which is usually assumed on the basis of Lesbian), its ο for α with liquids (*qe-to-ro-po-pi*, *to-pe-za*), υ from ο (*a-pu-do-si*) and *po-si* go with Thessalian, and its ἱερός (*i-je-re-u* etc.) instead of ἱαρός and Ἄρτεμις (*a-te-mi-to*) instead of Ἄρταμις with both; in addition, only Mycenaean and Arcado-Cyprian have the third person singular primary verbal ending -τοι (Myc. *-to* as in *e-u-ke-to*). That Mycenaean provides examples of both thematic and athematic inflection of contract verbs (thematic: *to-ro-qe-jo-me-no* = τροπεόμενος; athematic: *te-re-ja*, 3rd person sing. < *τελείαμι)[38] indicates that it was fixed in writing when the old thematic forms had not yet been completely superseded by the new athematic ones, and the same seems to be true of the coexistence of μετά and πεδά in the Mycenaean texts (see also below, pp. 141–2).[39] The genitives in *-a-o* = -αο and *-o-jo* = -οιο and patronymic suffixes in *-i-jo* = -ιος, which are attested in both Mycenaean and dialects of the Aeolic group, as well as in the Homeric poems, are obviously common retentions, and the datives -αισι/-οισι and -αις/-οις are still functionally distinct in Mycenaean. Finally, Mycenaean treatment of the labiovelars clearly shows that the Linear B tablets are of earlier date than the elimination of the labiovelars. On the whole, there is no reason to doubt that Mycenaean represents an early state of Arcado-Cyprian, and this is indeed the majority opinion as regards the position of this dialect.[40] Another dialect that Mycenaean closely resembles is Lesbian (cf. the respective positions of Arcado-Cyprian and Lesbian within the dialect continuum); yet, the Mycenaean *o-te* and *po-si* suggest a closer association of this dialect with Arcado-Cyprian (cf. Lesb. ὅτα and πρός <

---

38 Cf. Chantraine 1958: 505.

39 The fact that the Mycenaean *po-se-da-o* agrees with the Ionic Ποσειδάων rather than with the Arcadian Ποσοιδάν poses no real problem: as was pointed out in Ruijgh 1958: 115, Ποσεδάων obviously presents the original (cf. West Greek Ποτειδάν) and Ποσοιδάν the late form, created from Ποσειδάων as a result of assimilation. Considering that the Arc.-Cypr. ἰν = ἐν is generally seen as a late innovation (which affected also Pamphylian and Cretan, see below, pp. 140–1 n. 1), the discrepancy between the Mycenaean ἐν and Arcado-Cyprian ἰν can also be accounted for along these lines. Cf. also Duhoux 1988: 67–8.

40 See e.g. Ventris and Chadwick 1973: 73–5; Thumb-Sherer 1959: 325–6; Cowgill 1966: 93; Ruijgh 1967: 35–41 and 1996: 116–17; Duhoux 1983: 40–50, 58 and 1988: 64–7; Peters 1986: 303 and passim.

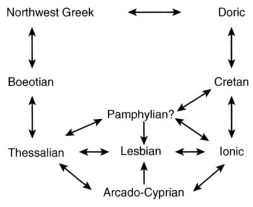

Figure 11. The general scheme of the dialect continuum.

προτί), whereas Arcado-Cyprian πός seems to be a direct derivative of Mycenaean *posi.*

As a result of the above analysis, the continuum of the Greek dialects can be tentatively reconstructed as in Fig. 11. Such is therefore the scheme of purely linguistic relations between the attested dialects. Our next task is to interpret these relations in terms of geography.

THE DIALECT GEOGRAPHY OF GREECE IN THE SECOND MILLENNIUM BC

In assigning geographical positions to the prehistoric Greek dialects, I have primarily been guided by their respective positions within the dialect continuum. I have also taken the following into consideration.

First, it is generally agreed that some of the historic dialects present features that cannot be consistently interpreted in terms of the dialects in question. This first of all concerns West Greek dialects. Thus, for example, the Laconian Ποhοιδᾶν agrees with the Arcadian Ποσοιδᾶν rather than with the West Greek Ποτειδᾶν, and the dative plural -εσσι, which occasionally emerges in the Northwest Greek dialects of Locris, Phokis and Elis, agrees with Aeolic rather than with Northwest Greek proper. By studying such features, which can only be due to the influence of a heterogeneous dialect substratum, we can sometimes learn where the dialects associated with this substratum had been spoken. Thus, the examples adduced above would certainly indicate that the speakers of

Laconian Doric settled in regions inhabited by the speakers of Arcado-
Cyprian and that the regions in which the speakers of the Northwest
Greek dialects of Locris, Phokis and Elis settled had been inhabited by
speakers of Aeolic.

Second, there is considerable literary evidence concerning the original
locations of the speakers of historic Greek dialects. Some of this evidence,
for example the *communis opinio* which saw in the Ionians of Attica and
the Arcadians of the Peloponnese the only Greek tribes that had never
changed their original places of settlement, can be accepted as trustworthy; some may be less so. In any case, it would be illuminating to
confront this material with the linguistic evidence at our disposal.

We have no reason to doubt the authenticity of the tradition according
to which the Ionians of Attica inhabited this region even in the Heroic
Age.[41] Put in linguistic terms, this would mean that *Ionic* or, to be more
exact, the ancestor of the historic Attic-Ionic, was spoken in Attica in the
Bronze Age. The real question, however, is not whether Ionic was spoken
in Attica, but in what other regions this dialect was spoken. Our sources
have preserved Greek traditions concerning Ionian settlement in Euboea,
East Boeotia, Megaris, the Argolic Akte, Cynuria and Achaea.[42] This is
why Buck wrote in *The Greek Dialects*:

> . . . we cannot doubt that the Ionians before the migration were not confined to
> Attica. The close relations of Epidaurus and Troezen with Athens, in cult and
> legend, are significant for the Argolic Acte, and it is reasonable to assume that at
> least the entire shore of the Saronic Gulf was once Ionic.[43]

The presence of Ionians in Euboea agrees with the fact that Ionic was
spoken on this island in the historic period, whereas their presence in East
Argos (the Akte) can be corroborated by the results of the first and the
second compensatory lengthening, which split the Doric of Argos in such
a way that East Argolic went with Ionic and West Argolic with Arcadian,
and we can actually be certain that the first and the second compensatory
lengthening took place in the first centuries of the Dorian colonisation of
the Peloponnese.[44] Note that the Ionian presence in the northeastern

---

41 Hdt. 1.56; 7.161; Thuc. 1.2; Str. 9.1.5, p. 392.
42 Euboea: Str. 10.1.3, p. 445; 10.1.6, p. 446; Megaris: Str. 9.1.5, p. 392; Paus. 1.39.4; Argos in general:
   Paus. 2.37.3; Epidaurus: Paus. 2.26.1; Cynuria: Hdt. 8.73; Boeotia: Hdt. 5.58; Achaea: Hdt. 1.145;
   7.94; cf. Thuc. 7.57; Str. 8.1.2, p. 333; 8.7.1, p. 383; Paus. 5.1.1; 7.1.3; 7.24.5; on the Ionians in the
   Peloponnese in general see Hdt. 8.73; 9.26; Str. 3.5.5, p. 171.
43 Buck 1955: 4. Cf. Thumb–Kieckers 1932: 65.
44 See Bartonek 1972: 27, 89, 113–15, 193–6; Peters 1986: 314–15. On the first and the second
   compensatory lengthening see also below, Chapter 7. As distinct from this, there is no linguistic

Peloponnese would be consistent with the peripheral position of this dialect in the dialect continuum.

Like the Athenians, the Arcadians are reported to belong to the pre-Doric population of Greece.[45] This tradition finds corroboration in the linguistic evidence, which strongly suggests that *Arcado-Cyprian* should be regarded as the dominant dialect of the Bronze Age Peloponnese. This conclusion follows from the presence in Peloponnese Doric and Northwest Greek of dialect forms that point in the direction of Arcado-Cyprian. Again, the Laconian Ποhοιδᾶν derives from the Arcadian Ποσοιδᾶν rather than from the West Greek Ποτειδάν; the Argolic πεδά agrees with the Arcadian, Lesbian and Cretan πέ/πεδά rather than with West Greek μετά,[46] and the emergence of the preposition ἰν = ἐν (Arcado-Cyprian, Pamphylian, Cretan only) on an inscription of the Achaean colony of Metapontum points in the same direction.[47] Actually, the only regions in the Peloponnese that show no signs of Arcado-Cyprian influence seem to be the Argolic Akte (see above under Ionic), Corinth and Elis (see below under Thessalian). It can be suggested, therefore, that Arcado-Cyprian was spoken in such Mycenaean centres as Pylos in Messenia, Amyclae in Lacedaemon and Mycenae and Tiryns in Argolis.

The occasional emergence of the dative plural in -εσσι in the Northwest Greek dialects of Locris, Phocis and Elis is generally recognised to indicate an Aeolic dialectal substratum.[48] The same also seems to be true of Corinth and the southern coast of Aetolia: for the former the dative plural -εσσι is attested whereas the latter was called 'Aeolis' in historic times. To quote Buck again, 'It is a natural presumption, on which there are some specific indications, that not only Thessaly and Boeotia but the intermediate lands of Phocis and Locris, and even southern Aetolia – in fact, all that portion of Greece north of Attica which plays a role in the legends of early Greece – was once Aeolic.'[49] It is significant in this

evidence as to the presence of the Ionic dialect in Cynuria and Achaea. This does not necessarily mean that the people who inhabited these regions were not Ionians by race. As Chadwick 1975: 814, appropriately remarks, tribal identity does not automatically involve the identity of the spoken idiom.

45 Hdt. 8.73; 9.26; Str. 8.8.1, p. 388; Paus. 5.1.1.
46 See Thumb–Kieckers 1932: 82, 112; Buck 1955: 8. In principle, the Argolic πεδά could also be due to an Aeolic influence, but the absence in the dialect of Argos of such a typical characteristic of the Aeolic substratum as dat. pl. -εσσι (see below) diminishes this option.
47 See Thumb–Kieckers 1932: 228, 234; Duhoux 1983: 56.
48 See Thumb–Kieckers 1932 237, 256–7, 262, 286; Buck 1955: 5, 89; Bartonek 1972: 69–71; Ruijgh 1988: 186–7 n. 65.
49 Buck 1955: 5. Cf. Thuc. 3.102; Str. 10.2.6, p. 451; 10.3.6, p.465 (quoting Ephorus).

connection that these are the very regions regarded in Greek tradition as having been inhabited by Aeolians.[50] Since Arcado-Cyprian, which borders on these regions, has been shown to be contiguous with *Thessalian*, this leads us to suggest that Thessalian was the Aeolic dialect spoken in Bronze Age Locris, Phocis, Elis, Corinth and southern Aetolia. It is difficult to say with certainty how far the Thessalian dialect spread to the north, but the fact that it was in contact with Boeotian, which was probably spoken in West Thessaly (Thessaliotis; see below), favours some region in South Thessaly (such as Malis) through which Thessalian could have been connected with Boeotian.[51]

The peripheral position of Boeotian, Doric and Northwest Greek within the dialect continuum suggests a geographical area on the fringe of Mycenaean Greece. Greek tradition is unanimous in that the homeland of the speakers of *Boeotian*, from which they invaded Central Greece, was in Thessaliotis in southwestern Thessaly,[52] whereas the homeland of the speakers of *Doric* and *Northwest Greek* is traditionally placed in northern Thessaly (Histiaeotis) and Epirus.[53] It goes without saying that these locations would well suit the respective positions of Boeotian, Doric and Northwest Greek within the dialect continuum.

The position of *Cretan* within the dialect continuum suggests a geographical area to the south of the Doric of Histiaeotis and to the north of the Ionic of Euboea. This seems to suggest Pelasgiotis as the place where Cretan was spoken in the Bronze Age.

Proceeding from the position of *Lesbian* within the dialect continuum, this dialect should be placed so as to be in contact with Ionic, Arcado-Cyprian and Thessalian. Boeotia, located to the west of the dialect area of Ionic, to the east of that of Thessalian and to the north of the dialect area of Arcado-Cyprian, would suit this description fairly well. The relevant linguistic evidence is as follows. As we saw above, the chain Lesbian–Thessalian–Boeotian forms a mini-continuum in which Thessalian

50 Elis: Str. 10.3.4, p. 464; Diod.Sic. 4.68.1; Central Greece in general: Str. 8.1.12, p. 333; Phocis: Hdt. 7.176; 7.35; Locris: Paus. 10.38.4.
51 Herodotus' statement (7.176.4) that the Thessalians arrived in 'Aeolis which they still occupy', that is, in historic Thessaliotis (see Hitschfelf in *RE* 1.1. 1034, s.v. 'Aiolis') from Thesprotia in Epirus allows us to suggest that the Thessalian migration at the end of the Bronze Age followed a western route. This suggestion finds an additional corroboration in the prominence of Thesprotia in the Greek tradition of *Nostoi* ('Returns') and in its association with Elis in the same tradition. See further Malkin 1998: 126–34; Finkelberg 2002: 245–9 and below, Chapter 7.
52 Thuc. 1.12; Str. 9.2.3, p. 401; 9.2.29, p. 411; Paus. 10.8.4.
53 Hdt. 1.56; Str. 9.5.17, p. 437; 10.4.6, pp. 475–6; Diod.Sic. 4.37.3; 5.80.2.

constitutes a bridge-dialect. Two features, however, do not fit into this picture: -σσ- in the future and aorist of the verb stems ending in a short vowel (ἐκάλεσσα) and the preposition πεδά = μετά, both of which are shared by Lesbian and Boeotian to the exclusion of Thessalian.[54] Comparison with other such cases of breaches in the continuum as Ποηοιδάν instead of Ποτειδάν in the Doric of Sparta or πεδά instead of μετά in Cretan and Argolic Doric suggests a similar explanation, namely, that the forms in question entered Boeotian from an earlier dialect substratum. In other words, we have reason to suppose that the former inhabitants of Boeotia spoke a dialect that had both ἐκάλεσσα and πεδά. Now although πεδά is both Lesbian and Arcado-Cyprian, ἐκάλεσσα is Lesbian alone. The combination of these two features in Boeotian and their absence in Thessalian strongly suggest that the Bronze Age population replaced by the Boeotians consisted of speakers of Lesbian.

The available literary evidence further supports the location of Lesbian in Boeotia. When Thucydides comments on more than one occasion that the inhabitants of Lesbos were Boeotian colonists, there can be no doubt that he is simply repeating what was taken for granted in his time.[55] This goes well with the tradition preserved by Strabo that the colonial expedition that brought Aeolians to Lesbos took place shortly after the so-called Boeotian invasion and started from Aulis in Boeotia.[56] Further, Herodotus tells us that with the coming of the Boeotians some aboriginal families fled to Athens, where even in his time their descendants continued to celebrate their native cults, among them the cult of Demeter Achaiia, in which the Athenians, Ionians by race, were not allowed to participate.[57]

Finally, the tentative position of *Pamphylian* between Cretan, Ionic, Thessalian and Lesbian suggests a location to the south of the Cretan of Pelasgiotis, to the west of the Ionic of Euboea, to the East of the Thessalian of South Thessaly and to the north of the Lesbian of Boeotia. The historic district of Achaia Phthiotis seems to answer this description fairly well.

As a result, the following dialect geography suggests itself (see Map 4). Ionic was spoken in the East (Euboea, Attica, the Argolic Akte) and was in

---

54 Cf. Buck 1955: 148; García-Ramón 1975: 68, 75. It is characteristic in this connection that Buck 1955: 107, suggests that in spite of the lack of evidence πεδά was actually present in Thessalian as well. On the preposition πεδά = μετά see also below, pp. 141–2.
55 Thuc. 3.2; 7.57; 8.100; cf. 3.5; 3.13.
56 Str. 9.2.3, p. 401; 9.2.5, p. 402; cf. 13.1.3, p. 582. Cf. also Thumb–Scherer 1959: 84.
57 Hdt. 5.57; 5.61; Cf. above, p. 36, on the Gephyraeans.

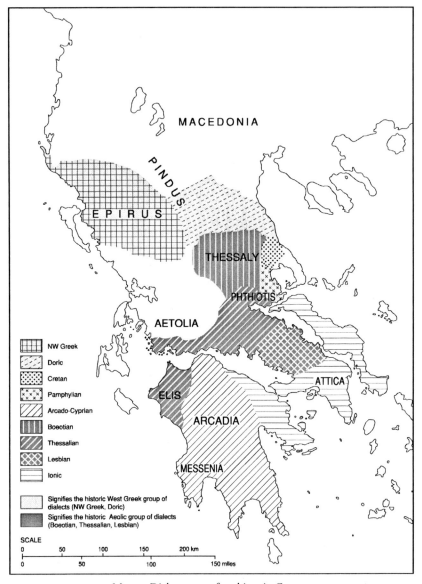

Map 4. Dialect map of prehistoric Greece.

contact with both Arcado-Cyprian, spoken in the greater part of the Peloponnese (West Argos, Sparta, Messenia, Arcadia, Achaea) and Lesbian, which was spoken in Boeotia. Both Arcado-Cyprian and Lesbian were in contact with Thessalian, which was spoken in the northwestern Peloponnese (Elis), on the opposite shore of Aetolia (Pleuron, Calydon), in Central Greece (Phocis, Locris) and in South Thessaly. It is through South Thessaly that Thessalian was connected with Boeotian, which was spoken in West Thessaly (Thessaliotis), while Boeotian was in turn connected with Northwest Greek, which was spoken in Epirus. Northwest Greek was in contact with Doric, spoken in Histiaeotis, and Doric with Cretan, spoken in Pelasgiotis. Finally, Cretan was in contact with both the Ionic of Euboea and Pamphylian, which was probably spoken in Phthiotis, while Pamphylian was in contact with Ionic, Thessalian and Lesbian.[58]

This picture of the dispersion of the Greek dialects would certainly allow for a dialect continuum in which, to repeat Bloomfield's words (p. 112), 'the difference from place to place is small, but, as one travels in any one direction, the differences accumulate, until speakers, say, from opposite ends of the country, cannot understand each other, although there is no sharp line of linguistic demarcation between the places they live.' This is especially true of the continuous distribution of such features as ὅκα/ὅτα/ὅτε or κα/κε/ἄ v: the Lesbian and Thessalian ὅτα proves to be a compromise form between the Boeotian and West Greek ὅκα on the one hand and the Ionic and Arcado-Cyprian ὅτε on the other, and the Lesbian, Cyprian and Thessalian κε a weak form of the Boeotian and West Greek κα. We can see now that the way these forms are distributed makes perfectly good sense not only linguistically but also geographically, especially when compared to the charts of distribution of the same features in the historic Greek dialects.[59]

---

58 This scheme of the Greek dialect interrelationships coincides in all the essentials with that drawn up by A. Thumb on his own grounds as early as 1909. See Thumb–Kieckers 1932: 51–2 (Pamphylian and Cretan were not treated in Thumb's classification). Yet, Thumb suggests a rather weak connection between Ionic and Arcado-Cyprian and between Arcado-Cyprian and Thessalian, whereas the connection between Ionic and Lesbian, according to his scheme, is next to negligible. Note also that Thumb's practice, based on empirical observation of relationships between the dialects, is at variance with his theory, which demanded a clear-cut classification: this seems to be why, after having admitted that 'infolge der . . . Verkettung der einzelnen Dialekte ist es unmöglich, eine scharfe Gliederung der Dialekte etwa in Form eines Stammbaumes zu gewinnen' (52), he proceeded to classify the dialects into 'mixed' and 'pure' (see esp. 59–61).

59 For the latter see e.g. Risch 1949: 19–28.

THE DIALECT AREAS AND THE TIME DEPTH OF THE
DIALECT CONTINUUM

Thanks to the decipherment of Linear B, today we know with certainty that
in the Late Bronze Age the Greek language was in use in such Mycenaean
centers as Pylos, Knossos and Thebes. The dialect continuum of Bronze
Age Greece as drawn above takes this evidence further in that it shows that
by the end of the second millennium BC Greek was spread without disruption over the entire territory of Greece, from Epirus in the north to
Lacedaemon in the south. This, however, still does not tell us much about
the sociolinguistic mechanisms at work. In Peter Trudgill's words,

> Dialectologists should not be content simply to *describe* the geographical
> distribution of linguistic features. They should also be concerned to *explain* – or
> perhaps, more accurately, to adduce reasons for – this distribution. Only in
> this way will we be able to arrive at an understanding of the sociolinguistic
> mechanisms that lie behind the geographical distribution of linguistic phe-
> nomena, the location of isoglosses, and the diffusion of linguistic
> innovations.[60]

And although the scarcity of evidence concerning Bronze Age Greece
severely impedes a full-scale explanation of the geographical distribution
of dialect phenomena in sociolinguistic terms, we may nevertheless try to
suggest several directions in which the evidence at our disposal may be
interpreted.

Among the isoglosses discussed above we can distinguish several
subgroups that are characteristic of some dialects to the exclusion of
others. This is an indication that the dialect continuum as reconstructed
above encompassed several dialect areas. These can be divided into three
main categories.

(a) Only Ionic, Arcado-Cyprian and Lesbian share the isoglosses ἱερός,
Ἄρτεμις, the vocalism *o* in the verb 'to wish', -σι from -τι, οἱ/αἱ as nom.
pl. of the article and ὅτε/ὅτα instead of ὅκα (nos. 3, 4, 6, 7, 12, 13; nos. 4,
6, 12 are shared by Pamphylian and Cretan and nos. 3, 4, 12, 13 by
Thessalian). On the basis of this evidence, Ionic, Arcado-Cyprian and
Lesbian should be seen as constituting a single dialect area to which
Pamphylian, Cretan and Thessalian were also attached.

(b) Only Arcado-Cyprian, Lesbian and Thessalian share the isoglosses
o for α with liquids and in other cases, υ for o, the modal particle κε in

---

60 Trudgill 1983: 54 (Trudgill's italics).

contrast to either ἄν or κα of the other dialects (the latter in Cyprian to the exclusion of Arcadian) and the athematic inflection of contract verbs (nos. 1, 2, 5, 16, 21; nos. 5 and 21 also in Pamphylian. and no. 1 also in Boeotian). On the basis of this evidence, Arcado-Cyprian, Lesbian and Thessalian should be seen as constituting a single dialect area to which Pamphylian and Boeotian were also attached.

(c) Only Lesbian, Thessalian and Boeotian share the isoglosses πε- from *$k^{w}e$- and -εσσι in dat. pl. of consonant stems (nos. 8, 11; no. 8 also in Cyprian and no. 11 also in Pamphylian.), as well as some other characteristically 'Aeolic' features (see above, n. 11). On the basis of this evidence, Lesbian, Thessalian and Boeotian should be seen as constituting a single dialect area to which Pamphylian and Cyprian were also attached.

Note that the dialect areas described above do not interfere with the dialect geography of Bronze Age Greece as outlined in the preceding section. Thus, although Thessalian does not participate in the dialect area formed by Ionic, Arcado-Cyprian and Lesbian (it lacks such hallmark characteristics of this area as -σι from -τι and the vocalism *o* in the verb 'to wish'), it nevertheless shows some features which are firmly associated with it, such as οἱ/αἱ as nom. pl. of the article, ὅτε/ὅτα instead of ὅκα, as well as ἱερός and Ἄρτεμις. This can only be explained by the territorial proximity of Thessalian to the dialect area in question; such proximity would be consistent with the position of Thessalian in the dialect continuum as reconstructed above (see Map 4). Again, although Boeotian lacks most of the features which characterise the dialect area formed by Arcado-Cyprian, Lesbian and Thessalian, it shows at least one feature firmly associated with this area, namely, o for α with liquids. This can only be explained, again, by the territorial proximity of Boeotian to the dialect area in question, which would be consistent with the position of Boeotian within the dialect continuum. All this indicates that the processes that led to the differentiation of the dialect continuum into dialect areas were not accompanied by breaches in the continuum. In other words, the consolidation of the dialect areas took place within approximately the same territorial boundaries, which suggests that it was due to sociolinguistic factors such as cultural and political barriers within a continuously settled territory rather than to migration or invasion from outside.[61]

---

61 On the distribution of isoglosses according to cultural and political factors see Bloomfield 1935: 341–3; Hockett 1958: 480–4; Chambers and Trudgill 1998: 6–7.

Further, the isoglosses are distributed in such a way that there is
considerable overlapping between the dialect areas they enclose. Thus,
Lesbian and Pamphylian are enclosed by each of the three groups of the
isoglosses, and Arcado-Cyprian and Thessalian by two each. The purely
linguistic division, then, is the one between the centre and the periphery.[62] That is to say, the dialects found in the centre of the dialect
continuum were, in virtue of their position, affected by the majority of
the linguistic changes that spread over the Greek-speaking territory. This
is especially the case of Lesbian and, probably, Pamphylian, the only
dialects that participate in each of the three dialect areas consolidated
within the dialect continuum; this conclusion goes well with the central
position of both Lesbian and Pamphylian within the dialect continuum.
Dialects located at the periphery of the dialect continuum were affected
by only part of the changes or even not affected at all. This is especially
the case of Doric and Northwest Greek, the only dialects that participated
in none of the three dialect areas consolidated within the dialect continuum; again, the conclusion is consistent with the peripheral position
of Doric and Northwest Greek in the dialect continuum.[63]

The overlap between the dialect areas, as well as the fact that the
consolidation of the dialect areas caused no breaches in the dialect
continuum, allow us to suggest that the areas in question relate to each
other diachronically, that is, that they represent successive stages of
differentiation of the dialect continuum. The chronological and sociolinguistic parameters for this differentiation are supplied first of all by the
evidence of Mycenaean.

Since Mycenaean shows such features as -σι from -τι (*di-do-si* etc.),
ὅτε rather than ὅκα (*o-te*), ἱερός rather than ἱαρός (*i-je-re-u* etc.),
Ἄρτεμις rather than Ἄρταμις (*a-te-mi-to*), we have good reason to conclude that this dialect participated in dialect area (a) formed by Ionic,
Arcado-Cyprian and Lesbian. Since Mycenaean shows such features as o
for α with liquids (*qe-to-ro-po-pi*, *to-pe-za*), υ for o (*a-pu-do-si*) and the
athematic inflection of contract verbs (*te-re-ja*), we have good reason to
conclude that it participated also in dialect area (b) formed by Arcado-
Cyprian, Lesbian and Thessalian. We saw too that by the time Mycenaean

62 Cf. Crossland 1971: 804.
63 Although it is true that a considerable number of the dialect features of Northwest Greek and
   West Greek in general are merely retentions of the original forms, this does not mean that the
   peripheral dialects, West Greek among them, developed no innovations of their own. However,
   these made their appearance over an area that did not overlap any of those in which other
   innovations were developing.

was fixed in writing the old thematic forms had not yet been completely superseded by the new athematic ones (p. 126). This seems to indicate that dialect area (b), to which this isogloss belongs, is younger than dialect area (a). Finally, the fact that Mycenaean shows no features characteristic of dialect area (c), formed by Lesbian, Thessalian and Boeotian, such as the dative plural -εσσι and πε- from *$k^{w}e$-, can only entail that it took no part in the dialect area in question. At the same time, the Mycenaean treatment of the labiovelars demonstrates that the Linear B tablets are earlier than the elimination of the labiovelars, which was contemporary to the formation of the so-called Aeolic group of dialects. This can only mean that dialect area (b) is older than dialect area (c). Accordingly, the process of the consolidation of the dialect areas can tentatively be reconstructed as follows.

Stage A – consolidation of the dialect area comprising the future Ionic, Arcado-Cyprian and Lesbian, contiguous with Pamphylian and Thessalian, and opposed to the dialect area comprising the future West Greek and Boeotian. Note that it is this stage that is accounted for by the classification of Porzig and Risch who, proceeding from its characteristic isoglosses, came to the conclusion that in Bronze Age Greece only two dialects existed, one comprising the future Ionic and Arcado-Cyprian and the other the future West Greek, Boeotian and Thessalian.

Stage B – consolidation of the dialect area comprising the future Arcado-Cyprian, Lesbian and Thessalian, contiguous with Pamphylian and Boeotian, and opposed to both West Greek and, significantly, Ionic, which becomes isolated as an independent idiom. Note that this stage in turn is accounted for by the older scholars' tripartite classification of the Greek dialects: proceeding from its characteristic isoglosses, they united Arcado-Cyprian and Aeolic into a single dialect and thus arrived at a division of the Greek dialects into West Greek, Central Greek and Ionic.

Stage C – consolidation of the dialect area comprising the future Lesbian, Thessalian and Boeotian, contiguous with Cyprian and Pamphylian, and opposed to West Greek, Ionic and, significantly, Arcadian, which becomes isolated as an independent idiom. Note that this stage is accounted for by the widely accepted classification of the Greek dialects into four groups – Ionic, Aeolic, Arcado-Cyprian and West Greek.

It follows, then, that the position of a Greek dialect can only be properly assessed if we approach it through two dimensions – synchronic, relating to its position in the dialect continuum, and diachronic, relating to its participation or non-participation in each of the dialect areas outlined above. With this in mind, let us try to determine with a greater precision both the chronological boundaries of each of the dialect areas and the factors responsible for their formation.

We have seen that Stage B is characterised by consolidation of the dialect area comprising Lesbian, Arcado-Cyprian and Thessalian, and that Mycenaean as fixed in the Linear B archives of Pylos, Knossos and Thebes also properly belongs here.[64] In view of this, it is reasonable to suppose that, when taken chronologically, Stage B of the dialect continuum would correspond to Mycenaean Greece. This conclusion, implying as it does the isolation of Ionic, goes well with the much discussed issue of under-representation of Athens in Greek heroic tradition; it also throws light on the fact that, in spite of being generally recognised to be descended from the pre-Dorian population of Greece, the Athenians and the Ionians in general have never been identified as 'Achaeans'.[65] At the same time, if our reconstruction of the dialect geography of Bronze Age Greece is correct, the dialect area in question would embrace such mainland centres of the Mycenaean civilisation as Mycenae, Tiryns, Pylos, Amyclae, Thebes and Pleuron.

Taking 1200 BC as a conventional date for the beginning of the disintegration of Mycenaean Greece (see below, p. 145), we can suggest this same date as the beginning of what we have defined as Stage C, a stage whose characteristic features are the isolation of Arcadian and the consolidation of the Aeolic group of dialects. This allows us to see Stage C as contemporary with the processes that led to the end of Mycenaean Greece. This stage will be discussed in detail in Chapter 7.

As distinct from Stages B and C, there is no linguistic or extra-linguistic evidence to assist us in establishing the chronological limits of Stage A, the stage that preceded Mycenaean Greece and was characterised by the consolidation of the dialect area comprising Ionic, Lesbian and Arcado-Cyprian. But it seems reasonable to suppose that the formation of Stage A and the dialect continuum as a whole was contemporary with the beginning of Greek settlement in Greece. Indeed, since it is likely that Stage A, Stage B and Stage C of the dialect continuum existed within approximately the same territorial boundaries and that these boundaries, as far at

---

64 Note that this conclusion goes well with the fact that the written idiom of Mycenaean Thebes as it comes to light from the recently discovered archives seems to be identical to that used at Pylos and Knossos. On the language of the Theban archives see Aravantinos, Godart and Sacconi 1995: 829–33; Lejeune and Godart 1995: 272–7; Duhoux 1997: 17–18. For the texts see Aravantinos, Godart and Sacconi 2001 and 2002.
65 The insignificance of Athens: Page 1959: 145–6; Finkelberg 1988: 36–7; the Ionians not to be identified as Achaeans: Hdt. 5.61; Thuc. 3.92.

least as Stages B and C are concerned, were definitely those of Greece, taking the beginning of Stage A as contemporary with the beginning of the dispersal of Greek-speaking tribes over Greece seems the only conclusion that would fit the linguistic data at our disposal. Since the arrival of the Greek-speaking tribes is normally placed ca. 2050–2000 BC, we can adopt this date as a conventional *terminus post quem* for the beginning of Stage A and the dialect continuum as a whole. The analysis of the Greek dialects thus entails that the dialect continuum of the Greek language, which can be shown to have been spread over the territory of Greece by the end of the Bronze Age, took shape in the period which began with the arrival of the Greek-speaking tribes at the end of the third millennium BC and ended with the collapse of Mycenaean Greece at the end of the second millennium.

CHAPTER 7

The end of the Bronze Age

LINGUISTIC EVIDENCE FOR THE COLLAPSE OF MYCENAEAN GREECE

In showing that in the second millennium BC a dialect continuum characteristic of long-settled areas was spread over most of the territory of Greece, the evidence of the Greek dialects corroborates the archaeological evidence, which suggests little or no break in continuity in the material culture in the same period. We saw that Greek genealogical tradition suggests a similar picture. Yet, all this changes dramatically at the end of the second millennium. The destruction levels and depopulation attested at many Mycenaean sites testify to a sharp break in continuity, and the myth of the destruction of the Race of Heroes obviously purports to account for the same events. The evidence of the dialects not only substantiates this picture but also points towards the factors responsible for the collapse of Mycenaean Greece.

We have seen that the last stage of the dialect continuum is contemporary with the processes that led to the formation of the dialect map of Greece as known to us from the historic period. Comparison of the dialect continuum of Bronze Age Greece as reconstructed above (Map 4) with the dialect geography of Greece in the historic period (Map 3) shows that the main changes which brought about the fragmentation of the dialect continuum were as follows:

a. Ionic, Lesbian, Cyprian and Pamphylian were pushed from the Greek mainland to their new habitats in the Eastern Mediterranean;
b. Doric replaced Arcado-Cyprian in Sparta and Messenia;
c. Doric and Cretan replaced Arcado-Cyprian in West Argos;[1]

---

1 The Cretan combination of ἰν and πεδά strongly suggests Arcadian influence, whereas the results of compensatory lengthening make Cretan indistinguishable from West Argolic. It can be inferred from this that the speakers of Cretan came to the Peloponnese together with the Dorians and that

d. Doric replaced Ionic in East Argos and the northeastern Peloponnese in general;

e. Northwest Greek replaced Arcado-Cyprian on the southern shore of the Corinthian gulf (the later Achaea);

f. Northwest Greek replaced Thessalian in Central Greece (Locris, Phocis), in Corinth and in the northwest Peloponnese (Elis);

g. Boeotian replaced Lesbian in what became known as Boeotia;

h. Thessalian replaced Boeotian in West Thessaly (Thessaliotis; see above, p. 130 n. 51).

To determine the end of the dialect continuum in chronological terms, we have to turn to the dialect features not yet discussed.

The first compensatory lengthening, which simplified the intervocalic groups consisting of *s* with liquids and nasals, split the Greek dialects into three groups. Thus, the inherited *ἐσμί became ἔμμι in Lesbian and Thessalian, ἠμί in Arcado-Cyprian, Doric and Boeotian[2] and εἰμί in Ionic, East Argolic Doric and Northwest Greek. Note now that the distribution of the different forms produced by the first compensatory lengthening would no longer allow a continuum between, say, Ionic, Arcado-Cyprian and Thessalian, which have εἰμί, ἠμί and ἔμμι, respectively: Ionic goes with the Doric of East Argos and Northwest Greek, Arcado-Cyprian with Doric and Boeotian, while Thessalian still goes with Lesbian. As far as I can see, the only way to account for these developments is to assume that they were contemporary with processes that led to the disintegration of the dialect continuum. Judging by the way in which the isoglosses are distributed among the dialects, these processes must have been triggered by emergence of Doric, Northwest Greek and Boeotian in Central Greece and the Peloponnese.

The preposition πεδά as distinct from μετά is most probably an innovation, which properly belongs to Arcadian and Lesbian alone (Arc. πέ). As indicated by the evidence of Mycenaean, this dialect, whose

---

they settled in West Argos, whence Crete was colonised. This reconstruction finds some support in the tradition concerning the colonisation of the island. Cf. e.g. Str. 14.2.6, p. 653: 'While some of the Dorians who founded Megara after the death of Kodros stayed there, others participated with Althaimenes the Argive in the colonisation of Crete . . .' It is not out of the question that the Pamphylian migration followed a similar route (cf. Pamph. ἰν, ἰς), but the linguistic evidence concerning this dialect is too scarce to allow us to arrive at a definite conclusion.

2 Since Boeot. α stands for original η (cf. Boeot. μα = μη) and Boeot. ι stands for original α (cf. Boeot. ἐπί = ἐπεί), Boeot. εἰμί should be treated as representing original *ἠμί < *ἐσμί, see Buck 1955: 25, 29, 31, 153–4; Lejeune 1972: 229–30, 232–3, 236–7. This point was overlooked by Risch 1955: 75, who gives εἰμί < *ἐσμί for Boeotian.

idiom is close to both Arcado-Cyprian and Lesbian (see above), still hesitates between the two forms. The fact that Cyprian, as distinct from Arcadian, shows only the inherited μετά strongly suggests that the speakers of this dialect emigrated to Cyprus before the innovation πεδά had been firmly established; the Cyprian retention of θάρσος instead of the innovation θέρσος, introduced in Arcadian, Lesbian, Thessalian and Boeotian, points in the same direction.[3] The emergence of πεδά in Boeotian and Cretan, together with its absence in Thessalian and Cyprian, disrupts the continuous distribution of isoglosses among Ionic, Lesbian and Thessalian; among Ionic, Arcado-Cyprian and Thessalian; and among Ionic, Cretan and Doric. The evidence of Argolic Doric, whose πεδά instead of the common Doric and West Greek μετά can only be explained as due to the influence of an Arcadian substratum, may serve here as an effective check. That is to say, the Boeotian and Cretan πεδά should be interpreted as produced by the influence of Lesbian and Arcadian, replaced by Boeotian and Cretan in the period of the great migrations.

Compare now the configuration produced by the second compensatory lengthening, which consisted in simplification of the group -*ns(-) in the intervocalic and final position. The extent of the fragmentation is best illustrated by the fact that the elimination of -*ns(-) split the Greek dialects into no fewer than five groups, cf. τόνς, τός, τούς, τώς, τοίς, the five variants of the accusative plural of the article.[4] This time Lesbian not only no longer goes with Thessalian (see Lesb. παῖσα as against Thess. πάνσα or Lesb. τοῖς as against Thess. τός) but is also isolated from the other dialects. As far as I can see, the only way to account for these facts is to assume that the second compensatory lengthening took place after the separation of Lesbian from the rest of the dialects, including the so-called Aeolic dialects with which it had been closely connected.

Fortunately, we can say with certainty that the first compensatory lengthening took place before the Attic-Ionic change α > η (cf. Att.-Ion. σελήνη from *σελασνα), whereas the change α > η can safely be dated as having occurred not earlier than 900 BC.[5] This gives us 900 BC as a conventional *terminus ante quem* for the end of the last stage of the dialect

---

3 On θέρσος = θάρσος see Buck 1955: 45 (par. 49.2).
4 For the chart of their distribution see Risch 1949: 27; for a comprehensive chart of the first and the second compensatory lengthening see Hainsworth 1982: 863.
5 In so far as the Persian *Mada* became Μῆδα in Ionic, and it is hardly possible that the Greeks could have known the Medes before the ninth century BC at the earliest. See Lejeune 1972: 222–3 and 235 n. 2; Risch 1955: 64–5; Chadwick 1956: 42.

continuum, a stage which began with the decline of Mycenaean Greece and ended with the disintegration of the dialect continuum that followed the emergence of northern Greek tribes in Central Greece and the Peloponnese and the great migrations to the East. Let us examine these two events.

THE DORIANS AND THE MYCENAEANS

In the most recent assessment of the archaeological record relating to the late eleventh–tenth centuries BC we read:

It is beyond question, however, that both the tradition and the archaeological record, supported by the linguistic evidence, reflect movement of people during the course of the Late Helladic IIIC and Sub-Mycenaean periods. Some of the Aegean regions were abandoned, while others were populated and then destroyed or abandoned again. People went as far as Cyprus and Cilicia looking for better and safer places to live. This mobility is well documented in the archaeological record and had an important effect in the crystallization of conditions in the Aegean and the Eastern Mediterranean at the end of the Late Bronze Age.[6]

The breaches in the dialect continuum not only go extremely well with this picture but, in that they unequivocally demonstrate the intrusive character of Doric and other West Greek dialects, vindicate the tradition of the so-called Dorian invasion. Let us dwell briefly on the tradition in question.

As distinct from the model of gradual infiltration, which prevailed in the traditional account of the population movements that took place during the Heroic Age (see Chapter 2), the tradition of the Dorian invasion supplies us for the first time with a clear-cut model of a population movement effected by force. The Dorians' first attempt to enter the Peloponnese is envisaged as an advance of the full-scale army led by the Heraclid Hyllos; yet, joint forces of the Peloponnesians succeeded in stopping the invaders at the Isthmus of Corinth, where Hyllos was killed by the Arcadian Ekhemos in single combat. It was only three generations later that the Dorians actually conquered the Peloponnese. They did not come now through the Isthmus but crossed from Naupaktos to Rhion, being guided on their way by the Aetolian Oxylos; the latter brought with him many Aetolians who occupied what was to become Elis, and made Oxylos king. The Dorian leaders on their part divided the territory of the peninsula by throwing lots: this is how the historic regions of Messenia,

---

6 Lemos 2002: 193.

Sparta and Argos were created. Finally, the population of the Peloponnese fled before the invaders and concentrated in new areas, first and foremost in Achaea and Attica.[7]

At the same time, it is important to keep in mind that the term 'Dorian invasion' or, which seems more preferable, 'the coming of the Dorians', relates to miscellaneous population movements from the periphery to the centre of the Mycenaean world, by no means all of them associated with the Dorians proper. Both the dialect evidence and the evidence of Greek tradition indicate unequivocally that, side by side with 'the coming of the Dorians', we should also speak of 'the coming of the Boeotians', 'the coming of the Northwest Greeks' and probably also of 'the coming of the (prospective) Cretans'.[8]

A massive wall across the Isthmus, the construction of which was initiated in the latter part of Late Helladic IIIB and which, in Jeremy Rutter's words, 'was evidently intended to seal off the Peloponnese from invasion by land forces from the north', indicates that there may be more than a kernel of truth in the tradition of the Dorians' attempt to enter the Peloponnese via the Isthmus.[9] The tradition that the population of the southern Peloponnese fled to what was to become the district of Achaea, as well as to Attica and other places, has also been supported by the archaeological record. This, for example, is how V. R. d'A. Desborough describes what happened to the population of the Peloponnese after the first wave of destruction ca. 1200 BC:

As a result of this destruction and desertion there was a movement of population to less dangerous and, in some cases, originally less populous areas. Achaea in the Northwest Peloponnese and the island of Cephallenia are examples of areas where a considerable increase in the Mycenaean population is to be observed. But the east coast of Attica now becomes more fashionable than previously, and it is fairly clear that a sizeable body of refugees made their way to Cyprus and to Taurus in Cilicia. Of these movements we can speak with some confidence; other groups may have gone elsewhere.[10]

---

7 Hdt. 9.26.2; Diod.Sic. 4.58.1–5; Apollod. 2.8.2–5; Paus. 1.44.10; 2.18.6–7; 4.3.3–5; 5.3.5–4.2; 8.5.1; 8.5.6; 8.45.3.
8 Boeotians: Thuc. 1.12; Northwest Greeks: Paus. 5.3–4; Cretans: Diod.Sic. 5.80.2; Str. 14.2.6, p. 653.
9 See Rutter 1996: Lesson 28 (with bibliography). Cf. Hammond 1975: 686.
10 Desborough 1964: 222. Cf. Rutter 1996: Lesson 28; Lemos 2002: 194–5, 197–200. On the migration of the Bronze Age population of the southern Peloponnese into Achaea see Hdt. 1.145; 7.94; 8.73; Polyb. 2.41; Str. 8.1.2, p. 333; 8.5.5, p. 365; 8.7.1, p.383; 8.7.4, p. 385; Paus. 3.22.6; 5.1.1; 7.1.3–4; 7.6.1; 7.18.3; 7.24.4. On the migration into Cyprus, Taurus and Cilicia see the next section.

According to Greek tradition, the Dorian invasion took place in two stages: after the first attempt to conquer the Peloponnese, the Dorians turned back to their base on the plain of Marathon, only to return and to complete the attack after three generations.[11] This again finds corroboration in that the first wave of destruction, which took place ca. 1200 BC and left no trace in terms of the influx of new population, was followed by a period of what Desborough described as 'the apparently undisturbed survival of the Mycenaeans in the Argolid', which 'perhaps lasted nearly three generations'.[12] The Granary within the Citadel of Mycenae was destroyed ca. 1150 BC, but it was not prior to ca. 1050 that the final destruction of the Mycenaean civilisation, accompanied this time by material evidence indicating the presence of new settlers from the north, took place. According to Paul Cartledge, archaeological evidence, especially the changes in ceramics, testify to a sharp cultural break after c. 1050 BC in most Dorian regions of the Peloponnese; this, side by side with the West Greek affinities of Laconian Protogeometric pottery, allowed him to conclude that 'had we not been told that newcomers made their way to Laconia some time after 1200, we would have to invent them to explain their pottery'.[13]

Still, many archaeologists are unhappy with the idea of the Dorian invasion, their main argument being that, although the break in continuity at the end of the second millennium BC is incontestable, 'the coming of the Dorians' as such has not been sufficiently corroborated by the archaeological record. Even when the evidence supplied by the dialects is mentioned in archaeological literature, it usually remains unaccounted for. Thus, for example, although Anthony Snodgrass admits that the population movements described in Greek tradition 'obviously find some ulterior confirmation in the distribution of dialects in historical times', he eventually discards the tradition in question on purely archaeological grounds with no further reference to the dialects.[14] It seems, however, that when solid evidence provided by one discipline is met by an *argumentum ex silentio* offered by another, the burden of proof should lie with the deniers of the Dorian invasion, the more so as this is far from being the only case in which archaeology fails to provide clear-cut evidence as regards population movements. To take two

---

11 Diod.Sic. 4.58.1–5; Apollod. 2.8.2; Paus. 8.5.1.   12 Desborough 1964: 231, 241.
13 Cartledge 1979: 87.
14 Snodgrass 1971: 302, 311–13. An excellent analysis of the issue from the archaeological point of view (with no reference to the dialects) is given in Rutter 1996: Lesson 28. The evidence of the dialects is taken into account in Drews 1988: 203–25; 1993a: 62–5.

well-known examples, neither the Galatian invasion of Anatolia (third century BC) nor the Slavic invasion of Greece (sixth century AD), both undisputed historic events, have been archaeologically attested. Invaders whose cultural level is lower than that of the inhabitants of the area they invade often do not leave behind any sign of their presence other than a destruction level and evidence of drastic depopulation.[15]

At this point, it is appropriate to ask whether the archaeological evidence is the only kind of evidence that should be taken into account in such cases. As I hope to have shown, the evidence supplied by the Greek dialects, in that it demonstrates the intrusive character of Doric and other West Greek dialects, is clear-cut to such a degree that it urges us to postulate the 'coming of the Dorians' whether or not a tradition of the Dorian invasion is available. As C. D. Buck put it, 'even if there were no tradition of a Dorian invasion such a movement would have to be assumed'.[16] In addition, the institutions of the Dorians and their way of life were so different from those of the other Greeks that it is difficult to find a better explanation than the Dorians' initial cultural difference from the other Greeks. Small wonder, therefore, that the situation among the historians differs from the current archaeological consensus.[17] To quote Irad Malkin, 'Deniers of a Dorian invasion must also explain away distinct dialects, Dorian *nomima* (characteristic features of political, social and religious organization), civic organization of Dorian cities (such as Argos), where the existence of a non-Dorian tribe emphasizes the Dorian aspect of the other three, and so forth.'[18] The characteristically Dorian model of hereditary kingship affords an additional example of the Dorians' cultural distinctiveness.

According to Greek tradition, the Dorian kings who entered the Peloponnese were the Heraclidae Temenos, who became king of Argos; his brother Kresphontes, who became king of Messenia; and their nephews Eurystheus and Prokles, who became kings of Sparta.[19] Kresphontes

---

15 See Desborough 1964: 224; Winter 1977: 60–76; Cartledge 1979: 79. For the discussion see Rutter 1996: Lesson 28; J. Hall 1996: 128–9 and 2002: 73–82.
16 Buck 1926: 18.
17 Cf. Lemos 2002: 191–2.
18 Malkin 1994: 44. Cf. Drews 1988: 203–25, and 1993a: 62–5. It is often claimed that, by the time the northern Greek tribes entered Central Greece and the Peloponnese, Mycenaean civilisation had already been destroyed by somebody else, the so-called Sea Peoples being a frequently mentioned candidate. Yet, in view of the new assessment of the provenance of at least some of the Sea Peoples, which will be discussed in the following section, this seems a highly unlikely scenario.
19 For convenient summaries see Diod.Sic. 4.58.1–5; Apollod. 2.8.2–5; Paus. 2.18.6–7; 4.3.3–5; 5.3.5–6; 8.5.1; 8.45.3.

married Merope, the daughter of the Arcadian king Kypselos; considering that this marriage was accompanied by the founding of Stenykleros, a new royal capital close to the Arcadian border, it can be suggested that it was Kresphontes' marriage to Merope that allowed him to settle in northern Messenia without a struggle. Nothing is known of the marriages of Eurysthenes and Prokles, but the most prominent of the first generation of the Dorian kings, Temenos of Argos,

openly employed Deiphontes, the son of Antimachos son of Thrasyanor son of Ktesippos son of Heracles, as the commander of the army instead of his own sons, and consulted him on every matter. Even before that, he had made this same man his son-in-law. Since he loved Hyrnetho best of all his children, there was a suspicion that he would transfer the kingship to her and Deiphontes. Because of this his sons contrived a conspiracy against him, and the eldest of them, Keisos, took over the throne.[20]

According to a slightly different version, Temenos did succeed in establishing Deiphontes as his heir, but the latter was deprived of royal status upon the death of his wife Hyrnetho, brought about by her own brothers. Temenos' son Keisos became king; he was succeeded by his son Medon and the latter's descendants in the male line till the dissolution of kingship at Argos in the ninth generation after Medon.[21]

As we saw in Chapter 5, Hyrnetho's status would depend on whether she was born by a Heraclid princess whom Temenos had brought with him from Doris or by a daughter of the local king. In the first case, Hyrnetho's city, either Argos or Epidauros, would have been treated as a Dorian colony and her descendants as genuine Heraclidae; in the second, she would have become priestess of the local goddess (Hera of Argos?) and the ancestor of a mixed clan. Since she became the eponym of the Argive tribe Hyrnathioi, which was universally regarded as non-Dorian, Hyrnetho must have been a daughter of a local princess the marriage to whom granted Temenos sovereignty over Argos. This would mean that, in conformity with the rules of matrilinear succession, Temenos' daughter Hyrnetho was a representative of the local matriliny, and this was sufficient to make her husband Deiphontes the king's heir. At the same time, the struggle of the sons of Temenos to succeed their father indicates that they were guided by a concept of royal succession differing sharply from the one in accordance with which Temenos and his son-in-law acted. Thus, for the first time in our sources, we see a clash between two

20 Paus. 2.19.1–2; see also 2.26.1.   21 Apollod. 2.8.5; Paus. 2.19.2; 2.28.3.

conflicting concepts of kingship, kingship by marriage on the one hand and patrilinear accession to the throne on the other.

Like his Bronze Age predecessors, Temenos probably assumed kingship over Argos by marrying the daughter of the local ruler, and the same was true of his brother Kresphontes who became king of Messenia. Yet, as the case of Temenos' sons shows, the model of kingship by marriage was abandoned in the next generation in favour of the model of hereditary kingship, probably not dissimilar to the one established in Sparta. The same seems to be true of Messenia, where Kresphontes is said to have been murdered by the Heraclid Polyphontes who married Kresphontes' widow Merope and succeeded him on the throne. Kresphontes' son Aipytos avenged his father's death. He became king of Messenia and founder of a clan whose representatives succeeded him in the male line till Messenia lost its independence to Sparta in the Messenian wars.[22] Thus, although the first Dorian rulers of Argos and Messenia acted in accordance with the indigenous practices of kingship by marriage, their descendants adopted the model of hereditary kingship based on strict clan endogamy that the Dorians brought with them (cf. above, p. 100). The Dorians thus seem to have been the first newcomers to Greece to whom the widespread model of Indo-European dispersal can be applied: 'the Indo-European immigrants would have achieved kingship by marrying the local "matriarch", as did so many heroes of Greek legend who succeeded to thrones in Anatolia by marrying the daughter of the local king and, having done so, sought to establish their own patriarchal system.'[23]

Needless to say, the Mycenaean Greeks on the one hand and the Dorians and their allies on the other did not start their mutual history as complete strangers to each other. If anything, the dialect continuum of Bronze Age Greece shows that, rather than being a purely artificial product of genealogical speculation, the Archaic Age subsuming of both the Mycenaean Greeks and the Dorians under the stemma of Hellen amounted to a post-factum recognition of the substantial affinity of all Greek tribes, both those who took part in Bronze Age Aegean civilisation and those who stayed beyond its borders. The former must have been related to the latter as the Romanised Gauls were related to their much less civilised Celtic kinsmen. From now on, the newcomers from the northern parts of Greece and the descendants of the Mycenaeans

---

22 Apollod. 2.8.5; cf. Paus. 4.3.7–4.1; Hygin. *Fab.* 184.
23 Gurney 1973b: 667; cf. above, p. 72.

were to negotiate anew the terms of their coexistence. This will be the focus of my discussion in Chapter 8.

The destruction levels and depopulation attested at many Mycenaean sites for the end of the second millennium BC testify to a sharp break in the cultural continuity. Undoubtedly, we are facing the end of an era, and the same is true of other sites all over the Eastern Mediterranean.[24] The Greek myth of the destruction of the Race of Heroes bears witness to the fact that Greek heroic tradition was well aware of these events. Let us try for a moment to look at the great watershed at the end of the Bronze Age through the eyes of this tradition. Consider first a shorter version of the myth of the end of the Heroic Age as it emerges in the scholiast's quotation from what was almost certainly the lost proem of the Cyclic *Cypria*:

Once upon a time the countless tribes of men as they wandered over the land began to oppress by their weight the surface of deep-bosomed Earth. Zeus saw it and took pity on her and in his wisdom resolved to relieve all-nurturing Earth of the burden of mankind by unleashing the great strife of the Ilian War, so that death should lessen the burden. And so the heroes were falling at Troy, and the plan of Zeus was being fulfilled.[25]

But it is above all Hesiod's *Works and Days* that provides what has become the standard version of the destruction of the Race of Heroes:

The godlike race of heroes who are called demigods, those who lived before us on the boundless earth. They were partly destroyed by evil war and terrible fighting, some at seven-gated Thebes, the land of Kadmos, when they fought for the flocks of Oedipus, and others it brought in ships over the great depth of the sea to Troy for the sake of fair-haired Helen, and there the end of death enwrapped some of them. But to others father Zeus the son of Kronos granted a livelihood and abode apart from men, and settled them at the ends of the earth. And they dwell with carefree hearts in the Islands of the Blessed alongside the deep-swirling Ocean, happy heroes for whom the grain-giving soil bears its honey-sweet produce as it flourishes thrice a year.[26]

In Hesiod, two main factors are responsible for the disappearance of the Race of Heroes: their destruction in the wars of Thebes and of Troy and their migration to the 'ends of the earth' (πείρατα γαίης). The two events are inextricably connected in the Trojan saga in that, instead of

---

24 For the overall picture see Drews 1993a: 8–30.   25 *Cypria* fr. 1 Bernabé.
26 Hes. *Erga* 159–73.

returning home, most heroes who survived the war went elsewhere, eventually to become founders of new settlements all over the Mediterranean. The entire epic genre, entitled somewhat incongruously *Nostoi*, or *Returns*, was created to deal with this event. Most of the poems that belonged to this genre are now lost, but the fragmentary information available concerning some of them – such as, for example, the epic *Melampodia* usually ascribed to Hesiod – gives us a pretty good impression of the range of the *Nostoi* phenomenon. Teukros son of Telamon went to Cyprus where he founded Salamis; Agapenor, the leader of the Arcadians in Homer, also settled in Cyprus where he founded New Paphos; Amphilochos son of Amphiaraos went to Pamphylia and Cilicia where he founded Mallos; Diomedes went to the Adriatic where he became the founder of numerous cities; Philoktetes went to the region of Croton in Italy where he colonised Cape Krimissa, and so on. 'The entire ethnography of the Mediterranean could be explained as originating from the Big Bang of the Trojan War and the consequent Nostos diffusion.'[27]

Everything suggests that originally the myth of the Heroes who dispersed to the 'ends of the earth' referred to the great migrations by which the historic cataclysm that marked the end of the Bronze Age was accompanied. The extent of the Mycenaean diaspora is immediately obvious in the East, where the locally made Mycenaean IIIC:1b pottery is found in abundance along the entire Mediterranean coast from Tarsos in the north to Ashkelon in the south (see below). But in the West too, after the first wave of destruction in the Peloponnese ca. 1200 BC, a considerable population influx was attested not only for Achaea in the northwest Peloponnese but also for the Ionian islands, in particular for the island of Kephallenia (see above, p. 144).[28] But in only one case does the rich Greek tradition of Returns find external corroboration. I refer to the legendary hero Mopsos, who properly belongs to the Theban cycle of the tradition about the end of the Race of Heroes.[29]

27/ Malkin 1998: 3. Malkin, who deals with the western *Nostoi* only, analyses the migrations of Philoktetes and Diomedes, see ibid. 214–26 and 324–57.

28 Significantly, it is as the leader of the Kephallenians that Odysseus figures in the Homeric Catalogue of Ships (*Il.* 2.631–35). The association of Odysseus and his men with Kephallenia, which at the end of the Bronze Age was apparently flooded by refugees from the Peloponnese, makes it likely that the story of Odysseus' wanderings was once meant to evoke the Mycenaean migration into this region. See further Finkelberg 2002.

29 For comprehensive summaries of the relevant evidence see Houwink ten Cate 1965: 44–50; Barnett 1975: 363–6; Hammond 1975: 679–80; Hawkins 1979: 153–7 and 1982: 429–31.

Mopsos is known in Greek legend as son of the Theban prophetess Manto daughter of Tiresias, and was himself a prophet. As the Theban saga has it, after the destruction of Thebes at the hands of the Epigoni Manto led the refugees to Kolophon in Asia Minor, where together with her Cretan husband Rhakios she founded the oracle of Apollo at Klaros. In the next generation, her son Mopsos led the immigrants not only into Pamphylia, where he founded Aspendos and Phaselis, and Cilicia, where together with Amphilochos he founded Mallos, but also into Syria and Palestine:

Herodotus says that the Pamphylians descend from the peoples led by Amphilochos and Kalkhas, some mixed hordes who accompanied them from Troy (μιγάδων τινῶν ἐκ Τροίας συνακολουθησάντων), and that, while most of them remained in Pamphylia, some were dispersed in different places all over the region. But Callinus says that Kalkhas died in Klaros and that the peoples passed over the Taurus being led by Mopsos: some of them remained in Pamphylia; as to the rest, some settled in Cilicia and others in Syria as far even as Phoenicia.[30]

According to the fifth century BC Lydian historian Xanthos, Mopsos (whom he calls 'Moxos') reached as far south as Ashkelon.[31] In historic times, Mopsos' name was commemorated in the Cilician place-names Mopsouhestia ('Mopsos' hearth') and Mopsoukrene ('Mopsos' spring'). The story of Mopsos' migration and his competition in divination at Klaros with Kalkhas, Agamemnon's seer in the *Iliad*, was an integral part of early Greek tradition about the end of the Heroic Age.[32]

The bilingual Phoenician–Hieroglyphic Luwian inscription that H. Bossert discovered in 1946 at Karatepe in Cilicia (the very one that eventually led to the decipherment of Hieroglyphic Luwian) is alternatively dated to either the ninth or seventh century BC.[33] It is written in the name of one Azatiwatas who boasts that he ensured the accession to the throne of Awarikus, styled 'king of the Danuniyim' in the Phoenician and 'king of the city of Adana' in the Luwian part of the inscription. Azatiwatas also refers to the fact that Awarikus' family belonged to the house of Muksas; the Phoenician rendering of the name as *Mpš* allows the

---

30 Str. 14.4.3, p. 668. Cf. Hdt. 7.91: Οἱ δὲ Πάμφυλοι οὗτοι εἰσὶ τῶν ἐκ Τροίης ἀποσκεδασθέντων ἅμα Ἀμφιλόχῳ καὶ Κάλχαντι.
31 765 F 17 Jacoby.
32 The tradition of the migration of Mopsos, Amphilochos and Kalchas was treated in the *Melampodia*. See Hes. fr. 278, 279 M-W.
33 According to Hawkins 1982: 431, the options for dating would be: (1) before 860 BC; (2) ca. 820–740 BC; (3) after 705 BC. He adds, however, that 'recent analysis of sculptural style and motifs supports a late dating, which agrees with the evidence of paleographic analysis.'

identification of Awarikus' forefather with the Mopsos of Greek legend (cf. also the form 'Moxos' recorded by the Lydian historian Xanthos).[34] The possible identification of the Danuniyim with the Greek Danaoi has also been suggested. Above all, however, the emergence of Muksas-Mopsos in the text of the Karatepe inscription allowed scholars not only to explain the Cilician and Pamphylian toponyms bearing his name (cf. also Moxoupolis in Southern Phrygia) but also to provide the tradition of Mopsos' wanderings over Asia with a proper historical background. Bossert's discovery thus 'made a historical contribution of unusual importance by transforming for the first time a figure of Greek legend, Mopsos, into an undeniable historical personality'.[35]

The importance of establishing the Mopsos-Muksas correspondence lies first of all in that it gives us reason to suppose that other traditions relating to the migrations of Greek heroes may also have a historic core. The 'Achaean' population of Pamphylia naturally comes to mind in this connection, but the elusive Hypachaioi of Cilicia, the Achaioi and Heniochi of Colchis and the Achaioi of Pontus may also be relevant.[36] At the same time, it can be seen that Greek tradition is similarly correct in that, with the sole exception of the Mycenaean settlers in Cyprus, all those Achaean migrants from Mycenaean Greece who dispersed all over the Mediterranean were irrevocably lost to the new Greek world that replaced Mycenaean Greece. It is only recently that the extent of their presence along the coasts of the Eastern Mediterranean has begun to be unveiled.

The end of the Bronze Age was the time of great population movements in the Levant. The characteristic feature of the new population groups which settled along the Mediterranean coast from Tarsos in the north to Ashkelon in the south is the so-called Mycenaean IIIC:1b pottery, of which the characteristic 'Philistine pottery' is a later development. The presence in ancient Canaan of the locally made Aegean pottery associated with the so-called Sea Peoples who attacked Egypt in the twelfth century BC is thus a well-established archaeological fact.[37] It seems to be more than a mere coincidence that this pottery is

---

34 The Phoenician *Mps* must have been borrowed from the Greek speakers of Cilicia and Pamphylia who were already using the later Greek form, which reflected the change in the spelling of the labiovelars (cf. again the Cilician place-names Mopsouhestia and Mopsoukrene).
35 Barnett 1975: 365.
36 On the Hypachaioi see Hdt. 7. 91; on the Achaioi and Heniochi of Colchis see esp. Str. 2.5.31, p. 129; 11.2.1, p. 492; 11.2.12–14, pp. 495–7; 17.3.24, p. 839; on the Achaioi of Pontus see Str. 9.2.42, p. 416. See now also Asheri 1998: 265–85 (with bibliography).
37 See esp. Hankey 1982: 167–71; Dothan 1989: 59–70; Dothan and Dothan 1992: 89–92, 159–70; Killebrew 2000; Barako 2003: 28–30. Besides the 'Pelesher', that is, the biblical Philistines proper,

found along the same route that was associated in Greek tradition with the migration of Mopsos and his people.[38]

The importance of the fact that the Mycenaean-type pottery found in abundance in ancient Canaan was locally produced is hard to overestimate. The example of the late Bronze Age settlers of Cyprus, who also produced Mycenaean IIIC pottery and who undoubtedly were speakers of Greek, may serve here as the most effective corroborration. Already in 1985, Amihai Mazar summed up the situation as follows:

We thus face a contradiction: the Philistines, the PLST of the 'Sea Peoples' mentioned by Ramesses III, use, in the first phase of their settlement in Philistia, locally produced Myc. IIIC:1b pottery, while the contemporary people settling in Cyprus and producing the same distinctive pottery are not defined as 'Sea Peoples' but as Greek immigrants! I believe that such divergent definitions of two ethnic groups who produced almost identical pottery are not justified. I would not hesitate to see in the Philistine immigration part of the same wave of civilized immigrants from the Mycenaean world that settled in Cyprus in the early twelfth century BCE.[39]

Although the association of Mycenaean IIIC pottery with the Philistines is a well-established archaeological fact, and although the excavations of Ashdod, Ekron and Ashkelon have shown that at least at these Philistine sites not only this pottery but also the distinctive Aegean-style cooking-pots were locally produced and used,[40] it is doubtful whether the impact of this discovery has been fully realised. That is to say, if the people who arrived in the Levant at the end of the Bronze Age brought with them not only the Mycenaean pottery but also the technology of its production, it is difficult to avoid the conclusion that the people in question could have been none other than the Mycenaeans or, to be more exact, 'Achaeans' who, as we have seen, probably stood for the Hellenised multi-ethnic

there were also the Shikalaya who bordered on the Philistine territory at least as far north as Dor, the Shardana who dwelt even farther to the north and probably also other groups. See further Singer 1988: 239–50; Dothan and Dothan 1992: 209–19. On the Sea Peoples in general see Sandars 1985.

38 This ancient land route was recently proposed in Yasur-Landau 2003: 37–8, as the most likely one to be taken by Mycenaean migration to Canaan. At the same time, it is important to keep in mind that it was Mopsos' mother Manto rather than Mopsos himself who was represented in Greek tradition as having actually emigrated from Greece. This seems to suggest that the migration that had eventually brought Mopsos and his people to Canaan was seen as having taken more than one generation.

39 Mazar 1985: 104–5; cf. Mazar 1990: 307–8.

40 On the latter see esp. Killebrew 1998; Barako 2003: 30.

population of Bronze Age Greece. Yet, though not a few students of the ancient Near East have in fact admitted as much, most Hellenists seem still unaware of this development. As far as I can see, it is mainly the history of Aegean archaeology itself that is responsible for this situation.

The Mycenaean provenance of the twelfth-century BC Aegean pottery found in ancient Canaan became clear to Duncan Mackenzie, Evans' fellow excavator at Knossos, as early as 1912. This is how Trude and Moshe Dothan summarise the conclusion which he reached as a result of the second season of the British excavations of Beth Shemesh to the west of Jerusalem:

> For the first time in the excavations, Mackenzie began to see that the true historical context of the Philistines was not in their connection to sun worship or to the Minoans, but to the Achaeans and to the repercussions of the great economic, social and political changes that transformed the Bronze Age Aegean world.[41]

Subsequent studies of the Philistine ware, especially those by W. A. Heurtley in the 1930s and A. Furumark in the 1940s, showed that in this specific respect at least the Philistine settlements in Canaan not only properly belonged to the Mycenaean world but in fact remained the only place where the ceramic traditions of this world were still being perpetuated after they had ceased to exist everywhere else, including Cyprus. To quote the Dothans again,

> . . . only in Philistia did the Late Mycenaean style continue. The twelfth-century BC potters of the mainland, of the Ionian Islands, of Crete, Rhodes, and Cyprus had all abandoned Mycenaean traditions in favour of the newer Granary style, a style completely absent from Philistine ware. The Philistines appear to have been cut off from the rest of the Aegean world for some still unexplained reason, maintaining Mycenaean styles long after they have disappeared from the Aegean itself.[42]

It is not only that neither Mackenzie in 1912 nor Heurtley in 1936 or Furumark in 1941 could possibly have known that the Mycenaeans were speakers of Greek: it is above all the authority of Sir Arthur Evans and his belief that for all practical purposes the Late Bronze Age civilisation of the Greek mainland was no more than an offshoot of the Minoan civilisation of Crete that for decades impeded the correct assessment of the relationship between the two. The story is well known, as well as the fact that Evans' influence remained all-pervasive even after his death in

41 Dothan and Dothan 1992: 40.　　　42 Dothan and Dothan 1992: 51–2.

1940. This, for example, is how John Chadwick related the history of the publication in 1953 in the *Journal of Hellenic Studies* by Michael Ventris and himself of the 'Evidence for Greek dialect in the Mycenaean archives', where the decipherment of Linear B was first made public:

The most daring choice was the use of 'Mycenaean' rather than Linear B; it was our intention to state plainly a fact boggled at or sidestepped by almost all who had written on the subject. The label 'Minoan' had been out of date as far as Linear B was concerned since 1939 [the year of the discovery of the Pylos archives]; the usual remedy was to ignore the fact that Pylos was a Mycenaean, not a Minoan site; or to camouflage the difficulty under a hybrid name like Minoan-Mycenaean or Creto-Mycenaean. With our conviction that Linear B contained Greek went the irresistible conclusion that Knossos in the Late Minoan II period formed part of the Mycenaean world. This is perhaps what, more than anything else, stuck in the throats of the archaeologists. But the insistence was justified, and the name Mycenaean, originally a label for the culture of the Greek mainland in the Late Helladic period, is now generally extended to the Linear B script and the dialect it contains.[43]

Characteristically, Evans himself was ready to admit that 'it is by no means impossible that an actual Hellenic or Hellenized Minoan element was included under the Philistine name'.[44] Although the evidence as regards the identity of the Mycenaeans and the nature of the relationship between Cyprus and Philistia that has accumulated since then is surpassingly greater than what Evans had at his disposal, contemporary archaeologists hardly go much farther than that statement of his. Thus, to take the Proceedings of a recent conference dealing with the period of transition from the Bronze to the Iron Age in the Eastern Mediterranean, although C. G. Doumas says unequivocally that 'the cultural affinity of the Aegean immigrants/refugees in Cyprus with the arrivals to the Palestinian coast, the Philistines, is now known beyond any shadow of doubt, thanks to the exhaustive investigations of our Israeli colleagues', he nevertheless uses the vague 'Aegean' rather than the unambiguous 'Achaean' or 'Greek' when referring to the cultural background of the Philistines. In a similar vein, Maria Iacovou, while speaking of the Philistines and 'their near kin in Cyprus, the descendants of the Greek-speaking Aegean newcomers', makes a reservation to the effect that 'we will probably never know what language they [the Philistines] spoke when settling in Palestine and before making the Canaanite-Hebrew language their own', while Shlomo Bunimovitz is extra-cautious in saying that

43 Chadwick 1967: 72–3.   44 Evans 1909: 77 n. 3.

'the "Achaean" immigrants to Cyprus and the Sea Peoples who settled coastal Canaan are seen now as culturally, if not ethnically, related'. The least ambiguous was Wolf-Dietrich Niemeier, who stated in his contribution that 'the evidence for the existence of the Mycenaean kitchen kit, of Mycenaean industries and of Mycenaean religious and cult patterns, form criteria which appear to point to actual Mycenaean settlement in Philistia.'[45]

According to the biblical tradition, the origins of the Philistines should be traced back to Kaphtor, a geographical name which is widely attested in the ancient Near Eastern sources and which almost definitely referred to Crete.[46] Upon the discovery of the Minoan civilisation, the biblical genealogy for the Philistines gave rise to numerous speculations concerning the association of the Sea Peoples with Minoan Crete. It should be kept in mind, however, that the formative stage of the biblical tradition is dated to the beginning of the first millennium BC at the very earliest, that is, a period when the Minoan civilisation had been inexistent for nearly five hundred years. As Chadwick pointed out in the above quotation, for the most part of this period, that is, before having been colonised by Dorians, Knossos formed part of Mycenaean Greece, which replaced the Minoan civilisation on Crete as well as in other places. It follows, then, that the biblical tradition could only refer to the Mycenaean settlers of the island, the 'Achaeans' mentioned by Homer in the *Odyssey:*

There [in Crete] people speak a mixture of different languages: there are Achaeans there, there are the Eteocretans [True Cretans] of great heart, there are the Cydonians and the Dorians divided into three parts, as well as the godlike Pelasgians.[47]

45 See Doumas 1998: 130–1; Iacovou 1998: 332, 339; Bunimovitz 1998: 103; Niemeier 1998: 48.
46 See esp. Amos 9:7; Jeremiah 47:4; cf. Gen. 10:14; Deut. 2:23. On the Philistines in the Bible see now Machinist 2000, Finkelstein 2002.
47 *Od.* 19.175–7. Another mysterious tribe dwelling along the Mediterranean coast of Canaan were the Cheretites, or *Kretim* (Ezekiel 25:16; Zephaniah 2:5). An association of the Cheretites with Crete naturally suggests itself and indeed has often been made, cf. Dothan and Dothan 1992: 8; Machinist 2000: 66. Considering that they often figure as mercenaries of David and probably also of other Israelite kings (I Sam. 30:14; II Sam. 8:18; 15:18; 20:7; 20.23; I Kings 1:38; 1:44), the Cheretites should probably be regarded as more at home in the early Iron Age milieu with which the composers of the Bible were well acquainted than in the Bronze Age. If this is so, this may well mean that the name 'Cheretites' stood for the Dorian Greek settlers of Crete who came to the island at the beginning of the first millennium BC and who, like other Greek communities of the period, very soon became suppliers of mercenary soldiers all over the Eastern Mediterranean. Cf. Finkelstein 2002: 148–50. Cf., however, West 1997: 617 n. 99, according to whom the *Kretim* 'will not have been Greeks from Crete but members of a tribe from that island which had settled in coastal Palestine with the Philistines around 1200'.

A recent discovery on the territory of ancient Canaan throws additional light on the issue of the Philistines' identity. In 1996, the excavators of Tel Miqne discovered a royal dedicatory inscription that mentions Ekron, thus confirming the tentative identification of the site with one of the cities of the Philistine pentapolis – Ekron, Ashkelon, Ashdod, Gaza and Gath. This well-preserved seventh-century BC alphabetic inscription is written in a Canaanite dialect and runs as follows:

The temple (which) Achish son of Padi son of Ysd son of 'Ada son of Ya'ir ruler of Ekron built for PTGYH [or PTNYH or PTYH, see below], his Lady. May she bless him and keep him and prolong his days and bless his land.[48]

Achish king of Ekron is known from the contemporary Assyrian records as *Ikausu*; this is also the name of a Philistine ruler of neighbouring Gath who is mentioned in the Bible and is dated to ca. 1000 BC. The name itself is not Semitic: parallels both with Aeneas' father Anchises and with the ethnonym 'Achaios' have been suggested. Thus, according to Joseph Naveh, 'the equation Ikausu = אכיש indicates that the vocalisation should rather be *Ikayus*, which eventually leads us to *Akhayus*, i.e. Ἀχαιός or "Achaean", meaning "Greek".'[49] With this in mind, let us turn to the name of the goddess whom the ruler of Ekron addresses as his divine protector.

The reading of the third letter in the goddess' name is problematic, and although Naveh, the editor of the inscription, eventually identified it as *gimel*, he nevertheless dotted it. Naveh, whose preferred reading is thus PTGYH, wrote in this connection: ' פתגיה was surely the name of a goddess of non-Semitic origin, perhaps some unknown Philistine or Indo-European deity'.[50] The tentative normalisation of the word as *Potigaia* (= Greek 'Potnia Gaia') or *Puthogaia* ('Gaia from Pytho') has been suggested in the scholarly literature.[51] According to the identification

---

48 Tr. A. Demsky; first published in Gitin, Dothan and Naveh 1997: 8–9.
49 Gitin, Dothan and Naveh 1997: 11 and n. 29; cf. Naveh 1998: 35. It should be recalled in this connection that the rendering *a* of the initial laryngeal' (= *aleph*) of the version 'Achish' given in the Bible is purely conventional. The vowel notation of biblical Hebrew originated in the work of the Masoretes in the second half of the first millennium AD, and it therefore postdates the consonantal text by a very considerable margin, see Moscati *et al.* 1980: 49; cf. Naveh in Gitin, Dothan and Naveh 1997: 11 n. 29 and 1998: 36. It seems to me, however, that, when taken side by side with the Assyrian version *Ikausu*, the spelling 'KYS would rather lead to *Iqeias* or something to this effect, that is, to a kind of name that eventually resulted in Greek *Hippias*, cf. Linear B *i-qo* and *i-qo-jo*, nominative plural and genitive singular of ἵππος < *ekwos*, 'horse', or Linear B *i-qe-ja*, 'She of Horses', which is one of the epithets of the Potnia, and so on.
50 Gitin, Dothan, Naveh 1997: 11.
51 *Potigaia* in Yasur-Landau 2001; *Pythogaia* in Schäfer-Lichtenberger 2000.

proposed by Aaron Demsky, the third letter of the divine name should be interpreted as an aborted *nun*, allowing one to read the name as PTNYH, that is, as identical to Greek *Potnia*. Demsky also pointed out that, in accord with the recognised function of Mycenaean Potnia, the goddess of Ekron also functions as the divine protector of the king.[52] However that may be, the Semitic word that directly follows the name of the goddess is *'dth*, 'his lady', or 'his mistress', thus giving a meaning which would exactly correspond to the meaning of Greek *potnia*.[53] It may be suggested in view of this that the reason why the Greek word became corrupted was that, although the person responsible for the inscription had a clear idea of the word's meaning, he possessed no knowledge of Greek and therefore misspelt the goddess' name.

The Mycenaean-style clay figurines of a seated goddess (the so-called 'Ashdoda') uncovered in cities of the Philistine pentapolis also seem to speak in favour of identification of the Ekron goddess with Mycenaean Potnia.[54] Interestingly, it was in Ashkelon, one of the cities of the Philistine pentapolis, where according to Xanthos Mopsos threw the queen Atargatis and her infant son Ichthys ('Fish') into the nearby lake. A similar story told in Argos of king Perseus' pursuit of Dionysos and his female attendants was associated with the foundation of Dionysos' temple and cult. Since Atargatis is the same as Derketo, a goddess who in historic times was regarded as dwelling in this very lake and worshipped under the form of half woman half fish, Xanthos' story seems to imply that Mopsos was regarded as the founder of the cult of the 'Askalon goddess'.[55]

The Ekron inscription is a good illustration of the cultural processes that determined the outcome of Mycenaean colonisation in the East. On the one hand, the discovery of the Aegean goddess-figure in a temple dedicated by a Philistine ruler some five hundred years after the migration of the Philistines into these parts of the Mediterranean shows how persistent certain traditions concerning cult and ritual could actually be. On the other hand, the cultural assimilation of the Philistines into their Canaanite milieu could not be more thorough: their supreme god was neither Zeus nor Poseidon but the Canaanite Dagon, and the very name

---

52 Demsky 1998: 57–8; cf. Schäfer-Lichtenberger 2000: 86–7. Demsky also examines and rejects the possibility that the Canaanite word could stand for PTYH = Gr. *Pytheiē*.
53 Cf. Mycenaean *po-ti-ni-ja*, 'for the Mistress', KN 172.
54 On the 'Ashdoda' figurines see Dothan 1982: 234–6; Mazar 1990: 323 and 2000: 223; Dothan and Dothan 1992: 153–7; Singer 1992: 440–2, 445–7; Yasur-Landau 2001.
55 On Perseus and Dionysos see Burkert 1983: 176, referring to Paus. 2.22.1; 2.20.4; 2.23.7–8 and Schol. T *Il.* 14.319; on the 'Askalon goddess' see Xanthos 765 F 17 Jacoby; Diod.Sic. 2.4.2–3. See also Fontenrose 1951: 132–3.

of the non-Semitic goddess was cast in a Canaanite dialect and executed in a Canaanite script.[56] The Philistines, who started as Mycenaean settlers on the southern coast of Canaan, ended as a Near Eastern people who worshipped the local gods, spoke the local language, used the local script and in due course produced pottery indistinguishable from the local ware. As Moshe Dothan put it, 'their Aegean heritage was almost forgotten, and local influences became predominant after a century and a half of assimilation'.[57] This compares well with other cases of cultural assimilation known to us from later periods. Athenaeus' account of the history of the Greek settlers of Poseidonia (Paestum), immortalised in 'The Poseidonians' by Cavafy, is especially illuminating:

. . . the Poseidonians residing in the Tyrrhenian gulf who, though initially Hellenes (ἐξ ἀρχῆς "Ελλησιν οὖσιν), turned into barbarians, having become Tyrrhenians or Romans, and changed their speech and the rest of their habits. Yet they observe one Greek festival even today: in the course of this festival they assemble together and recall to memory their ancient names and customs and then, lamenting loudly to each other and weeping, they go home.[58]

When taken in this context, the Mycenaean migrants in the East prove to be a rather ordinary case of a colonisation movement eventually assimilated into the native population. At the same time, the Mycenaean migrants were special in that they lost contact with the mother country already at an early stage of their settlement. This is probably why they were remembered in Greek tradition as the last survivors of the Race of Heroes who retired to the ends of the earth, never to be seen again.

The loss of contact with the former homeland seems also to be the reason why, while the presumed descendants of the refugees from Mycenaean Greece were habitually identified as 'Achaeans', not all of them were also identified as 'Hellenes'. Only those of the Achaeans who became part of the new Greek world that replaced Mycenaean Greece counted as both Achaeans and Hellenes at one and the same time. Such double identity would apply not only to the Achaeans of Achaia Phthiotis[59] or

---

56 Cf. Demsky 1998: 58. On the language and script of the Ekron inscription see Gitin, Dothan and Naveh 1997: 12–15; on Dagon see Singer 1992.
57 Dothan and Dothan 1992: 177; cf. also ibid. 174–5.
58 Ath. 14.31 Kaibel, quoting the fourth-century BC philosopher and musicologist Aristoxenus of Tarentum. See also Str. 5.4.4, p. 243 (on Cumae); 5.4.7, p. 246 (on Neapolis); 6.1.2, p. 253 (on Magna Graecia in general).
59 It is not out of the question that the reference to Achilles' contingent from Achaia Phthiotis in the Homeric Catalogue of Ships as 'they were called Myrmidons, as well as Hellenes and Achaeans' (*Il.* 2.684 Μυρμιδόνες δὲ καλεῦντο καὶ "Ελληνες καὶ Ἀχαιοί) should be interpreted in this vein. On the anachronistic geography of the Catalogue of Ships see below, pp. 170–1.

Achaea in the northern Peloponnese but also to those descendants of Mycenaean migrants who, as for example the Aeolians of Asia Minor, not only had not lost contact with the new Greek civilisation but even actively participated in its creation. In other words, like other descent groups discussed in Chapter 2, while some of the Achaeans 'became reckoned among Hellenes' others did not. This shows again that, rather than primordial ethnic groups, both 'Achaeans' and 'Hellenes' were self-created cultural identities under which the heterogeneous population groups that inhabited Greece first in the Bronze and then in the Iron Age were subsumed.

CHAPTER 8

Continuities and discontinuities

THE NEW BEGINNINGS

The period that followed the end of the Bronze Age (ca. 1050–ca. 800 BC) represented a sharp break from the Mycenaean civilisation and was characterised by deep recession in material culture. It is true that archaeological discoveries of the last decades, first and foremost the famous Lefkandi tomb, have shown that there were pockets of continuity even in the so-called Dark Age.[1] Yet, this evidence, indicative as it is of the complex mixture of continuities and discontinuities that characterised the transition to the Iron Age, cannot affect the general assessment of the relationship between Dark Age Greece and its Mycenaean predecessor, let alone account for the contrast with the epoch subsequent to it. The growth of population and a considerable increase in prosperity, which are discernible in the archaeological record since the early eighth century BC, fully justify singling out the Dark Age as a separate historical period.[2] This is not yet to say that recession in material culture was the only feature by which the Dark Age was characterised.

Let us consider an additional version of the destruction of the Race of Heroes, the one found in the concluding part of the *Catalogue of Women*. This corrupted passage, which immediately follows the description of Helen's wedding,[3] runs as follows:

And all the gods were split over the strife. For this was the time when Zeus high-thundering contrived wondrous deeds, to stir up and mix {...} over the boundless earth, and he was already most eager to wipe out the race of mortal men, and declared that he would destroy the lives of the demigods [...}, that the

---

1 On the Lefkandi tomb. see e.g. Blome 1991; Antonaccio 1995: 236–43; Lemos 2002: 140–6, 165–8.
2 Cf. Cartledge 1979: 92.
3 The version of the end of the Heroic Age given in the Cyclic *Cypria* also emphasised the role of Helen in the destruction of the Race of Heroes in that she was made daughter of Zeus and Nemesis. See *Cypria* fr. 9 Bernabé.

children of gods [should not mix] with wretched mortals, seeing [. . .] with his own eyes, but that the blessed [gods] should keep their own company and lead their lives apart from men even as before. And so Zeus [inflicted] suffering upon suffering on those who [were born] of immortals and of mortal men.[4]

Although both the *Cypria* and the *Works and Days*, the two other traditional poems which refer to the end of the Heroic Age (above, p. 149), take it for granted that the Race of Heroes was that of demigods, ἡμίθεοι, only the *Catalogue of Women* explicitly treats the cataclysmic events at the end of the Heroic Age as directly connected with Zeus' intention to put an end to unions between gods and mortals. This is not to say that the *Catalogue*'s version of the end of the Heroic Age has no parallels in other sources. As Jenny Strauss Clay has shown, the *Homeric Hymn to Aphrodite* implicitly associates the end of the Heroic Age with the termination of the unions between gods and mortal women: 'The final upshot of Zeus's intervention is to make Aphrodite cease and desist from bringing about these inappropriate unions between the gods and mortals, which, in turn, will mean the end of the age of heroes.'[5] Another version of the same story emerges, rather unexpectedly, in Genesis 6: 1–5, just before the Flood episode:

When people began to multiply on the face of the earth, and daughters were born to them, the sons of God saw that the daughters of men were fair; and they married such of them as they chose. . . The Nephilim were on the earth in those days, and also afterward, when the sons of God came in to the daughters of men, and they bore children to them. These were the mighty men that were of old, the men of renown. Then the Lord saw that the wickedness of man was great on the earth etc.

The commentators of the Bible, both ancient and modern, have had much difficulty handling this puzzling passage.[6] Yet, the Genesis passage makes perfectly good sense when taken against the background of Greek heroic tradition. Its similarity to the passage from the *Catalogue of Women* quoted above is especially noteworthy. This seems to indicate that versions of the myth of the destruction of the Race of Heroes, probably a reflection of the historical cataclysm that accompanied the end of the

---

4 Hes. Fr. 204.95–105 M-W.
5 *Hymn. Hom. Ven.* 247–53, cf. ibid. 45–52; Strauss Clay 1989: 166.
6 Cf. Kugel 1997: 108: 'It is hard to know what to make of this strange passage even today. In any case, ancient readers saw in these words a hint that the immediate cause of the flood (and perhaps of other ills) had been the mating of the "sons of God" (generally interpreted to mean some sort of angel or heavenly creature) with the "daughters of men". The flood must have come about, directly or indirectly, as a result of this union.' See also ibid. 108–14; cf. West 1997: 117–18.

Bronze Age, circulated not only in Greece but also in wider regions of the Eastern Mediterranean.

The divinely sanctioned cataclysm with which the end of the Heroic Age was associated is thus directly connected with putting an end to the practice of producing the mixed offspring of gods and mortal women – that is, the same *nothoi* issuing from the exogamous marriages of females whose status was discussed in Chapter 5. This seems to indicate that at least one of the functions of the myth of the destruction of the Race of Heroes was to commemorate a great cultural change that spread over Greece and probably also over wider regions of the Aegean and Western Asia at the beginning of the Iron Age. The essence of this change seems to have been the abolition of the Bronze Age marriage practices, first and foremost female exogamy.

In her *Prolegomena to the Study of Greek Religion,* Jane Harrison drew attention to a version of the famous story of the rivalry between Athena and Poseidon preserved by Saint Augustine. Both men and women of Athens participated in the vote: the women exceeded the men by one and Athena prevailed. To appease the wrath of Poseidon, the men inflicted on women a triple punishment: 'they were to lose their vote, their children were no longer to be called by their mother's name, and they themselves were no longer to be called [after their goddess] Athenians.'[7] Characteristically, the Athenian king Kekrops who summoned the citizens to the vote is credited in Greek tradition with what Harrison calls 'the introduction of the patriarchal form of marriage'. Namely, Kekrops is said to have been the first 'to join one woman to one man: before connections had taken place at random and marriages were in common – hence, as some think, Kekrops was called "of double form" (διφυής), since before his day people did not know who their fathers were, on account of the number [of possible parents].'[8]

The 'double form' of Kekrops is explained by the Suda as due to his being of double sex and by Diodorus Siculus as due to his being of double race;[9] the most popular explanation, treating Kekrops as half-man and half-serpent, obviously also relates to his being of the mixed Greek and indigenous descent. There can be little doubt that here we have traces of yet another traditional story relating to the abolition of the Bronze Age marriage practices whose main fault was seen in that they involved female

7 Harrison 1903: 261; *De civitat.* 18.9 (Harrison's translation).
8 Athen. 13. 2, p. 555 (quoting Klearchos); cf. Tzetzes *Chil.* 5.19.650. See Harrison 1903: 262.
9 Diod. Sic.1.28; Suid., s.v.; cf. LSJ, s.v.

exogamy. We have seen indeed that the individuals and population groups that sprang from the exogamous marriages of females were conspicuous in that they had no male progenitor to whom their descent could be traced. This is why it is hard not to agree with Harrison's assessment of the Athenian myth: 'The myth is aetiological, and it mirrors surely some shift in the social organization of Athens.' To be sure, this shift by no means concerned Athens alone.

The abolition of female exogamy was universally accompanied by the abolition of the institution of kingship by marriage. As we have seen, it is likely that the queen was the source of sovereignty by virtue of her status as the priestess of the goddess of the land (pp. 88–9). This would entail that the institution of kingship by marriage was much more at home in the context of settled populations than among nomads. It is indeed reasonable to suppose that the central position of Mother Goddess and her priestess as known to us from Bronze Age societies should ultimately be traced back to the civilisations of Neolithic agriculturalists of Western Asia and the Aegean. The Neolithic populations of Anatolia and the Aegean handed down their matrifocal practices to the Bronze Age newcomers to their lands, among them the Mycenaean Greeks. Even if these new population groups started as nomads and pastoralists alien to the issue of sovereignty, rather than replacing indigenous social practices, including matrifocality, they and their descendants eventually adjusted themselves to these practices as a direct result of their intermingling with the indigenous population. All this changed dramatically with the influx of fresh nomadic populations at the end of the Bronze Age. The transition from the matrilinear to the patrilinear succession among the Dorians of Argos, discussed in Chapter 7, provides a good illustration of this development.

By the end of the Dark Age, almost everywhere in Greece the institution of kingship, either by marriage or otherwise, was replaced by the political system of the city-state. The erosion in the status of the priestess-queen, which directly issued from the abolition of the Bronze Age system of kingship (above, p. 90), is reflected in an analogous change in the status of the female deities with whom the priestess had initially been associated. Take for example the case of Hera. As has been observed more than once, an irresolvable contradiction exists between Hera the wife and sister of Zeus as represented in Homer and Hesiod and Hera of the Greek cult, who is not only not envisaged as Zeus' wife but also displays all the characteristic features of the ancient figure of the Great Goddess. According to Joan O'Brien, the transformation of Hera the fertility and protection goddess into the wife and sister of Zeus was ultimately due to her emerging Pan-Hellenic role; this transformation can also be seen in the switch from the aniconic *xoana* as the cult representation of Hera to the iconic images of the goddess.[10] The same with other goddesses. Artemis, the virgin daughter of Zeus in the Olympian religion, emerges at Ephesos as a great fertility goddess, who is, again, not subordinated to any male authority whatsoever, while Athena, another Greek goddess conspicuous for her virginity, was worshipped at Elis under the title of the Mother.[11]

This is not to say that Bronze Age marriage practices disappeared without trace. Consider for example the following. In the course of the spring festival of the Anthesteria, the wife of the archon basileus, 'king-ruler', one of the three highest offices in Athens, who was in charge of all the religious duties of the former kings, turned for one night into the 'queen' (βασίλισσα or βασίλιννα) and was given in marriage to the god Dionysos to whom the festival was dedicated. Walter Burkert, who studied this ritual in *Homo Necans*, comments on it as follows:

The details of the sacred marriage were kept a secret, 'unspeakable'. Our sources are uniformly silent and offer no assistance in deciding between the two possible explanations: was there a symbolic union with a statue, a herm, or did a mortal represent the god - most likely the 'king' himself?[12]

The Anthesteria ritual is only one of many examples of the mixture of continuities and discontinuities that characterised the social and religious life of historic Greece. On the one hand, the role the wife of the archon basileus temporarily performed was none other than, again, that of the spouse of god, which as we saw was an inseparable part of the Bronze Age marriage practices. On the other hand, the ancient ritual of the union of a mortal woman and god had for ever lost its primeval force for the simple reason that this union was no longer supposed to lead to any special kind of progeny of 'double form' on a par with the demigods of Greek legend. A ritual that originally embodied the Bronze Age ideas of marriage[13]

---

10 O'Brien 1993: 25, 30–1. On the incomplete character of Hera's integration into the Olympic Pantheon see Aloni-Ronen 1998: 11–15; on the iconic and aniconic cult images of the same deities see Finkelberg 2001b.

11 Paus. 5.3.2; cf. Rose 1958: 110.

12 Burkert 1983: 234; cf. Burkert 1985: 239–40.

13 As Burkert 1983: 213, has shown, the fact that the Athenians shared the festival of the Anthesteria with all Ionians makes it practically certain that this festival existed even before Ionian migration to Asia Minor.

became subordinate to the political and religious norms of the city-state and was preserved only in its outward form.

The developments described above cannot be taken separately from the establishment of the Olympian pantheon, which accompanied the emergence of the city-state. The Pan-Hellenic cult of Zeus and other Olympians; the Olympian games and other Pan-Hellenic festivals in which these cults found their fullest expression; the free-standing temple with the cult statue of an Olympian deity within it; the canonic epics of Homer and Hesiod celebrating these very deities – all these were hallmark features of the new age. As the cases of Hera and the Anthesteria ritual demonstrate, the new worship partly superseded and partly absorbed the old cultic and religious practices. But it is not only in the transformation of the old political and religious system that sharp discontinuities between Mycenaean and historic Greece can be observed. The same discontinuities can also be seen in the radical change in artistic style; in the complete abandonment of the palace economy; in the development of an innovatory system of warfare; in the adoption of a new system of writing – in short, the entire social texture was transformed beyond recognition. As the new self-definition 'Hellenes' and the new chronology introduced during this very period indicate, the Greeks were highly conscious of the fact that the religious and social developments that took place in the first centuries of the first millennium BC signalised the beginning of a new era.

It is not surprising, therefore, that the Greeks of the historic period had a far from adequate understanding of their past. 'This [the Mycenaean collapse] ushered in a long period, lasting to the dawn of Greek history, in which traditional culture was transformed by the incorporation of many new elements, so absolutely basic to the later Greeks' way of life that, as their legends show, they could not imagine the past without them.'[14] The gap dividing Mycenaean and classical Greece has become especially obvious after the decipherment of Linear B. The picture of Mycenaean society that gradually emerged as a result of the decipherment has led scholars to an increasing recognition that Greek tradition, and first and foremost the poems of Homer, cannot be seen as an adequate reflection of the institutions and society of Bronze Age Greece (see also above, pp. 2–3).

To sum up, the fall of Mycenaean Greece brought about a radical break in cultural continuity. We saw that the Greece of the second millennium BC cannot be taken separately from the larger world of the ancient Near East, so much so that our habitual categorisation into 'East' and 'West'

14 Dickinson 1994: 309. Cf. Drews 1993a: 4.

can hardly be applied with profit to the historic period in question (Chapter 3). But the Greece of the first millennium BC was different. The disastrous events at the end of the Bronze Age led to the collapse of the eastwards-oriented Mycenaean civilisation and severed the centuries-long ties between Greece and Western Asia. When the eastern contacts were re-established, they were more akin to the external influences discussed in Burkert's *Orientalizing Revolution* than to the systemic affinity that existed in the Bronze Age.[15] The situation thus created resulted in that, rather than directly continuing their Bronze Age past, the Greeks of the Dark and Archaic Age laid the foundations of a new civilisation, the one known today as the civilisation of Classical Greece. The dichotomy into 'East' and 'West' did not emerge before this development. The Greeks themselves became aware of this dichotomy and started elaborating on it ideologically only from the moment of their first confrontation with the Persians at the end of the sixth and the beginning of the fifth century BC. But everything points in the direction that all the materials needed for its construction had existed long before, and in any case not later than the eighth century BC, the time of the rise of the polis and its characteristic institutions.

THE MYTH OF THE HEROIC AGE

In spite of the break in cultural continuity that the passage to the Iron Age involved, the narrative of the past adopted by the new Greek civilisation that replaced Mycenaean Greece was the narrative of the Heroic Age and its end in the Trojan War. It is at this point that we encounter for the first time a major discrepancy between Greek heroic tradition on the one hand and archaeology and linguistics on the other. It is obvious indeed that, whatever the nature of the historic events underlying the Trojan saga,[16] they cannot account for the destruction levels and depopulation in mainland Greece. The momentous events that brought about the end of the Mycenaean civilisation were replaced in the mainstream Greek tradition by the story of the Trojan War that destroyed the Race of Heroes — a mythological construction that was apparently considered as offering a more satisfactory explanation of the transition of Greece from

15 Burkert 1992; cf. S. Morris 1992; West 1997: 625.
16 According to the contemporary assessment of the relevant archaeological data, the destruction of Troy VIIa postdates that of Mycenae and Pylos. This conclusion rests on the presence of Late Helladic IIIC pottery in that level, see Wood 1985: 224; Easton 1985: 189; Drews 1993a: 10 n. 6; Hood 1995: 25. I am grateful to Martin West for drawing my attention to this evidence.

prehistory to history. Neither the 'coming of the Dorians' nor the migration to the East, the two events mainly responsible for the radical changes that brought about the emergence of the political and dialectal map of historic Greece, became part of the standard Greek narrative about the end of the Heroic Age as found in the traditional poetry associated with the names of Homer and Hesiod.

This is not to say that these events passed unnoticed in Greek epic tradition as a whole. Thus, we have good reason to suppose that the lost traditional epic *Aigimios* dealt with the coming of the Dorians, whereas the tradition of the migration to the East was certainly treated in the lost epic poem *Melampodia*.[17] And, judging by the evidence of the literary sources, the Dorian tradition of the 'Return of the Children of Heracles' gave the Dorians' own distinct version of the population movements that shook Greece at the end of the Bronze Age.[18] Thus, although the mainstream epic tradition did not treat the coming of the Dorians or the great migrations in any considerable detail, this does not mean that Greek traditional poetry as a whole was unaware of these events. One may conclude that the silence of Homer and Hesiod on the issue of the 'Return of the Children of Heracles' and the migrations to the East was anything but incidental. How may we account for this phenomenon?

One result of the population movements that changed the face of the Eastern Mediterranean at the end of the Bronze Age was that the Early Iron Age population of Greece was manifestly heterogeneous. While the collapse of Mycenaean Greece was accompanied by a fresh influx of Greek-speaking tribes to Central Greece and the Peloponnese, it did not bring about the complete disappearance of the Bronze Age population of these lands. As we saw in Chapter 7, while some Bronze Age population groups were replaced by northwestern tribes and left Greece altogether, others changed their places of settlement without leaving Greece, and there were also those who remained in their original habitats in spite of the turmoil that followed the collapse of the Mycenaean civilisation. This meant that some regions, notably Attica, Arcadia and Achaea, remained inhabited by non-Dorian populations, whereas in

---

17 See Hes. frs. 270–9, 294–302 M-W. Aigimios (below, n. 18) is also mentioned in Hes. fr. 10a. 6–19 M-W, a genealogical fragment which probably belonged to the *Catalogue of Women*, see West 1985: 57.

18 According to this tradition, the Dorian king Aigimios adopted as his son Hyllos son of Heracles; the latter became the founder of the tribe of Hylleis, one of the three Dorian tribes, and progenitor of the Dorian kings in subsequent generations. For useful summaries of Greek tradition of the Dorian invasion see Hammond 1975: 681–706; J. Hall 1997: 56–7; on the Dorian charter myth see above, p. 100 n. 30.

others the Dorians settled side by side with the original inhabitants to form a symbiosis which in some cases lasted till the end of antiquity. The non-Dorian tribe of Argos, the Hyrnathioi, immediately comes to mind in this connection, but a considerable 'Achaean' population was also present in Triphylia, formally part of Dorian Messenia, and in Laconia itself, where several cities, most notably Amyclae, were captured from 'Achaeans' as late as the beginning of the Archaic Age.[19]

Sooner or later, the heterogeneous population groups present in Greece since the beginning of the Iron Age had to negotiate the terms of their coexistence. This seems to be the reason why, side by side with such other formative events as the establishment of Pan-Hellenic cults and festivals, the tradition of the Trojan War rose to Pan-Hellenic circulation. That this tradition originated among the refugees from Mycenaean Greece who settled along the Aegean shore of Asia Minor shows clearly enough that not only the populations of mainland Greece but also large parts of Greek diaspora had become integrated by this time into the new Greek world that emerged out of the Dark Age.[20] The painful historical events that accompanied the end of Mycenaean Greece were replaced in this tradition by the story of a war specially designed by Zeus to put an end to the Race of Heroes. As a result, it was the Trojan War rather than the population movements that shook Greece at the end of the second millennium BC that became universally envisaged as the main if not the only factor responsible for the catastrophe that brought about the end of the Heroic Age.

It is not out of the question that at least to some extent this remarkable instance of collective amnesia was due to what Jack Goody defined as 'homeostatic transformation', or selective forgetting and remembering, which he regards as a characteristic feature of oral societies:

There are, of course, techniques for preserving special kinds of information. But unless deliberately directed, memory bends to other interests, tending to set aside what does not fit. This feature of oral storage and transmission constitutes one aspect of the relatively homogeneous character of such [sc. oral] cultures, in which uncomfortable dissonances tend to get overridden by the healing powers of oblivion while memory works with those experiences that link with others.[21]

---

19 For the initial period of the Dorian settlement in the Peloponnese see Hammond 1982: 705–38; for the presence of non-Dorian *phylai* in Dorian states see J. Hall 1997: 9–10.

20 Cf. Snodgrass 1971: 456: 'For me, the decisive moment comes when the Greek world can be seen to be moving forward *as a whole*, when the beneficial or disruptive developments in one centre are swiftly reflected in most parts of central and southern Greece, in the islands and in Ionia.' (Snodgrass' italics.)

21 Goody 2000: 44–5. On homeostasis see also above, pp. 10–11.

At the same time, there is good reason to suppose that homeostatic transformation cannot account in full for the entire range of the phenomena involved. Consider, for example, the so-called Catalogue of Ships, introduced in the second Book of the *Iliad*. This much-discussed document ostensibly offers a comprehensive survey of the political geography of Greece in the Heroic Age. No wonder, therefore, that quite a few geopolitical maps of Mycenaean Greece have been drawn with its assistance (see e.g. Map 5). On the whole, however, while it cannot be denied that the Catalogue of Ships mentions a fairly large number of genuine Bronze Age sites, the problems of historical interpretation raised by this document are generally regarded as insurmountable. This changes as soon as the Catalogue of Ships is compared to the political map of Archaic Greece. The most significant points arising from such a comparison are as follows.

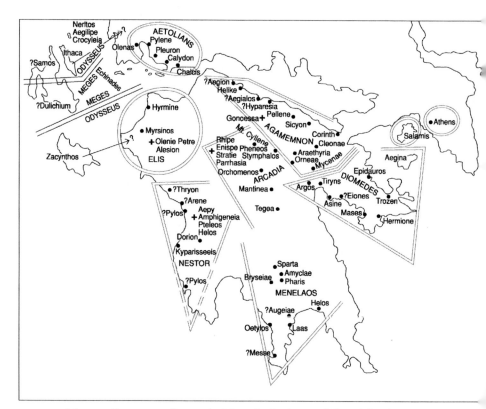

Map 5.   Greece according to the Homeric Catalogue of Ships (after Page 1959).

1. Homer's picture of Attica, with Athens as its only city, projects onto the Heroic Age the synoecism of Attica, that is, its unification under Athens; this, although consistent with the official ideology of Athens, could by no means have taken place earlier than the Archaic period.

2. Megara, the historic rival of Athens, is completely deleted from the map, making it possible to represent the island of Salamis, to which both Athens and Megara laid claim, as dissociated from the latter.

3. The Argos of Diomedes is represented as spreading over the entire territory of northeastern Peloponnese. This picture corresponds fairly well to what were claimed to have been the original domains of Dorian Argos (the so-called 'lot of Temenos'), presumably restored under king Pheidon in the seventh century BC.[22] The Heroic Age Argos as it emerges in Homer thus reflects this state's geopolitical aspirations in the historic period.[23]

4. The territory of Messenia, a Dorian state annexed by Sparta in the seventh century BC, emerges on the Homeric map as a blank space between Nestor's Pylos and Menelaus' Sparta.

The case of Messenia is especially illuminating, because today we know with certainty that this territory was densely populated in Mycenaean times.[24] Hence, if the Catalogue of Ships provides, as many are still ready to believe, a reliable picture of the political geography of Mycenaean Greece, we can reasonably ask where the towns and leaders representing this territory are to be found in this document. As Homer's mention of the seven Messenian towns of Agamemnon in *Iliad* 9 and the leaders of one of them in *Iliad* 5 indicates,[25] his failure to place Messenia on his map of Heroic Greece could hardly have resulted from obliteration of memory. It is therefore much more likely that the answer to the questions raised by the Catalogue of Ships should rather be sought in the political agenda of the leading states of Archaic Greece. If Argos finds its claim to the 'lot of Temenos' satisfied; Sparta sees Messenia deleted from the map; and Athens ascertains that Megara is altogether missing and the synoecism of Attica under Athens completed even before the Trojan War, there is every reason why these dominant Greek states should be content with the map of Heroic Greece that the *Iliad* offers.

---

22 Athens: *Il.* 2.546–56; Salamis: 557–8; Argos: 559–68. On the 'lot of Temenos' see Str. 8.3.33, p. 358 (following Ephorus); Hammond 1982: 715; J. Hall 1995: 586–7.

23 The *Catalogue of Women*, in which the same territories are represented as belonging to Ajax's Salamis, obviously did not undergo a similar revision; see Hes. Fr. 204 M-W and Finkelberg 1988.

24 See e.g. the map of Mycenaean sites adduced in Blegen 1975: between 171 and 172.

25 *Il.* 9.149–53 and 291–5; 5.541–60.

Note also that, although the Dorians as such are hardly mentioned by Homer,[26] not only does the Argos of Diomedes roughly correspond as we saw to Dorian Argos, but the Sparta of Menelaus corresponds fairly well to Dorian Sparta. Yet, such geopolitical realities as Argos or Sparta do not properly belong to the Heroic Age.[27] The centres of the relevant territories were Mycenae, Tiryns and Amyclae, all of them abundantly represented in Greek legend. Characteristically, Mycenae, an insignificant town in historic times, is the only one of the three whose treatment is historically consistent, in that it was made the capital of the antiquarian kingdom of Agamemnon. Tiryns and Amyclae, whose key position in Greek legend shows that their function as administrative and cult centres of pre-Dorian Greece was well known to the Greeks of the Archaic Age, have been replaced by the more up-to-date Argos and Sparta and, accordingly, marginalised. That is to say, although it was a matter of common knowledge that the Dorians were newcomers into the Peloponnese, they could nevertheless easily locate themselves on the map of Heroic Greece provided by the Catalogue of Ships.

The need to consolidate the heterogeneous population groups that inhabited Greece since the beginning of the first millennium BC seems also to be the reason why at approximately the same period the collective name 'Hellenes', meant to embrace both the descendants of the Bronze Age population of Greece and the Iron Age newcomers to their lands, became generally accepted. Let us return for a moment to the genealogy of Hellen as discussed in Chapter 2. We saw that of Hellen's three sons, Aiolos, Doros and Xouthos, only the latter is a mythological figure in his own right rather than just an eponym. But Xouthos in turn is father of two sons, Ion and Achaios, whose names are clearly eponymous. It looks as if the figure of Xouthos mainly served the purpose of preserving the three-son pattern archetypical to most genealogical traditions,[28] whereas the relevant taxonomy is the one that takes into account four descendants of Hellen – Aiolos, Doros, Ion and Achaios, neatly reflecting the conventional division of the Hellenic body in historic times. As Jonathan Hall put it, 'In making the eponymous Aiolos, Doros, Ion and Achaios sons and grandsons of the Hellenic *Urvater*, Hellen, the "Hellenic Genealogy" sought to project the view that a single, undifferentiated population of Hellenes had existed prior to a series of subdivisions that resulted in the

---

26 The only explicit reference to the Dorians is *Od.* 19.177 (quoted above, p. 156).
27 Cf. Cartledge 1979: 93, about the site of classical Sparta.
28 On the three-son pattern see West 1985: 27–8.

principal ethnic groups of the historical period.'[29] We have seen, however, that it is likely that both Ionians and, especially, Achaeans were in fact multi-ethnic entities and therefore not suitable to be unconditionally subsumed under the stemma of Hellen.[30] It is at this point that the artificial character of the initial group comprising Hellen and his sons becomes obvious. In that it is an 'empty' group typical of artificially lengthened genealogies, it contrasts sharply with the 'bushy' stemmas of Aiolos and Inachos, which as we saw would account much more satisfactorily for the complex ethnic situation in Greece in the second millennium BC.[31] Needless to say, the result is an artificial and inherently inconsistent system, not dissimilar to the inconsistent account of the Greek past found in the Homeric epics.

Furthermore, the poets' strategy of updating the past in accordance with the contemporary agenda cannot be considered separately from large-scale developments that took place at the same period and that are sometimes given the collective name of the 'eighth-century Renaissance'.[32] The emergence of the hero-cult is the most conspicuous example. This characteristically Greek cult, closely connected with the cult of the dead, consisted in the worship of personages of Greek legend – many of whom were the heroes celebrated in the poems of Homer and Hesiod – which concentrated around ancient tombs supposed to be the places of their burial. This remarkable coincidence between the traditional poetry on the one hand and the new religious practice on the other has even given rise to the suggestion that the hero-cult developed under the direct influence of the epic tradition, above all of Homer.[33] However, it seems more plausible that both expressed the same tendency towards establishing continuity between prehistoric and historic Greece that became dominant at that period. To quote François de Polignac: 'The coincidence of the diffusion of both epic poems and offerings in ancient tombs, far from pointing to a

29 J. Hall 2002: 56.
30 The inferior status of Ion and Achaios as descending from a son of Hellen rather than from Hellen himself was probably intended to meet this difficulty. Note also that both Ion and Achaios are in fact *nothoi* born to Xouthos by the daughter of the Athenian king Erechtheus, cf. Hes. fr. 10a M-W; Apollod. 1.7.3.
31 On artificial lengthening of genealogies by the inclusion of 'spurinyms' (toponyms, eponyms and patronyms) see Henige 1974: 46–4; on 'bushy' stemmas see Vansina 1985: 183 and above, p. 32.
32 On 'the eighth-century Renaissaince' see Snodgrass 1971: 416–36; Coldstream 1976: 8–17 and 1977: 341–57, 367–9; Hiller 1983: 9–15; de Polignac 1995: 128–49; Whitley 1988: 173–82; I. Morris 1988: 750–61.
33 Farnell 1921: 340; Coldstream 1976: 8–17; for the discussion see Whitley 1988: 173–82; Antonaccio 1995: 242–3.

strictly causal relationship, testifies rather to a general interest in the memory of the "heroic ages" that took two close but separate forms.'[34]

In his 1988 assessment of the hero-cults of Attica and the Argolid James Whitley wrote:

The significance of the emergence of 'hero-cults' . . . seems . . . to be much more directly political than some other authors have allowed for . . . Offerings in Mycenaean tombs . . . were part of the means by which the city defined its territorial limits and established a beneficial relationship to a usable, ideological past.[35]

That not only Attica but also predominantly Dorian Argolid were engaged in hero-worship clearly indicates that the new practice of establishing 'a beneficial relationship to a usable, ideological past' concerned also those who, unlike the inhabitants of Attica, had no reason whatsoever to see themselves as descendants of the Mycenaeans.[36]

In the late eighth century Dorian Mycenae inaugurated the cult of Agamemnon, and the cult of Menelaus was established at approximately the same time at the Mycenaean citadel of Therapne near Sparta.[37] We have seen that epic geography draws a similar equation between the kingdom of Menelaus and historic Sparta. Some hundred years later, the Spartans made a considerable effort to locate and to bring to their city the bones of Menelaus' son-in-law Orestes, whom they also made a recipient of a hero-cult.[38] For the Spartans, Orestes was again first and foremost king of Amyclae, which by then had become part of their state. But it was the same Orestes who was generally believed to have been the last pre-Dorian ruler of what was to become Dorian Sparta and whose descendants led the Achaeans, whom the Dorians expelled from their lands, to what was to become the district of Achaea in the northern Peloponnese and to Asia Minor.[39] The Spartans' identification with

---

34 de Polignac, 1995: 139.
35 Whitley 1988: 181; cf. Antonaccio 1995: 8.
36 On Dorian hero-cults see also Coldstream 1976: 14 and 1977: 347–8; I. Morris 1988: 756.
37 Snodgrass 1971: 192; Coldstream 1977: 347, 383; Antonaccio 1995: 147–52, 155–66. The eighth-century attribution of the Mycenae cult to Agamemnon was challenged in J. Hall 1995: 601–3.
38 Hdt. 1.67–8; Paus. 3.3.5–7; 8.54.4.
39 Pi. *N.* 11.34–5; Hellan. F 32 Jacoby. In his short summary of the early history of the Achaean *ethnos* Polybius, himself an Achaean, adduces what was in all probability the standard Achaean version: 'Their first king was Tisamenos. Although a son of Orestes, on the Return of the Heraclidae he was driven out of Sparta and then conquered Achaea.' Polyb. 2.41; cf. Str. 8.7.1, p. 383; Paus. 7.1.2. In addition, the founders of the Aeolian colonies in Asia Minor claimed to be descendants of Orestes' son Penthilos, see Str. 9.2.3, p. 401; 9.2.5, p. 403; 13.1.3, p. 582; Paus. 2.18.6; 3.2.1; cf. 7.6.1–2.

Orestes, the ruler of the population that they replaced, clearly indicates the direction in which the updating of the past proceeded at this period.[40] We have seen that the mainstream Greek tradition marginalised the epic traditions that offered alternative versions of the end of Mycenaean Greece. There is reason to suppose that at some later stage a similar thing happened both to the tradition represented in the Cyclic epics, which had also once been credited with Homeric authorship,[41] and to the traditional poetry associated with the name of Hesiod. Take for example the theme of the destruction of the Race of Heroes, prominent in the Hesiodic tradition as well as in the poems of the Cycle. According to these sources, the Heroic Age came to an end in two great wars, the Theban and the Trojan, which were especially designed by Zeus to put an end to the Race of Heroes. Although Homer was also engaged in perpetuating the glorious memory of the Trojan War, the theme of the End of Heroes is conspicuously absent in his poems. As Ruth Scodel put it in an important article, 'In Homer, the continuity of history from the heroes to the poet's contemporaries is complete.'[42] It is clear that Homer's suppressing of the traditional myth of the destruction of the Race of Heroes was again part of a cultural strategy purporting to establish continuity with the heroic past.

Let me emphasise once again that we have no reason to doubt that the Greeks of the Archaic Age were fully aware that the inhabitants of Heroic Age Greece were called 'Achaeans' rather than 'Hellenes' or that the Dorians were not part of the Heroic Age milieu. Yet this awareness did not prevent them from ignoring such facts for the sake of creating, whenever they saw fit, a bluntly anachronistic picture of heroic Greece. As a result, it became possible to represent the Trojan War as a common Hellenic enterprise in which all the elements that formed historic Greece took part. In Anthony Snodgrass' words, 'The great unifying force was the "Heroic Age", in which almost all elements claimed a share, unprejudiced by their later movements.'[43] This picture of prehistoric Greece became the standard if not the only account of their past that the Greeks

---

40 Malkin 1994: 30, interprets the reburial of the bones of Orestes and other cases of the Spartans' appropriation of the pre-Dorian past as indicative of their 'political use of cult and myth vis-à-vis other Greeks'. Yet, the fact that the same practices are also paralleled in the Homeric poems strongly suggests that there was a broad Pan-Hellenic consensus in favour of crediting the Spartans and other Dorians with a Heroic Age past for the sake of their fuller integration into the body of the 'Hellenes'.

41 Cf. Nagy 1990: 72–3.

42 Scodel 1982: 35. Cf. Finkelberg 2004.   43 Snodgrass 1971: 299.

could envisage – so much so that even such a critically minded historian as Thucydides took it for granted that the Trojan War was the first genuinely Pan-Hellenic enterprise in Greek history.[44]

There is thus reason to suppose that, although it is not out of the question that the comprehensive revision of the past in Greek historical memory was to some degree rooted in the spontaneous dynamics of homeostatic transformation, the latter could hardly be the only factor involved. Rather, what is being dealt with is, to use Goody's words again, 'deliberately directed' memory, that is, a self-conscious cultural strategy aiming to establish a new image of the Greek civilisation that replaced Mycenaean Greece. The uniformity and the Pan-Hellenic circulation of the Trojan tradition point in the same direction. This is why, borrowing the expression coined by the Old Testament scholar Nadav Na'aman, I would prefer to characterise the phenomenon under discussion as 'the shaping of collective memory'.[45]

It is difficult to tell what Pan-Hellenic authority could have lain behind the strategy of updating the past in accordance with the contemporary agenda that the Greeks of the Archaic Age adopted. The only thing that can be said with certainty is that the poems of Homer and Hesiod were both a by-product of this strategy and its most effective vehicle. Once it began to be communicated, the new image of the past became universally accepted. There were several reasons for its success. The bearers of this image, epic poets, were in a position to spread it. The recipients were willing to adopt it, both because it answered their own needs and because of the prestige of the bearers. By having thus modified the inherited picture of the past, the new Greek civilisation not only acquired the unity it initially lacked but also established imagined continuity between Greece of the Bronze Age and historic Greece. From now on, the myth of the Heroic Age will provide this civilisation with a foundation upon which the collective identity common to all those who have chosen to identify themselves as 'Hellenes' will be built.[46]

---

44 Thuc. 1.3, quoted above, p. 30.
45 Na'aman 1996: 449–72. See now also Na'aman 2002; cf. Finkelberg 2003: 79–85. It is difficult to avoid the impression that Ephorus of Cyme (fourth century BC), who polemically started his universal history with the events that took place after the Return of the Heraclidae rather than with the standard mythological account of Greek past, was well aware of the strategy in question. See Diod.Sic. 4.1.3.
46 Cf. Smith 1986: 136, on territorial nations: 'In practice, this meant that territorial nations must also be cultural communities. The solidarity of citizenship required a common "civil religion" formed out of shared myths and memories and symbols, and communicated in a standard language through educational institutions. So the territorial nation becomes a mass educational enterprise. Its aim is cultural homogeneity.'

Appendix

The so-called *Testament of Hattusili* is a Hittite–Akkadian bilingual inscription which contains Hattusili's address to the Hittite nobles at the end of his reign. The passage concerning the royal succession runs as follows:[1]

The young Labarna I proclaimed to you (*nu-us-ma-as TUR-la-an la-ba-ar-na-an te-nu-un*), saying 'He shall sit upon the throne'; I called him my son (*DUMU-la-ma-an*), embraced (?) him, and cared for him continually. But he showed himself a youth not fit to be seen . . . The word of the king he has not laid to the heart, but the word of his mother, the serpent, he has laid to heart . . . Enough! He is my son no more . . . Then his mother bellowed like an ox: 'They have torn asunder the womb in my living body! They have ruined him and you will kill him!' Have I, the king, done him any evil? . . . Behold, I have given my son Labarna a house, I have given him [arable land] in plenty, [sheep in] plenty I have given him. Let him now eat and drink. [So long as he is good] he may come up to the city. [But] if he stand forward (?) as [a trouble-maker(?) . . . then he shall not come up, but shall remain [in his house].

Behold, Mursili is now my son . . . [When] three years have elapsed, he shall go on a campaign . . . [The daughter has disgraced my person] and my name . . . A father's word she has cast aside . . . Now she [is banished from the city] . . . In the country [a house has been assig]ned to her; she may eat and drink, [but you] must not do [her harm]. She has done wrong; I will not do [wrong in return]. She [has not called] me father, I will not call her my daughter . . .

The nomenclature of the roles played by participants in the events described in this and related documents would be as follows:

1. the reigning king, Labarna Hattusili I;
2. Hattusili's sister's son, Young Labarna, whom the king proclaimed as his heir, but later disinherited;

---

1 *HAB* Col. II 2–Col. III 24.

3. Hattusili's sister who supported her son against the king;
4. Hattusili's daughter who also acted against the king and was in consequence sent into exile;
5. Hattusili's son or grandson Mursili whom he adopted as his heir (see also above, pp. 76–7);
6. Mursili's sister Harapsili;
7. Hantili, the husband of Harapsili, who was responsible for Mursili's assassination and succeeded him on the throne (see also above, p. 77).

As we see in the passage quoted above, Hattusili's daughter was sent into exile because she rebelled against her father. The same happened to Hattusili's sister's son, who was his original heir. Now, according to the reconstruction proposed in Chapter 4, the king's heir ought to be not only his sister's son but also his son-in-law, because it is only by virtue of his marriage to the queen's daughter that he can become king (see Fig. 4). If this is correct, then Hattusili's nephew and daughter must have been husband and wife, the Labarna and the Tawananna who should have succeeded Hattusili and his queen on the throne.

When we turn to Hattusili's actual successor Mursili, we should keep in mind that not all the terms of kinship used in the early Hittite documents can be taken at face value. It has been observed, for example, that in the most ancient Hittite texts the logogram DUMU ('son') assumes the meaning 'heir' and is actually equivalent to 'sister's son'.[2] It seems that the term 'grandson' applied to Mursili is also far from unambiguous. In this connection, the following passage, again from the *Testament of Hattusili*, deserves to be quoted in full:[3]

My grandfather had proclaimed his son Labarna ([*la-ba-a]r-na-an DUMU-sa-an* . . . *is-ku-na-ah-hi-is*) in Sanahuitta, [but afterwards] his servants and the leading citizens spurned (?) his words and set Papahdilmah on the throne. Now how many years elapsed and [how many of them] have escaped their fate?

It can be seen that the situation described in the phrase 'My grandfather had proclaimed his son (DUMU) Labarna', has much in common with

---

2 Gurney 1973b: 667–8, based on Dovgyalo 1963: 72–83. Cf. Bryce 1983: 118–19: 'As far as we can judge from the early sections of the *Testament*, if a king wished to appoint someone outside his immediate family line, he first of all adopted this person as his son. Hattusili names as his son (DUMU) and successor first his nephew, and subsequently his grandson.' Sürenhagen 1998: 75–94, bases his entire reconstruction of royal succession in the Old Hittite Kingdom on this assumption. On a similar use of kinship terminology in ancient Egypt see Troy 1986: 104–5.
3 *HAB* Col. III 41–5.

what took place later between Hattusili himself and his nephew, the Young Labarna.[4] In both cases, the reigning king publicly proclaims his heir (Labarna, Young Labarna), who is also styled as his son (DUMU). According to the reconstruction of the succession scheme proposed in Chapter 2, the 'son' proclaimed by Hattusili's 'grandfather' as his successor must have been his sister's son and son-in-law.[5] By the same token, Hattusili who succeeded Labarna II and who is styled in this document as Labarna I's 'grandson', must in fact have been the sister's son and son-in-law of Labarna II and the biological son of Labarna I.[6] That is to say, although the king is actually succeeded by his nephew (his sister's son), from the dynastic point of view the latter is regarded as his son, whereas his biological son, who will succeed the king's successor, is regarded as the king's dynastic grandson. In that case, the reference to Mursili as Hattusili's grandson should also be understood in the dynastic rather than the strictly biological sense; on this interpretation, he must have been Hattusili's biological son.[7]

When taken in this perspective, the relations between Hattusili and his two successors appear to be as follows. By proclaiming his sister's son his 'son' and the next Labarna, Hattusili was only following the regular scheme of royal succession according to which the king's legitimate heir, viz. his sister's son, would be his dynastic son.[8] As distinct from this, in disinheriting his dynastic son and legitimate successor Hattusili prompted what was probably the worst constitutional crisis of his reign. As far as I can see, it is in this vein that the following passage in the *Testament* should be interpreted:

[Consider] my son Huzziya. I, the King, [made him master] of (the town of) Tappasanda. But they took him and conspired with him and [oppos]ed [me]: 'Rebel against the person of your father . . .'

---

4 Cf. Macqueen 1959: 184; Bryce 1983: 117.
5 Cf. Bryce 1983: 119.
6 Bryce 1998: 69 n. 20, also places Labarna I in the generation of Hattusili's grandparents; however, as distinct from Bryce, I take him as Hattusili's dynastic rather than his biological grandfather.
7 The view that Mursili was Hattusili's son (favoured, among others, by Goetze 1928/29: 64) finds additional corroboration in such expressions applied to Mursili in the *Testament of Hattusili* as 'The god will appoint only another lion to the place of the lion' (Col. II 37–41) and 'He is My Sun's own offspring' (ibid. 42–7) (tr. T. R. Bryce).
8 See Gamkrelidze and Ivanov 1995: 675, who take Hattusili's words 'let no one bring up his sister's son' (Col. II 2–3) as testifying 'to an ancient system of inheritance preserved by the Hittites until historical times'.

I, [the King], deposed (?) [Huzziya]. And the sons of Hatti [stirred up hostility in Hattusa (itself?)]. Then they took my daughter, and since she had [female]⁹ offspring, they opposed me: '[There is no son for] your father's [throne. A serv] ant will sit upon it. A servant [will become king!']

Thereupon she (my daughter) made Hattusa and the court [disloyal; and the noblemen] and my own courtiers opposed me. [And she incited the whole land to rebellion.]¹⁰

The passage is often interpreted as referring to events that preceded the period when the Young Labarna became Hattusili's dynastic son and legitimate heir.¹¹ However, taking this episode in the perspective of kingship by marriage would allow us to identify the king's 'son' Huzziya as his nephew and legitimate heir and thus to render the entire episode directly relevant to the main subject of the *Testament of Hattusili*. As far as the king can only be succeeded by his son-in-law, and as far as everything points in the direction that Hattusili's legitimate successor stayed married to his daughter even after he had been disinherited by the king, this could only mean that the country remained with no legitimate heir to succeed the reigning king. The only heir who can be taken into account in a situation like this is the future husband of Hattusili's daughter's daughter. This is how, I believe, the accusations that the 'sons of Hatti' levelled at their king should be interpreted. Let us consider them once again: 'Then they took my daughter, and since she had [female] offspring, they opposed me: "[There is no son for] your father's [throne. A serv]ant will sit upon it. A servant [will become king!"].'

In so far as the king is succeeded by his son-in-law, it is perhaps desirable but by no means imperative that the successor should be a member of the king's own family. When no king's relatives fit to marry the woman of royal matriliny are available, anyone will do as her husband and, accordingly, the next king. This is apparently how the threat 'a servant will sit upon the throne' should be interpreted.¹² To avoid this unwelcome consequence, Hattusili proclaimed his son Mursili, obviously

---

9 Usually completed with 'male', but this does not make sense in the context of royal succession through the female line, see further below.
10 *HAB* Col. II 63–74 (tr. T. R. Bryce).
11 See Bryce 1983: 109–10. Cf. Gurney 1973a: 246–7.
12 Cf. Bryce 1983: 116: 'I suggest that . . . the sentence "A servant will become king" simply expresses the concern that the king will choose a successor outside his immediate family line.' The election of Roman kings seems to have followed this latter strategy, cf. Cornell 1995: 143: 'From our sources, then, we can gather that the king was an outsider, sometimes a foreigner, but in any case chosen from outside the patrician aristocracy, and that his election was a complex process involving the previous king, the patricians, the people, and the gods.'

still an adolescent,[13] as his successor on the throne (and, accordingly, as the future husband of the 'offspring' of Hattusili's daughter). On this interpretation, the *Testament of Hattusili* aimed to commemorate what the old king saw as a successful solution of a major constitutional crisis which threatened to undermine not only his own reign but also the entire system of royal succession in the Old Hittite Kingdom.[14]

In proclaiming his biological son and dynastic grandson Mursili his dynastic 'son', Hattusili sought to accelerate the sequence of generations demanded by the pattern of alternate succession by skipping the rule of his nephew who was also his son-in-law. With this in mind let us turn to Mursili's sister Harapsili. On the assumption that Mursili was Hattusili's son, Harapsili must have been the old king's daughter, either the one who, together with her husband, 'the Young Labarna', rebelled against her father and was sent into exile, or one of her sisters.[15] Note that Hantili's being married to Mursili's sister would render him a legitimate claimant for the throne, if not the sole heir to it. In other words, Hantili's assumption of the throne amounted not only to a restoration of the order of succession which had been disrupted as a result of Hattusili's acceleration of the sequence of generations but also to a restoration of the king's daughter Harapsili to her legitimate place within the succession of Tawanannas.

Accordingly, the course of events in the Hittite royal house can be tentatively reconstructed as follows. After Hattusili's sister's son and son-in-law Huzziya had been considered his legitimate heir for some time, he was disinherited by the king who proclaimed his own son Mursili his heir. Both the king's sister, who had been the wife of his predecessor and was the mother of the king's legitimate heir, and the king's daughter, who was already married to the legitimate heir, opposed this measure but failed. Hattusili's son Mursili (probably already dynastically married to his sister's daughter) became king. Some time after this, Mursili was

---

13 See esp. *HAB* Col. II 42–7: 'In three years' time he shall enter the battlefield. In the meantime I shall make him into a [Hero-King]. Yet even before this, [he must be honoured as a king (??)]. He is my Sun's own offspring, and you must honour him as a Hero-King. If you take him to the field [while still a youth], you must bring him back [safe and sound] etc.' (tr. T. R. Bryce).

14 Cf. the colophon which concludes the Akkadian version of the *Testament*: 'Tablet of Tabarna, the Great King, when the Great King Tabarna fell ill in Kussara and named the young Mursili as successor to the throne' (tr. T. R. Bryce).

15 There is no indication that the dynastic reckoning was the same for daughters as for sons. Indeed, since the king always married into the next generation, this kind of reckoning would have involved his styling his wife his 'daughter', which is hardly possible for obvious reasons. In view of this, it seems wise to suppose that the dynastic reckoning of kinship as distinct from the biological one was kept only in the male line.

assassinated, and Hattusili's 'legitimate heir' in the proper sense of the word, that is, the husband of his daughter, assumed the throne.

In a royal decree dated to the end of Hattusili's reign, we read:

> In future let no one speak the Tawananna's name . . . Let no one speak the names of her sons or her daughters. If any of the sons of Hatti speaks them they shall cut his throat and hang him in his gate. If among my subjects anyone speaks their names he shall no longer be my subject. They shall cut his throat and hang him in his gate.[16]

Since the office of Tawananna was retained for life and could only be inherited by the new king's wife on the death of her predecessor (see above, Chapter 4), the royal decree must have been directed against Hattusili's sister.[17] Nevertheless, severe as these measures certainly were, the king's authority was evidently still not enough to deprive his sister of the title of Tawananna.

16 KBo III 27. 5–12 (tr. T. R. Bryce).
17 The same conclusion was reached by Bryce on other grounds, see Bryce 1983: 123; cf. Bryce 1998: 98.

References

Adrados, F. R. (1956) 'Achäisch, Jonisch und Mykenisch', *IF* 62: 240–8.
(1989) 'Etruscan as an IE Anatolian (but not Hittite) language', *JIES* 17: 363–83.
Albright, W. F. and T. O. Lambdin (1970) 'The evidence of language', in *CAH*, 3rd edn. vol. I 1: 122–55.
Aloni-Ronen, N. (1998) 'Marrying Hera: incomplete integration in the making of the Pantheon', in *Les Panthéons des cités: des origines à la Périégèse de Pausanias* (*Kernos*, Suppl. 8), ed. V. Pirenne-Delforge. Liège: 11–22.
Antonaccio, C. M. (1995) *An Archaeology of Ancestors. Tomb Cult and Hero Cult in Early Greece.* Lanham, Maryland.
(2001) 'Ethnicity and colonization', in Malkin (2001): 113–57.
Aravantinos, V., L. Godart and A. Sacconi (1995) 'Sui nuovi testi del palazzo di Cadmo a Tebe', *Rendiconti (Accademia nazionale dei Lincei. Classe di scienze morali, storiche e filologiche)*, s. 9, vol. VI: 829–33.
(2001) *Thèbes. Fouilles de la Cadmée, I: les tablettes en linéaire B de la Odos Pelopidou.* Pisa and Rome.
(2002) *Thèbes. Fouilles de la Cadmée, III: corpus des documents d'archives en linéaire B de Thèbes (1–433).* Pisa and Rome.
Asheri, D. (1977) 'Tyrannie et mariage forcé: essai d'histoire sociale grecque', *Annales ESC* 32.1: 21–48.
(1998) 'The Achaeans and the Heniochi. Reflections on the origins and history of a Greek rhetorical topos', in *The Greek Colonization of the Black Sea Area. Historical Interpretation of Archaeology*, ed. G. R. Tsetskhladze. Stuttgart: 265–85.
(ed.) (1988) *Erodoto. Le storie. Libro I.* Fondazione Lorenzo Valla.
Atchity, K. and E. J. W. Barber (1987) 'Greek princes and Aegean princesses: the role of women in the Homeric poems', in *Critical Essays on Homer*, ed. K. Atchity with R. Hogart and D. Price. Boston: 15–36.
Bader, F. (ed.) (1994) *Langues indo-européennes.* Paris.
Barako, T. (2003) 'How did the Philistines get to Canaan? One: by sea . . .', *BAR*, March/April 2003: 27–33 and 64.
Barber, E. J. W. (1991) *Prehistoric Textiles. The Development of Cloth in the Neolithic and Bronze Ages with Special Reference to the Aegean.* Princeton.

(1998) 'Aegean ornaments and designs in Egypt', in Cline and Harris-Cline (1998): 13–16.

(1999) *The Mummies of Ürümchi*. London.

(2001) 'The clues in the clothes: some independent evidence for the movements of families', in Drews (2001): 1–14.

Barnett, R. D. (1975) 'The Sea Peoples', in *CAH*, 3rd edn. vol. II 2: 359–78.

Bartonek, A. (1972) *Classification of the West Greek Dialects in the Time about 360 BC*. Amsterdam and Prague.

Bennet, J. (1997) 'Homer and the Bronze Age', in Morris and Powell (1997): 511–33.

Bin-Nun, S. R. (1975) *The Tawananna in the Hittite Kingdom*. Heidelberg.

Birnbaum, H. and J. Puhvel (eds.) (1966) *Ancient Indo-European Dialects. Proceedings of the Conference on Indo-European Linguistics Held at the University of California, Los Angeles, April 25–27, 1963*. Berkeley and Los Angeles.

Blegen, C. W. (1975) 'The expansion of the Mycenaean civilization', in *CAH*, 3rd edn. vol. II 2: 165–87.

Blome, P. (1991) 'Die dunklen Jahrhunderte – aufgehellt', in Latacz (1991): 45–60.

Bloomfield, L. (1935) *Language*. London.

Bremer, J. (1983) 'The importance of the maternal uncle and grandfather in Archaic and Classical Greece and Early Byzantium', *ZPE* 50: 173–86.

Briquel, D. (1994) 'Étrusque et indo-européen', in Bader (1994), 319–30.

Brixhe, C. (1976) *Le Dialecte grec de Pamphylie*. Paris.

Broadbent, M. (1968) *Studies in Greek Genealogy*. Leiden.

Brown, E. L. (1992/93) 'The Linear A signary: tokens of Luvian dialect in Bronze Age Crete', *Minos* 27/28: 25–54.

Bryce, T. R. (1983) *The Major Historical Texts of Early Hittite History*. Brisbane.

(1998) *The Kingdom of the Hittites*. Oxford.

(2002) *Life and Society in the Hittite World*. Oxford.

Buck, C. D. (1907) 'The interrelations of the Greek dialects', *CPh* 2: 241–76.

(1926) 'The language situation in and about Greece in the second millennium BC', *CPh* 21: 1–26.

(1955) *The Greek Dialects*. Chicago.

Bunimovitz, S. (1998) 'Sea Peoples in Cyprus and Israel: a comparative study of immigration processes', in Gitin, Mazar and Stern (1998): 103–13.

Burkert, W. (1983) *Homo Necans. The Anthropology of Ancient Greek Sacrificial Ritual and Myth*. Tr. P. Bing. Berkeley and Los Angeles.

(1985) *Greek Religion*. Tr. J. Raffan. Cambridge, Mass.

(1992) *The Orientalizing Revolution. Near Eastern Influence on Greek Culture in the Early Archaic Age*. Tr. M. E. Pinder and W. Burkert. Cambridge, Mass.

Carruba, O. (1977) 'L'origine degli etruschi: il problema della lingua', in *Paleontologia linguistica. Atti del VI convegno internazionale di linguisti*. Brescia: 137–53.

(1995) 'L'arrivo dei greci, le migrazioni indoeuropee e il "ritorno" degli Eraclidi', *Athenaeum* 83: 5–44.

Cartledge, P. (1979) *Sparta and Lakonia. A Regional History 1300–362 BC.* London.

Caskey, J. L. (1973) 'Greece and the Aegean islands in the Middle Bronze Age', in *CAH*, 3rd edn. vol. II 1: 117–40.

Cavalli-Sforza, L. L., P. Menozzi and A. Piazza (1996) *The History and Geography of Human Genes.* Abridged paperback edition. Princeton.

Chadwick, H. M. (1912) *The Heroic Age.* Cambridge.

Chadwick, H. M. and N. K. Chadwick (1932) *The Growth of Literature*, vol. I. Cambridge.

(1940) *The Growth of Literature*, vol. III. Cambridge.

Chadwick, J. (1956) 'The Greek dialects and Greek prehistory', *Greece and Rome* 3: 38–50, reprinted in Kirk (1964), 106–18.

(1967) *The Decipherment of Linear B.* 2nd edn. Cambridge.

(1975) 'The prehistory of the Greek language', in *CAH*, 3rd edn. vol. II 2: 805–19.

Chadwick, N. K. and V. Zhirmunsky (1969) *Oral Epics of Central Asia.* Cambridge.

Chambers, J. K. and P. Trudgill (1998) *Dialectology*, 2nd edn. Cambridge.

Chantraine, P. (1958) *Grammaire homérique*, vol. I. Paris.

Cline, E. H. (1994) *Sailing the Wine-Dark Sea. International Trade and the Late Bronze Age Aegean.* Oxford.

(1995) 'Tinker, tailor, soldier, sailor: Minoans and Mycenaeans abroad', in Laffineur and Niemeier (1995): 265–87.

Cline, E. H. and D. Harris-Cline (eds.) (1998) *The Aegean and the Orient in the Second Millennium. Proceedings of the 50th Anniversary Symposium. Cincinnati, 18–20 April 1997 (Aegaeum 18).* Liège.

Cohen R. and J. Middleton (eds.) (1970) *From Tribe to Nation in Africa. Studies in Incorporation Processes.* Scranton, Pa.

Coldstream, J. N. (1976) 'Hero-cults in the Age of Homer', *JHS* 96: 8–17.

(1977) *Geometric Greece.* Cambridge.

(1993) 'Mixed marriages at the frontiers of the early Greek world', *OJA* 12: 89–107.

Coleman, J. E. (2000) 'An archaeological scenario for the "coming of the Greeks" ca. 3200 BC', *JIES* 28: 101–53.

Coleman, R. (1963) 'The dialect geography of Ancient Greece', *TPhS* 58–126.

Cornell, T. J. (1995) *The Beginnings of Rome. Italy and Rome from the Bronze Age to the Punic Wars (c.1000–264 BC).* London and New York.

Cowgill, W. C. (1966) 'Ancient Greek dialectology in the light of Mycenaean', in Birnbaum and Puhvel (1966): 77–96.

Crossland, R. A. (1971) 'Immigrants from the North', in *CAH*, 3rd edn. vol. I 2: 824–76.

(1982) 'Linguistic problems of the Balkan area in the Late Prehistoric and Early Classical periods', in *CAH*, 2nd edn. vol. III 1: 834–49.

Davis, S. (1967) *The Decipherment of the Minoan Linear A and Pictographic Scripts.* Johannesburg.

Demsky, A. (1998) 'Discovering a Goddess', *BAR* 24 (5): 53–8.

Desborough, V. R. d'A. (1964) *The Last Mycenaeans and their Successors. An Archaeological Survey c.1200–c.1000 BC.* Oxford.

Dickinson, O. T. (1994) *The Aegean Bronze Age.* Cambridge.

Dothan, M. (1989) 'Archaeological evidence for movements of the early "Sea Peoples" in Canaan', *AASOR* 49: 59–70.

Dothan, T. (1982) *The Philistines and their Material Culture.* New Haven.

Dothan T. and M. Dothan (1992) *People of the Sea. The Search for the Philistines.* New York.

Dougherty, C. (1993) *The Poetics of Colonization. From City to Text in Archaic Greece.* New York and Oxford.

Doumas, C. G. (1998) 'Aegeans in the Levant: myth and reality', in Gitin, Mazar and Stern (1998): 129–37.

Dovgyalo, G. I. (1963) 'O perekhode k nasledovaniyu tsarskoi vlasti po otsovsko-pravovomu prinsipu (po materialam khettskikh klinopisnykh istochnikov XVII–XIII vv. do n.e.) ['On the transition to accession to kingship by patrilineal law (based on Hittite cuneiform sources of the seventeenth to thirteenth centuries BC)'], *Sovetskaya Ethnographiya* 6: 72–83.

Dow, S. (1973) 'Literacy in Minoan and Mycenaean lands', in *CAH*, 3d edn. vol. II 1: 582–608.

Dowden, K. (1992) *The Uses of Greek Mythology.* London and New York.
(1996) 'Homer's sense of text', *JHS* 116: 47–61.

Drews, R. (1983) *BASILEUS. The Evidence for Kingship in Geometric Greece.* New Haven and London.
(1988) *The Coming of the Greeks. Indo-European Conquests in the Aegean and the Near East.* Princeton.
(1993a) *The End of the Bronze Age. Changes in Warfare and the Catastrophe ca.1200 BC.* Princeton.
(1993b) 'Myths of Midas and the Phrygian migration from Europe', *Klio* 75: 9–26.
(1997) 'PIE speakers and PA speakers', *JIES* 25 :153–77.
(2001) 'Greater Anatolia: Proto-Anatolian, Proto-Indo-Hittite, and beyond', in Drews (2001): 248–83.
(ed.) (2001) *Greater Anatolia and the Indo-Hittite Language Family. Papers presented at a Colloquium Hosted by the University of Richmond, March 18–19, 2000.* Washington, DC.

Duhoux, Y. (1983) *Introduction aux dialectes grecs anciens.* Louvain-la-Neuve.
(1988) 'Les Éléments grecs non doriens du Crétois et la situation dialectale grecque au IIe millénaire', *CS* 1: 57–72.
(1997) 'Les Révélations des nouvelles tablettes en linéaire B de Thèbes', in *Seminaire de Delphes (4–16 août 1997). Exposés, Supplément au Bulletin d'information de la Fédération des Professeurs de grec et le latin* 109 (November–December 1997): 16–19.

(1998) 'Pre-Hellenic language(s) of Crete', *JIES* 26: 1–39.

Duhoux, Y., T. G. Palaima and J. Bennet (eds.) 1989. *Problems in Decipherment.* Louvain-la-Neuve.

Dunbabin, T. J. (1948). *The Western Greeks.* Oxford.

Easton, D. (1985) 'Has the Trojan War been found?' *Antiquity* 59: 188–96.

Eshet, Y. (1996) 'Micropalaeontological examination of a chalky bowl from Lachish', *Tel Aviv* 23: 208.

Etter, A. (ed.) (1986) *o-o-pe-ro-si. Festschrift für Ernst Risch zum 75. Geburtstag.* Berlin and New York.

Evans, A. J. (1909) *Scripta Minoa. The Written Documents of Minoan Crete*, vol. I. Oxford.

Farnell, L. R. (1921) *Greek Hero Cults.* Oxford.

Finkelberg, M. (1988) 'Ajax's entry in the Hesiodic *Catalogue of Women*', *CQ* 38: 31–41.

(1990/91) 'Minoan inscriptions on libation vessels', *Minos* 25/26: 43–85.

(1991) 'Royal succession in Heroic Greece', *CQ* 41: 303–16.

(1994) 'The dialect continuum of ancient Greek', *HSCPh* 96: 1–36.

(1997a) 'Anatolian languages and Indo-European migrations to Greece', *CW* 91: 3–20.

(1997b) 'The Brother's Son of Tawananna and others: the rule of dynastic succession in the Old Hittite Kingdom', *Cosmos* 13: 127–41.

(1998a) 'Bronze Age writing: contacts between East and West', in Cline and Harris-Cline (1998): 265–72.

(1998b) '*Timē* and *Aretē* in Homer', *CQ* 48: 15–28.

(1998c) *The Birth of Literary Fiction in Ancient Greece.* Oxford.

(1999) 'Greek epic tradition on population movements in Bronze Age Greece', in Laffineur (1999): 31–6.

(2001a) 'The language of Linear A – Greek, Semitic, or Anatolian?', in Drews (2001): 81–105.

(2001b) 'Two kinds of representation in Greek religious art', in *Representation in Religion. Studies in Honor of Moshe Barash*, eds. J. Assmann and A. L. Baumgarten. Leiden: 27–41.

(2002) 'Homer and the bottomless well of the past'. A review article of Malkin (1998). *SCI* 21: 243–50.

(2003) 'Homer as a foundation text', in *Homer, the Bible, and Beyond. Literary and Religious Canons in the Ancient Word*, eds. M. Finkelberg and G. G. Stroumsa. Leiden: 75–96.

(2004) 'The end of the Heroic Age in Homer, Hesiod and the Cycle'. *Ordia Prima* 3: 11–24.

Finkelberg, M., A. Uchitel and D. Ussishkin (1996) 'A Linear A inscription from Tel Lachish (LACH Za 1)', *Tel Aviv* 23: 195–207, reprinted (with revisions) in Ussishkin (2004): 1629–1638.

Finkelstein, I. (2002) 'The Philistines in the Bible: a late-monarchic perspective', *JSOT* 27: 131–67.

Finley, M. I. (1979) *The World of Odysseus*, 2nd edn. Harmondsworth.

Finnegan, R. (1977) *Oral Poetry. Its Nature, Significance and Social Context.* Cambridge.

Fol, A. (2000) 'A Linear A text on a clay reel from Drama, South-East Bulgaria?' *Praehistorische Zeitschrift* 75: 56–62.

Fontenrose, J. (1951) 'White Goddess and Syrian Goddess', *University of California Publications in Semitic Philology* 11: 125–48.

Fowler, R. (1998) 'Genealogical thinking, Hesiod's *Catalogue*, and the creation of the Hellenes', *PCPhS* 44: 1–19.

Fradenburg, L. O. (ed.) (1992) *Women and Sovereignty.* Edinburgh.

Franken, H. J. (1964) 'Clay tablets from Deir 'Alla, Jordan', *Vetus Testamentum* 14: 377–9.

Frazer, J. G. (1905) *Lectures on the Early History of the Kingship.* London.
   (1922) *The Golden Bough. A Study in Magic and Religion.* Abridged edition. London.
   (ed.) (1921) *Apollodorus. The Library* (2 vols.). Cambridge, Mass.

Frei, P. and C. Marek (1997) 'Die Karisch-griechische Bilingue von Kaunos. Eine zweisprachliche Staatsurkunde des 4. Jhs. v. Chr.', *Kadmos* 36: 1–89.

Gamkrelidze, Th. V. and V. V. Ivanov (1995) *Indo-European and the Indoeuropeans* vol I. Berlin and New York.

García-Ramón, J. L. (1975) *Les Origines post-mycéniennes du groupe dialectal éolien.* Salamanca.

Gates, C. (1995) 'Defining boundaries of a state: the Mycenaeans and their Anatolian frontier', in Laffineur and Niemeier (1995) 289–97.

Geiger, J. (2002) 'The Hasmoneans and Hellenistic succession', *Journal of Jewish Studies* 53: 1–17.

Gernet, L. (1921) 'Sur l'épiclérat', *REG* 34: 337–79.
   (1981) *The Anthropology of Ancient Greece.* Tr. J. Hamilton and B. Nagy. Baltimore and London.

Gimbutas, M. (1991) *The Civilization of the Goddess. The World of Old Europe.* San Francisco.

Gitin, S., T. Dothan and J. Naveh (1997) 'A royal dedicatory inscription from Ekron', *IEJ* 47: 1–16.

Gitin, S., A. Mazar and E. Stern (eds.) (1998) *Mediterranean Peoples in Transition. Thirteenth to Early Tenth Centuries* BCE. Jerusalem.

Godart, L. (1994) 'Les Écritures crétoises et le bassin méditerranéen', *CRAI* (1994): 707–73.

Goetze, A. (1928–29) 'Die historische Einleitung des Aleppo-Vertrages', *Mitteilungen der Altorientalischen Gesellschaft* 4: 59–66.
   (1957a) *Kleinasien*, 2nd edn. Munich.
   (1957b) 'On the chronology of the second millennium BC', *JCS* 11: 53–73.

Goody, J. (1970) 'Marriage policy and incorporation in northern Ghana', in Cohen and Middleton (1970): 114–49.
   (2000) *The Power of the Written Tradition.* Washington DC and London.

Graff, F. (1991) *Griechische Mythologie. Eine Einführung.* Munich and Zürich.

Graham, A. J. (1964) *Colony and Mother City in Ancient Greece.* Manchester.

Gray, D. (1947) 'Homeric epithets for things', *CQ* 41: 109–21, reprinted in Kirk (1964), 55–67.

Gray, R. and Q. Atkinson (2003) 'Language-tree divergence times support the Anatolian theory of Indo-European origin', *Nature* 426 (27 November): 435–8.

Gschnitzer, F. (1991) 'Zur homerischen Staats- und Gesellschaftsordnung: Grundcharacter und geschichtliche Stellung', in Latacz (1991): 182–204.

Gurney, O. R. (1954) *The Hittites*, 2nd edn. Harmondsworth.

(1973a) 'Anatolia *c*.1750–1600 BC', in *CAH*, 3rd edn. vol. II 1: 228–55.

(1973b) 'Anatolia *c*.1600–1380 BC', in *CAH*, 3rd edn. vol. II 1: 659–83.

Hainsworth, J. B. (1982) 'The Greek language and the historical dialects', in *CAH*, 2nd edn. vol. III 1: 850–65.

(1984) 'The fallibility of an oral heroic tradition', in *The Trojan War: its Historicity and Context*, ed. L. Foxhall and J. K. Davies. Bristol: 111–35.

Hajnal, I. (1987) 'Zur Sprache der ältesten kretischen Dialektinschriften', *IF* 92: 58–84.

(1988) 'Zur Sprache der ältesten kretischen Dialektinschriften', *IF* 93: 62–87.

Haley, J. and C. W. Blegen (1928) 'The coming of the Greeks', *AJA* 32: 141–54.

Hall, E. (1989) *Inventing the Barbarian. Greek Self-Definition through Tragedy*. Oxford.

Hall, J. M. (1995) 'How Argive was the "Argive" Heraion? The political and cultic geography of the Argive plain, 900–400 BC', *AJA* 99: 577–613.

(1997) *Ethnic Identity in Greek Antiquity*. Cambridge.

(2001) 'Contested ethnicities: perceptions of Macedonia within evolving definitions of Greek identity', in Malkin (2001): 159–86.

(2002) *Hellenicity: Between Ethnicity and Culture*. Chicago.

Hammond, N. G. (1975) 'The end of the Mycenaean civilization and the Dark Age: the literary tradition for the migrations', in *CAH*, 3rd edn. vol. II 2: 678–712.

(1982) 'The Peloponnese', in *CAH*, 2nd edn. vol. III 1: 696–744.

Hankey, V. (1982) 'Pottery and people of the Mycenaean III C period in the Levant', in *Archéologie au Levant. Recueil à la mémoire de Roger Saidah*, Lyons: 167–71.

Harrison, J. E. (1903) *Prolegomena to the Study of Greek Religion*. Cambridge.

Hawkins, J. D. (1979) 'Some historical problems of the Hieroglyphic Luwian inscriptions', *AS* 29: 153–67.

(1982) 'The Neo-Hittite states in Syria and Anatolia', in *CAH*, 2nd edn. vol. III 1: 372–441.

Helms, M. W. (1998) *Access to Origins. Affines, Ancestors and Aristocrats*. Austin.

Heltzer, M. and E. Lipinski (eds.) (1988) *Society and Economy in the Eastern Mediterranean (c.1500–1000 BC). Proceedings of the International Symposium held at the University of Haifa from the 28th of April to the 2nd of May 1985*. Louvain.

Henige, D. P. (1974) *The Chronology of Oral Tradition. Quest for a Chimera*. Oxford.

Herbert, M. (1992) 'Goddess and king: the sacred marriage in early Ireland', in Fradenburg (1992): 264–75.

Heubeck, A. (1961) *Praegraeca. Sprachliche Untersuchungen zum vorgriechisch-indogermanischen Substrat.* Erlangen.

Hiller, S. (1983) 'Possible historical reasons for the rediscovery of the Mycenaean past in the Age of Homer', in *The Greek Renaissance of the Eighth Century BC. Tradition and Innovation*, ed. R. Hägg. Stockholm: 9–15.

Hinz, W. (1973) 'Persia c.1800–1550 BC', in *CAH*, 3rd edn. vol. II 1: 256–88.

Hockett, F. (1958) *A Course in Modern Linguistics.* New York.

Hoenigwald, H. M. (1966) 'Criteria for the subgrouping of languages', in Birnbaum and Puhvel (1966): 1–12.

Hoffmann, I. (1984) *Der Erlass Telepinus.* Heidelberg.

Hood, S. (1995) 'The Bronze Age context of Homer', in *The Ages of Homer. A Tribute to Emily Townsend Vermeule*, ed. J. B. Carter and S. P. Morris. Austin: 25–32.

Hooker, J. T. (1979) *The Origin of the Linear B Script.* Salamanca.

Houwink ten Cate, Ph. H. J. (1965) *The Luwian Population Groups of Lycia and Cilicia Aspera during the Hellenistic Period.* Leiden.

Humphreys, S. C. (1974) 'The Nothoi of Kynosarges', *JHS* 94: 88–95.

Huxley, G. L. (1962) *Early Sparta.* London.

Iacovou, M. (1998) 'Philistia and Cyprus in the eleventh century: from a similar prehistory to a diverse protohistory', in Gitin, Mazar and Stern (1998): 332–44.

Imparati, F. and C. Saporetti (1965) 'L'autobiografia di Hattusili I', *Studi Classici e Orientali* 14: 44–85.

Isaac, B. 2004. *The Invention of Racism in Classical Antiquity.* Princeton.

Jameson, M. H. and I. Malkin (1998) 'Latinos and the Greeks', *Athenaeum* 86: 477–85.

Janko, R. (1982a) *Homer, Hesiod, and the Hymns : Diachronic Development in Epic Diction.* Cambridge.

(1982b) 'A stone object inscribed in Linear A from Ayos Stephanos, Laconia', *Kadmos* 21: 97–100.

Killebrew, A. E. (1998) 'Ceramic typology of Late Bronze II and Iron I assemblages from Tel Miqne-Ekron: the transition from Canaanite to Philistine culture', in Gitin, Mazar and Stern (1998): 379–405.

(2000) 'Aegean-style early Philistine pottery in Canaan during the Iron I Age: a stylistic analysis of Mycenaean IIIC:1b pottery and its associated wares', in Oren (2000) 233–53.

Kirk, G. S. (ed.) (1964) *The Language and Background of Homer.* Cambridge.

(1985) *The Iliad. A Commentary* vol. I. Cambridge.

(1990) *The Iliad: A Commentary* vol. II. Cambridge.

Konstan, D. (2001) '*To Hellenikon ethnos*: ethnicity and the construction of ancient Greek identity', in Malkin (2001) 29–50.

Kretschmer, P. (1896) *Einleitung in die Geschichte der griechischen Sprache.* Göttingen.

(1925) 'Die protoindogermanische Schicht', *Glotta* 14: 300–19.

(1940) 'Die vorgriechischen Sprach- und Volksschichten', *Glotta* 28: 231–79.

(1943) 'Die vorgriechischen Sprach- und Volksschichten', *Glotta* 30: 84–218.

Kugel, J. L. (1997) *The Bible as It Was*. Cambridge, Mass.

Laffineur, R. (ed.) (1999) *POLEMOS. Warfare in the Aegean Bronze Age. Proceedings of the 7th International Aegean Conference (Aegaeum* 19). Liège.

Laffineur, R. and L. Basch (eds.) (1991) *THALASSA. L'Égee préhistorique et la mer. Actes de la troisième Rencontre Égéenne Internationale de l'Université de Liège. (Aegaeum* 7). Liège.

Laffineur, R. and W.-D. Niemeier (eds.) (1995) *POLITEIA. Society and State in the Aegean Bronze Age. Proceedings of the 5th International Aegean Conference (Aegaeum* 12). Liège.

Laroche, E. (1957) 'Notes de toponyme anatolienne', in MNHMHΣ XAPIN. *Gedenkschrift Paul Kretschmer*, vol. II, ed. H. Kronasser. Vienna: 1–7.

(1961) 'Études de toponymie anatolienne', *RHA* 19: 57–98.

Latacz, J. (ed.) (1991) *Zweihundert Jahre Homer-Forschung*. Stuttgart and Leipzig.

Lefèvre, F. (1998) *L'Amphictionie pyléo-delphique. Histoire et institutions*. Paris.

Lejeune, M. (1972) *Phonétique historique du mycénien et du grec ancien*. Paris.

Lemos, I. S. (2002) *The Protogeometric Aegean. The Archaeology of the Late Eleventh and Tenth Centuries* BC. Oxford.

Lorimer, H. L. (1950) *Homer and the Monuments*. London.

Lurje, S. (1959) 'Burgfrieden in Sillyon', *Klio* 37: 7–20.

Lyle, E. (1990) *Archaic Cosmos*. Edinburgh.

(1992) 'A line of queens as the pivot of a cosmogony', in Fradenburg (1992): 276–89.

(1997) 'Age grades, age classes and alternate succession', *Emania* 16: 63–71.

Machinist, P. (2000) 'Biblical traditions: the Philistines and Israelite history', in Oren (2000): 53–83.

Macqueen, J. G. (1959) 'Hattian mythology and Hittite monarchy', *AS* 9: 171–88.

(1986) *The Hittites*, revised edition. London.

Malkin, I. (1987) *Religion and Colonization in Ancient Greece*. Leiden.

(1994) *Myth and Territory in the Spartan Mediterranean*. Cambridge.

(1998) *The Returns of Odysseus. Colonization and Ethnicity*. Berkeley.

(2001) 'Introduction', in Malkin (1991). 1–28.

(2003) *Ethnicity and Identity in Ancient Greece*. Tel Aviv [Hebrew].

(ed.) (2001) *Ancient Perceptions of Greek Ethnicity*. Cambridge, Mass.

Mallory, J. P. (1989) *In Search of the Indo-Europeans. Language, Archaeology and Myth*. London.

Matsas, D. (1991) 'Samothrace and the northeastern Aegean: the Minoan connection', *ST* 1: 159–79.

(1995) 'Minoan long-distance trade: a view from the northern Aegean', in Laffineur and Niemeier (1995): 235–47.

Mazar, A. (1985) 'The emergence of the Philistine material culture', *IEJ* 35: 95–107.

(1990) *Archaeology of the Land of the Bible. 10,000–586 BCE*. New York and London.

(2000) 'The temples and cult of the Philistines', in Oren (2000): 213–32.

McInerney, J. (1999) *The Fold of Parnassos. Land and Ethnicity in Ancient Phocis.* Austin.

(2001) 'Ethnos and ethnicity in early Greece', in Malkin (2001): 51–73.

Mee, C. (1998) 'Anatolia and the Aegean in the Late Bronze Age', in Cline and Harris-Cline (1998): 137–45.

Meillet, A. (1908) 'La Place du pamphylien parmi les dialectes grecs', *REG* 21: 413–25.

(1930) *Aperçu d'une histoire de la langue greque,* 6th edn. Paris.

Mellaart, J. (1958) 'The end of the Early Bronze Age in Anatolia and the Aegean', *AJA* 62: 1–31.

Mellink, M. (1991) 'The native kingdoms of Anatolia', in *CAH,* 2nd edn. vol. III 2: 619–65.

Merkelbach, R. and M. L. West (1967) *Fragmenta Hesiodea.* Oxford.

Michalidou, A. (1992/93) '"Ostrakon" with Linear A Script from Akrotiri (Thera). A non-bureaucratic activity?' *Minos* 27/28: 7–24.

Mitford, T. B. and O. Masson (1982) 'The Cypriot syllabary', in *CAH,* 2nd edn. vol. III 3: 71–82.

Morgan, C. (2001) 'Ethne, ethnicity, and early Greek states, ca. 1200–480 BC: an archaeological perspective', in Malkin (2001): 75–112.

Morpurgo Davies, A. (1988) 'Mycenaean and Greek language', in Morpurgo Davies and Duhoux (1988): 75–125.

Morpurgo Davies, A. and Y. Duhoux (1988) *Linear B: A 1984 Survey.* Louvain-la-Neuve.

Morris, I. (1986) 'The use and abuse of Homer', *CA* 5: 81–138.

(1988) 'Tomb cult and the "Greek renaissance": the past in the present in the 8th century BC', *Antiquity* 62: 750–61.

Morris, I. and B. Powell (1997) *A New Companion to Homer.* Leiden.

Morris, S. P. (1992) *Daidalos and the Origins of Greek Art.* Princeton.

Moscati, S., A. Spitaler, E. Ullendorff and W. von Soden (1980) *An Introduction to the Comparative Grammar of the Semitic Languages.* Wiesbaden.

Na'aman, N. (1996) 'Historiography, the shaping of collective memory and the creation of historical consciousness in the people of Israel at the end of the First Temple Period', *Ziyon* 60: 449–72 [Hebrew].

(2002) *The Past that Shapes the Present. The Creation of Biblical Historiography in the Late First Temple Period and After the Downfall.* Jerusalem [Hebrew].

Nagy, G. (1979) *The Best of the Achaeans: Concepts of the Hero in Archaic Greek Poetry.* Baltimore.

(1990) *Pindar's Homer. The Lyric Possession of an Epic Past.* Baltimore.

Naveh, J. (1987) *Early History of the Alphabet,* 2nd edn. Jerusalem

(1998) 'Achish-Ikausu in the light of the Ekron dedication', *BASOR* 310: 35–7.

Neumann, G. 1979. 'Phryger: Sprache', *Der Kleine Pauly,* vol. IV (1979): col. 824–5.

Niemeier, W.-D. (1991) 'Minoan artisans travelling overseas: the Alalakh frescoes and the painted plaster floor at Tel Kabri (Western Galilee)', in Laffineur and Basch (1991): 189–201.

(1996) 'A Linear A inscription from Miletus (MIL Zb 1)', *Kadmos* 35: 87–99.

(1998) 'The Mycenaeans in Western Anatolia and the problem of the origins of the Sea Peoples', in Gitin, Mazar and Stern (1998): 17–65.

Niemeier, W.-D. and B. Niemeier (1998) 'Minoan frescoes in the Eastern Mediterranean', in Cline and Harris-Cline (1998): 69–98.

Nilsson, M. P. (1932) *The Mycenaean Origin of Greek Mythology*. Berkeley.

(1933) *Homer and Mycenae*. London.

O'Brien, J. V. (1993) *The Transformation of Hera. A Study of Ritual, Hero, and the Goddess in the 'Iliad'*. Lanham, Maryland.

Ogden, D. (1996) *Greek Bastardy in the Classical and Hellenistic Periods*. Oxford.

(1997) *The Crooked Kings of Ancient Greece*. London.

Olivier, J.-P. (1988) 'Tirynthian graffiti', *AA* 17 (1988), 253–68.

Oren, E. D. (ed.) (2000) *The Sea Peoples and Their World. A Reassessment*. Philadelphia.

Oren, E., J.-P. Olivier, Y. Goren, Ph. P. Betancourt, G. H. Myer and J. Yellin (1996) 'A Minoan graffito from Tel Haror (Negev, Israel)', *CS* 5: 91–117.

Owens, G. A. (1996) 'Evidence for the Minoan language (1): the Minoan libation formula', *CS* 5: 163: 206.

Page, D. (1959) *History and the Homeric Iliad*. Berkeley.

Palaima, T. G. (1982) 'Linear A in the Cyclades: the trade and travel of a script', *Temple University* 7: 15–18.

(1988) 'The development of the Mycenaean writing system', in *Texts, Tablets and Scribes*, ed. J.-P. Olivier and T. G. Palaima. Salamanca: 269–342.

(1989) 'Cypro-Minoan scripts: problems of historical context', in Duhoux, Palaima and Bennet (1989): 121–87.

Pallottino, M. (1955) *The Etruscans*. Tr. by J. Cremona from the 3rd Italian edn. Harmondsworth.

Palmer, L. (1962) 'The language of Homer', in Wace and Stubbings (1962): 88–94.

(1965) *Mycenaeans and Minoans. Aegean Prehistory in the Light of the Linear B Tablets*, 2nd edn. London.

(1980) *The Greek Language*. London.

Parker, R. (1996) *Athenian Religion. A History*. Oxford.

Patterson, C. (1981) *Pericles' Citizenship Law of 451–50 BC*. New York.

Pembroke, S. (1965) 'Last of the matriarchs', *JESHO* 8: 217–47.

Peters, M. (1986) 'Zur Frage einer "achäischen" Phase des griechischen Epos', in Etter (1986): 303–19.

Polignac, François de (1995) *Cults, Territory, and the Origins of the Greek City-State*. Tr. by J. Lloyd. Chicago.

Porzig, W. (1954) 'Sprachgeographische Untersuchungen zu den altgriechischen Dialekten', *IF* 61: 147–69.

Puhvel, J. (1989) 'Hittite regal titles: Hattic or Indo-European?', *JIES* 17: 351–61.

Raaflaub, K. A. (1991) 'Homer und die Geschichte des 8. Jhs. v. Chr.', in Latacz (1991): 205–56.

Ramsay, W. M. (1928) *Asianic Elements in Greek Civilization*. London.

Ray, J. D. (1990) 'An outline of Carian grammar', *Kadmos* 29: 54–83.
Renfrew, C. (1987) *Archaeology and Language. The Puzzle of Indo-European Origins.* London.
(1998) 'Word of Minos: the Minoan contribution to Mycenaean Greek and the linguistic geography of the Bronze Age Aegean', *CAJ* 8: 239–64.
(1999) 'Time depth, convergence theory, and innovation in Proto-Indo-European "Old Europe" as a PIE linguistic area', *JIES* 27: 257–92.
(2001) 'The Anatolian origins of Proto-Indoeuropean and the autochthony of the Hittites', in Drews (2001): 36–63.
Renfrew, C. A. and W. C. Brice (1977) 'A Linear A tablet fragment from Phylakopi in Melos', *Kadmos* 16: 111–19.
Risch, E. (1949) 'Altgriechische Dialektographie?', *MH* 6: 19–28.
(1955) 'Die Gliederung der griechischen Dialekte in neuer Sicht', *MH* 12: 61–76, reprinted in Kirk (1964), 90–105.
Rohde, E. (1921) *Psyche. Seelencult und Unsterblichkeitsglaube der Griechen*, 7th edn. 1921.
Rose, H. J. (1958) *A Handbook of Greek Mythology*, 6th edn. London.
Roux, G. (1979) *L'Amphictionie, Delphes et le temple d'Apollon au IVᵉ siècle.* Lyons.
Ruijgh, C. J. (1958) 'Les Datives pluriels dans les dialectes grecs et la position du mycénien', *Mnemosyne* 11: 97–116.
(1961) 'Le Traitement des sonantes voyelles dans les dialectes grecs et la position du mycénien', *Mnemosyne* 14: 206–16.
(1967) *Études sur la grammaire et le vocabulaire du grec mycénien.* Amsterdam.
(1988) 'Le Mycénien et Homère', in Morpurgo Davies and Duhoux (1988): 143–90.
(1996) 'Sur la position dialectale du mycénien', in *Atti e Memorie del Secondo Congresso Internazionale di Micenologia*, ed. E. De Miro, L. Godart and A. Sacconi, vol. I. Rome: 115–24.
Rutter, J. (1996) (revised 1997, 1998, 1999, 2000) *The Prehistoric Archaeology of the Aegean.* projectsx.dartmouth.edu/history/bronze_age/.
Sandars, N. K. (1985) *The Sea Peoples. Warriors of the Ancient Mediterranean.* London.
Schachermeyr, F. (1967) *Ägäis und Orient. Die überseeischen Kulturbeziehungen von Kreta und Mykenai mit Ägypten, der Levante und Kleinasien unter besonderer Berücksichtigung der 2. Jahrtausends v. Chr.* Graz and Vienna.
Schäfer-Lichtenberger, C. (2000) 'The goddess of Ekron and the religious-cultural background of the Philistines', *IEJ* 50: 82–91.
Schoep, I. (1999) 'The origins of writing and administration on Crete', *OJA* 18: 265–76.
Scodel, R. (1982) 'The Achaean Wall and the myth of destruction', *HSCPh* 86: 33–50.
Singer, I. (1988) 'The origin of the Sea Peoples and their settlement on the coast of Canaan', in Heltzer and Lipinski (1988): 239–50.

(1992) 'Towards the image of Dagon the god of the Philistines', *Syria* 69: 431–50.

(2000) 'Cuneiform, linear, alphabetic: the contest between writing systems in the Eastern Mediterranean', in *Mediterranean Cultural Interaction*, ed. A. Ovadiah. Tel Aviv: 23–32.

(forthcoming) 'A fragmentary tablet from Tel Aphek with unknown script', in *Aphek II*, ed. M. Kochavi *et al.* Tel Aviv.

Slatkin, L. (1991) *The Power of Thetis. Allusion and Interpretation in the Iliad.* Berkeley.

Smith, A. D. (1986) *The Ethnic origins of Nations.* Oxford and Cambridge, Mass.

Snodgrass, A. M. (1971) *The Dark Age of Greece. An Archaeological Survey of the Eleventh to the Eighth Centuries* BC. Edinburgh.

(1974.) 'An historical Homeric society?' *JHS* 94: 114–25.

Sommer, F. and A. Falkenstein (1938) *Die hethitisch-akkadische Bilingue des Hattusili I (Labarna II).* Munich.

Sourvinou-Inwood, C. (1974) 'The Votum of 477/6 BC and the Foundation Legend of Locri Epizephyrii', *CQ* 24: 186–98.

(1995) *'Reading' Greek Death to the End of the Classical Period.* Oxford.

Southall, A. (1970) 'Incorporation among the Alur', in Cohen and Middleton (1970), 71–92.

Strauss Clay, J. (1989) *The Politics of Olympus. Form and Meaning in the Major Homeric Hymns.* Princeton.

Sürenhagen, D. (1998) 'Vervandtschaftsbeziehungen und Erbrecht im althethitischen Königshaus vor Telepinu – ein erneuter Erklärungsversuch', *AF* 25: 75–94.

Thomas, R. (1989) *Oral Tradition and Written Record in Classical Athens.* Cambridge.

(2001) 'Ethnicity, genealogy, and Hellenism in Herodotus', in Malkin (2001): 213–33.

Thumb, A. (1932) *Handbuch der griechischen Dialekte*, 2nd edn. vol. I ed. E. Kieckers. Heidelberg.

(1959) *Handbuch der griechischen Dialekte*, 2nd edn. vol. II ed. A. Scherer. Heidelberg.

Troy, L. (1986) *Patterns of Queenship in Ancient Egyptian Myth and History.* Uppsala.

Trudgill, P. (1983) *On Dialect. Social and Geographical Perspectives.* Oxford.

Tsipopoulou, M. and E. Hallager (1996) 'Inscriptions with Hieroglyphic and Linear A from Petras, Siteia', *SMEA* 37: 7–46.

Uchitel, A. (1988) 'The archives of Mycenaean Greece and the ancient Near East', in Heltzer and Lipinsky (1988): 19–30.

Ussishkin D. (ed.) (2004) *The Renewed Archaeological Excavations at Lachish (1973–1994)*, vol. III. Tel Aviv.

Vansina, J. (1985) *Oral Tradition as History.* Madison, Wisconsin.

Ventris, M. and J. Chadwick (1973) *Documents in Mycenaean Greek*, 2nd edn. Cambridge.

Vidal-Naquet, P. 1981. 'Slavery and the rule of women in tradition, myth and utopia', translation of 'Esclavage et gynéocratie dans la tradition, le mythe et l'utopie' (1970), in *Myth, Religion and Society*, ed. R. L. Gordon. Cambridge: 187–200.

Wace, A. J. B. and F. H. Stubbings (eds.) (1962) *A Companion to Homer*. London.

Walbank, F. W. (1967) *A Historical Commentary on Polybius*, vol. II. Oxford.

Walker, R. (1992) 'The relevance of Maori myth and tradition', in *Te Ao Hurihuri. Aspects of Maoritanga*, ed. M. King. Auckland: 170–82.

Wasserman, N. (2001) A review of West (1997). *SCI* 20: 261–7.

Webster, T. B. L. (1964) *From Mycenae to Homer*, 2nd edn. London.

Weingarten, J. (1990) 'The sealing structure of Karahöyük and some administrative links with Phaistos on Crete', *OA* 29: 63–95.

(1997) 'Another look at Lerna: an EH IIB trading post?', *OJA* 16: 147–66.

West, M. L. (1966) *Hesiod. Theogony*. Oxford.

(1985) *The Hesiodic Catalogue of Women*. Oxford.

(1988) 'The rise of the Greek epic', *JHS* 108: 151–72.

(1997) *The East Face of Helicon. West Asiatic Elements in Greek Poetry and Myth*. Oxford.

Whitley, J. (1988) 'Early states and hero cults: a re-appraisal', *JHS* (108), 173–82.

Winter, F. A. (1977) 'An historically derived model for the Dorian invasion', in *Symposium on the Dark Ages in Greece*, ed. E. Davis. New York: 60–76.

Wood, M. (1985) *In Search of the Trojan War*. London.

Woudhuizen, F. (1991) 'Etruscan and Luwian', *JIES* 19: 133–50.

Yasur-Landau, A. (2001) 'The mother(s) of all Philistines? Aegean enthroned deities of the 12th–11th century Philistia', in *Potnia. Deities and Religion in the Aegean Bronze Age. Proceedings of the 8th International Aegean Conference*, ed. R. Laffineur and R. Hägg (*Aegaeum* 22). Liege: 329–43.

(2003) 'How did the Philistines get to Canaan? Two: by land', *BAR*, March/April 2003: 35–39 and 66–67.

Zuidema, R. T. (1990) *Inca Civilization in Cuzco*. Austin.

Index of Passages Cited

General index

Achaean, the Achaeans 30, 107, 114, 129, 131, 138, 152, 153, 154, 155–156, 157, 159–160, 169, 173, 174, 175
Achaia Phthiotis 30, 131, 133, 159
Acusilaus of Argos 25, 35
Adrastos 27, 29, 32, 39, 66, 81, 82–83, 84
Aegean scripts 1, 57–61
    see also Linear A, Linear B
Aegean substratum 4–5, 8, 31, 42, 48–49, 50–52, 53, 54
Aeolians 32, 87–88, 129–130, 131, 160, 174
Aetolians 27, 28, 65, 143
Agamemnon 29, 33, 70, 83, 86, 151, 171–172, 174
Aiakos 35, 65, 66, 96
Aigimios 168
Aiolos 26, 27, 29, 31, 32, 39, 80, 94, 172–173; descendants of 32, 40, 41, 80, 85–86, 87, 89, 95
Alkmene 101
alphabets 59, 157
alternate succession 75, 77, 84, 86, 90, 180, 181
Alur of Central Africa 25, 35, 40
Amphiaraos 27, 29, 32, 39, 81, 82–84, 85, 150
Amphilochos 32, 150, 151
Amphitryon 36, 101
Amyclae 27, 32, 39, 83, 85–86, 87, 129, 138, 169, 172, 174
Anatolia, Anatolians 6, 23, 42–44, 47, 48, 54, 56, 57, 61, 72, 107–108, 164
    see also Western Asia
Anatolian languages 4, 5, 22, 47, 49–51, 52, 53–54, 63–64
    see also Carian, Hittite, Luwian, Lycian, Lydian, Palaic
Anthesteria 101, 165, 166
Antonnaccio, Carla 18, 21–22, 161, 173–174
Apollodorus 14, 28, 68, 85
Apollonius Rhodius 82, 102
Arcadians 33, 37, 57, 128, 129, 150
Argonauts, see Minyans

Argos 38, 39, 66, 71, 80–84, 86, 87, 105, 128, 129, 133, 140–144, 146–148, 158, 169, 171–172, 174; royal dynasty of 32, 63, 80–84, 103, 164
    see also Hera of A.
Aristotle 92–93, 104
Asante 26, 97
Asheri, David 15, 101, 102, 152
Ashkelon (Askalon) 150, 151, 152, 153, 157, 158
    See also Philistines
Athens, Athenians 14, 27, 29, 31, 33, 36, 37, 38, 39, 41, 66, 67, 92, 93, 94, 95, 96, 98, 103, 106, 107, 128, 129, 131, 138, 163–164, 165, 171
Atkinson, Quentin 22–23

Bacchiadae of Corinth 93, 95, 100
Barber, Elizabeth 8, 65, 68
Barnett, R. D. 150, 152
Bellerophon 63, 66, 67, 80
Bias 27, 32, 39, 80–84
biblical tradition, the Bible 47, 156, 157, 162
Blegen, Carl 1, 4, 8, 53, 171
Bloomfield, Leonard 112, 133, 135
Boghasköy archives 47, 48
    see also Anatolian languages
Bossert, H. 151–152
Brown, Edwin 52
Bryce, Trevor R. 54–55, 64, 72, 74, 75, 78, 99, 178–182
Buck, Carl Darling 50, 52, 109, 115–117, 128, 129, 131, 141, 142, 146
Bunimovitz, Shlomo 155–156
Burkert, Walter 5, 11, 158, 165, 167

Canaan 56, 59, 63, 148, 152–156, 157–159
Canaanite: container jars 55–56; dialect 157, 159; script 56, 59, 159
Carian 5, 42, 49
    see also Anatolian languages
Carruba, Onofrio 5, 50, 51, 53
Cartledge, Paul 145, 146, 161, 172
Caskey, John L. 6–7, 53